PALAEOLITHIC ARCHAEOLOGY IN IRAN

The American Institute of Iranian Studies Monographs: 1

Series Editors,
William L. Hanaway, Jr.
Brian Spooner

PALAEOLITHIC ARCHAEOLOGY IN IRAN

Philip E. L. Smith

Published for

THE AMERICAN INSTITUTE
OF IRANIAN STUDIES

by

THE UNIVERSITY MUSEUM
University of Pennsylvania
Philadelphia
1986

Design, production
Publications Division, The University Museum

Typesetting
The Sheridan Press
Hanover, Pennsylvania

Printing
Cushing-Malloy, Inc.,
Ann Arbor, Michigan

Library of Congress Cataloging in Publication Data
Smith, Philip E. L. (Philip Edward Lake)
  Palaeolithic archaeology in Iran.
  (American Institute of Iranian Studies monographs ; 1)
  Bibliography: p. 43
  1. Paleolithic period—Iran. 2. Iran—Antiquities.
I. Title.
GN772.32.I7S65   1986   935   85–20884
ISBN 0-934718-81-4
ISBN 0-9834718-73-3 (pbk)

To the Memory of

Glynn Ll. Isaac (1937–1985)

Philip E. L. Smith is Professor of Old World prehistory in the Department of Anthropology, University of Montreal, Montreal, Canada. He received a Ph.D. from Harvard University in 1962 and also studied at the University of Bordeaux in France. Most of his earlier research was focussed on the Palaeolithic, especially in France and Egypt where he excavated a number of sites. He has also conducted field work in Iraq, Mexico and the United States. Between 1965 and 1977 he investigated an early Neolithic site (Tepe Ganj Dareh) in the Zagros region of Iran, as well as making several archaeological surveys in the area. He is currently interested in the late Palaeolithic cultures and the development of early food-production in the Near East and elsewhere. He was elected a Fellow of the Royal Society of Canada in 1978.

Contents

Illustrations

Acknowledgments

My thanks go to the following colleagues who have read an earlier draft of this paper and have offered comments and criticisms, sometimes in considerable detail: I. A. Brookes, J. D. Clark, Z. M. Cooper, R. S. Davis, W. R. Farrand, F. Hole, B. Howe, the late G. Ll. Isaac, P. Mortensen, L. Rigazio, R. L. Solecki, R. S. Solecki, T. C. Young, Jr., and W. van Zeist. As far as possible I have incorporated their suggestions into the final version, but I take full responsibility for any misinterpretations of their opinions. I also thank N. Minugh-Purvis and E. Trinkaus for information about the allegedly human remains from Hunter's Cave at Bisitun and Tamtama Cave.

The maps and tables were prepared by L. Goupil, draftsman in the Department of Anthropology, University of Montreal.

Foreword

The American Institute of Iranian Studies was established in 1969 to support and encourage research in Iran. Through the 1970s the Institute's major role lay in the provision of a center in Tehran where scholars from North America could work, meet with Iranian colleagues, and organize the logistical details of their research programs. The first nine years of the Institute's existence were boom years for Iranian studies. The amount of basic research carried out in Iran increased annually, and expanded beyond the conventional study of Iranian culture and civilization into a number of disciplines in the social and the natural sciences.

In 1979 the boom ended. The political change brought with it changes not only in the administration of research but also in epistemology. Most projects were discontinued, and the Institute shifted the focus of its activities to North America, where the loss of opportunities for field research had been accompanied by a sharp reduction in the support for Iranian studies at home.

Research in Iran during the 1970s had produced large amounts of data, but the attraction of unlimited field opportunities had tempted scholars to put off the task of writing up their material. The 1980s promised to be a decade of writing rather than field research. In order to encourage and promote this new phase in the history of Iranian Studies, the Institute decided to commission a series of assessments of the state of research, in order to establish in a systematic manner where we stand as we begin to bring each field up to date.

Accordingly, the Institute requested a number of scholars to write monographs on the state of the study of Iran in their fields. Implicit in the planning of this project was the hope that the monographs would make clear not only what any given discipline has contributed to our knowledge of Iran, but also what the study of Iran has contributed to the advancement of that discipline. Authors have been encouraged to develop their own interpretation of their commissions and to take positions on the achievements and potential of the fields they define.

The Institute is happy to inaugurate its monograph series with the present volume, as one way of continuing its service to the field of Iranian studies. We are particularly grateful to Professor Philip E. L. Smith for preparing the first volume, and to Ezat O. Negahban, Visiting Curator of Iranian Archaeology, Near East Section, The University Museum for making the abridgement and Persian translation. Palaeolithic archaeology, as the study of the earliest human activity in the area covered by Iranian history and culture, makes a fitting opening to the series.

William L. Hanaway, Jr.
Brian Spooner
The Editors

Introduction

The purpose of this monograph is to describe and assess the Palaeolithic archaeology of Iran. In one sense the shortage of reliable data makes this an easy task. It would be possible to make facile generalizations without tripping over untidy details. In another sense, however, the job is difficult; there are so many gaps and weaknesses in our data that we can barely define the proper questions to ask, or choose between sometimes radically differing explanations. The result is perplexity about the significance of Iran in this period of prehistory.

Iran is by no means a total blank on the world map of the Palaeolithic, and indeed there are some regions of the Old World about which even less is known. But, compared to Europe, the Levant zone of Western Asia, some areas of Africa and even the Indian sub-continent, the Palaeolithic past of Iran is still uncharted. Since this circumstance will probably not change greatly in the near future, however, it is fruitless to deplore our present ignorance or to anticipate an early infusion of new field data. The most reasonable course is to discuss what is presently available while acknowledging and even emphasizing the lacunae. In this spirit I shall make a tentative interpretation of Iranian materials from the viewpoints of human adaptations within the territory and of relationships to other Palaeolithic materials outside it. The present enforced pause in field work gives the prehistorian a good opportunity to evaluate what we know, as well as to offer suggestions for the time when Palaeolithic research in Iran will resume.

Works of synthesis in prehistoric archaeology are generally ephemeral; they are quickly superseded by new discoveries and new interpretations. For better or worse, the rate of obsolescence of the present survey may be a little slower than most in view of the hiatus in field work that has now lasted about six years and whose end we cannot yet foresee.

It is hardly necessary to insist on the point that Iran cannot be studied in complete isolation from its neighbors. This is probably even more true for prehistoric than for historic times, and I suspect it is truest of all for that exceedingly long and complex period called the Palaeolithic when mankind lived by hunting and gathering. By the nature of their lives, hunters and gatherers are weakly anchored to given areas; although at times they can, at least in the short term, be remarkably sedentary if conditions permit, evidence from the several million years of the Palaeolithic shows a tendency for expansion beyond local territories and gradual infiltration into all zones of the world that would support the foraging manner of life. So, there is nothing astonishing in the view that the territory now called Iran underwent a continuous process of infiltration from outside, as well as the reverse, during the Palaeolithic. While Iran is perhaps a more naturally "closed" region than many others, with its mountain ranges enclosing a central basin and its large seas to the north and south, the land barriers were by no means insuperable at any time. A conscious effort will be made in this essay to place the Iranian Palaeolithic within the context of the Asian continent and particularly of the cultural events occurring in the lands adjacent to Iran.

Archaeologists also find it useful to attempt to define prehistoric culture areas. It is assumed that over long periods of time given geographical regions manifested certain features or themes—in large part the products of the natural environment and its resources—that mark them off from other regions, even those nearby and at the same level of cultural development. These local traditions presumably both represent stable and long-lasting adaptations to the conditions of the natural environment and reflect indigenous quirks and orientations that make up what the archaeologists and historians of a past age, or some geographers, would have called the "personality" or special character of a region. While this approach sometimes tempts the prehistorian to exaggerate the distinctiveness or uniqueness of his own particular region, it is nonetheless perfectly legitimate.

As cross-cutting perspectives these two ways of looking at the archaeological materials may bring us somewhat closer to understanding the role of Iran in the Palaeolithic world, both as an important geographical link in the Eurasian land mass and as a place in which peculiar environmental conditions may have helped evoke a distinctive response or set of responses among its human inhabitants.

It might also be pointed out that this essay is not a theoretical or methodological work. It is unfortunate that the information we have about the Iranian Palaeolithic today does not allow that kind of presentation. So there will be no attempts at building "models" to explain how the Palaeolithic occupants of Iran made their livings, utilized certain territories, evolved through time or obtained and transmitted ideas and things beyond the present frontiers. All this waits to be done by more fortunate investigators of the future. Instead, this is basically a descriptive account that tries to identify the main problem areas, and makes some suggestions about what we need to know to make further progress. It is written in the same spirit as my earlier attempt at synthesizing the Iranian Palaeolithic (Smith 1971), but is more detailed and longer and of course, more up to date where recent findings are concerned.

The deficiencies in our understanding of the Palaeolithic archaeology of Iran are the consequences of a number of interrelated factors which are briefly outlined here.

Two very obvious factors are the relatively limited amount of field work that has been done and the small number of sites that have been properly excavated. There is also a serious sampling bias resulting from the heavy emphasis on field work in the Zagros area at the expense of other regions. In good part this is no doubt due to the frequency and visibility of "closed" (cave and rock shelter) sites in the Zagros. Even here, however, the quality of excavations has not always been high, nor has the analysis of the excavated materials produced landmarks of archaeological method. It is significant that only one memoir or monograph-length report (Coon 1951) has yet appeared for an Iranian Palaeolithic site, although several shorter preliminary reports have been published. Some full reports may be expected in the near future, but as of the time of writing of this paper (1985) the results of most of the research carried out in the past several decades are still not fully available for discussion. A good many sites that have been tested or excavated have in fact received only a few lines in print. The writer admits his own culpability in this respect.

Closely linked to this handicap is our uncertainty about the absolute and relative chronologies of the Palaeolithic sequence. This is a weakness in our understanding of many other parts of the world, including the Levant, but in Iran it is even more apparent. Thus of the nineteen Iranian radiocarbon "dates" known, few can be accepted at face value, and in any case they refer only to the past 50,000 years or less. There are no methods yet applied to arrange in even approximate chronological order the many thousands of years of the earlier Palaeolithic cultures, although such methods (for example, potassium-argon, thermoluminescence, magnetic polarity chronology, and uranium-thorium series) have been successfully used in other parts of the world to date Palaeolithic sites. The events of the Pleistocene Epoch (the geological period which began nearly two million years ago and which saw the inception and development of the Palaeolithic cultural period) are not well understood in Iran. The terrestrial vestiges of former large-scale climatic events—the so-called glacial and pluvial environmental fluctuations of the Pleistocene Epoch—are thus poorly documented, although they should in principle furnish the prehistorian with a relative time-scale, however gross, in which to situate his cultural remains. Consequently, it is not possible to say with any precision how long any of the Palaeolithic cultures or traditions in Iran lasted, to what degree they overlapped with each other, and how they might be chronologically subdivided to document their internal changes.

There is also a great paucity of palaeoenvironmental and palaeoecological data. While it is true that prehistorians everywhere regularly and tediously deplore this deficiency, compared to Europe and North America, and even to the Levant region of the Near East, our knowledge of the past environmental events and processes in Iran remains relatively limited. Although some of the field studies, particularly in palynology, have been excellent, considering their restricted scope, their number has been small. We still cannot properly evaluate the environmental background of human activities in any single region of Iran, even in the comparatively well-studied Zagros mountains, let alone in the country as a whole.

The consequence of this failure is important. While giving due allowance for the probable differences between Pleistocene and modern environmental conditions, it is nevertheless reasonable to believe that there must have been considerable contrasts in physical environments, and hence in the resources available to human groups, within the territory today called Iran. Probably the interregional contrasts were as pronounced, at least at certain times, as those existing today. We might, therefore, expect great differences in the patterns of resource exploitation by the Palaeolithic peoples. Those living in Kerman or Baluchistan, for instance, may have had ways of life somewhat like those of the recent natives of the Australian desert, while the Zagros inhabitants may have resembled some of the recent hunter-gatherers of western North America; those living along the Caspian Sea undoubtedly had another and very different adaptation oriented to the exploitation of marine resources as well as to the usual terrestrial ones. Unfortunately, the lack of accurate data prevents us from doing much more than speculating on such topics at the present time. Indeed, this might be a convenient place to point out that Palaeolithic archaeologists in Iran (and for that matter in all of Southwest Asia) are handicapped to some degree because in this area there are no living or recent hunter-gatherer populations whose patterns of adaptation to local circumstances might serve as direct historical analogues of the archaeological materials. In our region (in contrast to parts of Africa, southern Asia, Siberia, and the New World) the hunting and gathering groups seem to have vanished as such during prehistoric times; archaeology is the poorer for this loss.

Finally, mention must be made of our ignorance of the anatomical features of the humans who were responsible for the cultural behavior that is the archaeologist's particular study. As will be discussed later, only a very small amount of authentic Palaeolithic human skeletal materials has yet been uncovered in Iran. Who the populations were in the various cultural periods, how they evolved physically, and to what degree we can speak of biological continuity from the Palaeolithic occupants of the country to the more recent inhabitants, are problems that await solution. The survey of the Iranian fossils made by Sunderland (1968) requires little modification today although some of his interpretations might be questioned.

I

The Palaeolithic: Some General Comments

Before we begin to discuss the Palaeolithic of Iran in more specific terms, something should be said about its definition and methods of classification. The term "Palaeolithic" was coined in the 19th century to signify, originally, the "Old Stone Age" when stone tools were chipped and flaked rather than ground and polished as they were in the later subdivision of the Stone Age, the "Neolithic" or New Stone Age. Gradually this technological definition was broadened to mean the very long period of the Pleistocene geological Epoch when people lived in small groups of hunter-gatherers before food production began in the Holocene (or Recent) Epoch among the Neolithic cultures. In Europe a "Mesolithic" was inserted as a transitional phase between the Palaeolithic and Neolithic around the turn of the century; this concept is sometimes employed in the Near East as well, although many prehistorians prefer the expression "Epipalaeolithic," a term that for some authors includes the final phase of the upper Palaeolithic back to ca. 16,000 B. C. or earlier, and extends forward to the earliest agricultural societies. But it was soon felt necessary to subdivide further the very long Palaeolithic period or age, and in Europe and Western Asia it has been the convention to define three somewhat arbitrary stages (see Fig. 15): the Lower Palaeolithic, which extends from the earliest local evidence of tool-using sometime in the late (?) Lower Pleistocene until roughly 100,000 years ago and is characterized in its material remains by typically heavy and often simple stone tools, especially hand axes and artifacts made on chipped pebbles and nodules; the Middle Palaeolithic, lasting from about 100,000 to about 40,000 years ago and producing, as a rule, smaller and more finely crafted stone implements, often made on flakes and showing much diversity in form; and the Upper Palaeolithic and Epipalaeolithic, which lasted until approximately 10,000 years ago in the Near East, and was characterized as a rule by stone tool assemblages strongly emphasizing implements made

on blades of various sizes (often microlithic), and, to a lesser extent, in some regions, those made on bone, antler and ivory and showing much greater regional diversity and specialization in the material culture and, probably, more emphasis on specialized activity sites than hitherto. These descriptions, it must be stressed, are very elementary and reality is far more complex, but they will do for the purposes of this study. It is usually difficult to determine just how much direct continuity there was from one stage to another, and the stages are neither universal nor precisely contemporaneous in all parts of the Old World.

This hallowed taxonomic framework has generally been adopted for Iran as for other parts of the Near East and Central Asia and, in recent years, India and Pakistan. In spite of certain drawbacks it is still useful when attempting correlations and comparisons from one region to another and it is the framework which will be adopted here—although Iran probably approaches the limits of viability of the system. We must of course always remember that these subdivisions, like the definition of the Palaeolithic itself, are largely based on technological and typological analyses of one class of human products: those made in stone. Much less is known about artifacts made of wood, plant fibers and leather, and even of bone and antler, which are often not preserved in archaeological contexts. It is also worth pointing out that some criteria customarily used in Europe to characterize the Upper Palaeolithic period, such as the presence of art on cave walls or on stone, antler, and bone, may be rare or completely absent in other regions. Such art is virtually unknown, for example, in the Near East.

Without going into the professional controversies concerning the nature of Palaeolithic archaeological materials (more particularly stone tools) and their interpretation, it is probably fair to say that an increasing number of prehistorians today no longer consider that the units they call "industries" are to be correlated closely with cultures in the ethnographic or sociological sense. There may, of course, be some degree of correspondence, but it is unlikely to be the one-to-one coincidence sometimes assumed in the past. Today the tendency among many prehistorians is to regard lithic industries as more abstract entities: a given assemblage found in a site or level may represent a complex of implements for performing certain tasks closely connected to subsistence as a rule but rather fluid according to time and place—for example, according to the season of the year or the kinds of activities involved. A single "ethnic" group, such as a band of foragers, might produce a variety of tool-kits, while quite distinct groups might utilize very similar ones. This controversy over the interpretation of Palaeolithic stone tools remains unsettled. I mention it here only to call attention to the fact that when we refer to industries such as the Acheulian, Mousterian, and Baradostian, we do not mean that these are homogeneous or distinct groupings in the ethnographic sense; and when we speak, for instance, of the "Zarzian people," this should not be understood as referring to a specific people in the social or ethnic sense but merely as the people who made and used the artifacts that archaeologists classify under the name "Zarzian."

Finally, we must also not be too quick to assume (as was often the case in the past) that the differences between the several stages of the Palaeolithic were the consequences simply of progressively increasing in-telligence or intellectual capacity in the people concerned. This may be a part of the explanation, but we cannot *a priori* assume it. Another common assumption is that each stage represents a progressive change in adaptive strategies and organizational abilities among groups with a growing capacity to communicate by verbal and nonverbal mechanisms; the transition from the Middle to the Upper Palaeolithic has been explained in such terms (e.g., Redman 1978:51–52). This hypothesis—which is really little more than a plausible postulate at this point—needs careful examination before it is incorporated permanently in our thinking. The causes of the cultural changes which undoubtedly took place during the several million years of our species' evolution are still largely unknown although they are the center of much debate and controversy among prehistorians today. The degree to which human groups became more proficient in their subsistence strategies and in the related technologies (and the extent to which the stone tools studied by the archaeologist reflect these advances), is a topic that unfortunately has not yet received much attention from Palaeolithic specialists in Iran. Indeed, we have virtually no information on the techniques the Palaeolithic populations of Iran may have used to gain a living—individual or group hunting, drives, ambushes, traps, snares, nets; types of weapons; collection, processing or consumption of plant foods.

The Development of Palaeolithic Research in Iran

Serious work in Palaeolithic archaeology began in Iran, as in neighboring Turkey, Iraq, and Afghanistan, considerably later than in the Syro-Palestine region of the Near East, where the earliest research goes back to the second half of the 19th century. The reasons for this no doubt lie in the relative remoteness of Iran and the rarity of visits by foreign scholars interested in Palaeolithic research. Probably the legal monopoly held on Iranian archaeology by the French from the 1890s to the early 1930s (Negahban 1981–82) was a contributing factor in discouraging prehistorians from other countries. Iran, unlike Iraq, Syria, Lebanon and Palestine, was of course not under a foreign mandate after World War I, and this also may be part of the explanation for the time lag in research.

At the close of the nineteenth century J. de Morgan, head of the French Archaeological Delegation, reported stone tools in a Pleistocene geological context in the Caspian area, but argued that the rest of Iran was covered with glaciers and lakes during this period and so uninhabitable (de Morgan 1907). In the 1930s surface finds of Palaeolithic implements were reported from Fars, near Shiraz (Field 1939:553–55). But, although the first Palaeolithic excavations in neighboring Iraq were made in 1928 (by the British prehistorian D. Garrod in the Zagros mountains) it was not until 1949 that such excavations were made in Iran (Coon 1951). Coon, an American, first dug in the Hunter's Cave at Bisitun and later in Tamtama Cave near Lake Urmia and in Khunik Cave in southern Khorasan near the Afghan frontier. In the same year he excavated the "Mesolithic" Belt Cave on the Caspian foreshore, and in 1951 he dug both Belt and the nearby Hotu Cave. Thus, in two years Iran was shown to have been occupied in at least the Middle Palaeolithic and "Mesolithic" periods. Only chance prevented Coon from identifying the Upper Palaeolithic (later to be known as the Baradostian cul-

ture) as well. He gives a well written and entertaining account of his pioneering investigations in his popular book *The Seven Caves* (1957).

Since those years a fair amount of Palaeolithic field work has been carried out in Iran by prehistorians from various foreign countries: Canada, Denmark, France, Great Britain, Italy, and the United States. Field made a survey in Luristan in 1950 (Field 1951). Braidwood's group excavated several Middle and Upper Palaeolithic sites at Kermanshah (now Bakhtaran) in 1959–1960 (Braidwood 1960). Hole and Flannery dug five sites near Khorramabad in Luristan in 1963 and 1965 (Hole and Flannery 1967), and Speth continued this in part in 1969 (Speth 1971). The writer briefly sounded Ghar-i-Khar at Bisitun in 1965, a cave visited but not tested by Coon in 1949 (Young and Smith 1966). McBurney (1964, 1968) excavated the Middle Palaeolithic cave of Ké-Aram I in Mazandaran in 1963, as well as undertaking "Mesolithic" investigations at Ali Tappeh near Behshahr on the Caspian in 1962 and 1964, and later (1969) investigated a Middle Palaeolithic cave in Luristan. In 1966–1967 Hume explored a number of surface sites in Baluchistan believed to be of early Palaeolithic age (Hume 1976), and J. Marucheck (1976) followed up on this in 1974–1975. Piperno reported (1972) on a large Middle Palaeolithic surface site discovered by W. Sumner in 1969, and in 1974 described flints from an Upper Palaeolithic rock-shelter near Shiraz, while in 1976 H. T. Wright investigated a number of other Palaeolithic sites in northeastern Khuzistan (Wright 1979). Meanwhile, in northern Iran Sadek-Kooros (1974) was attempting to identify early Palaeolithic artifacts in Pleistocene terraces in eastern Azerbaijan and to correlate them with geological events, while Ariai and Thibault (1975–77) were in Khorasan investigating what may be the earliest evidence of human presence in Iran. Mention should also be made of the research in many kinds of Palaeolithic sites in Luristan by Mortensen (1974*a*, 1974*b*, 1975), and of a survey made by Mortensen and the author in 1977 which located an enormous Palaeolithic open-air workshop area near Harsin in Kermanshah District. There have also been a few Palaeolithic surveys and collections by several other investigators in northwestern Iran, and particularly in Azerbaijan, by Solecki (1969) and by Singer and Wymer (1978).

These flurries of field work present us with a number of peculiarities. For the most part the work has been sporadic in nature with few extensive excavations lasting more than one or two seasons, and virtually no efforts at problem-oriented, multi-stage investigation or serious multidisciplinary research. As already mentioned there has been a heavy concentration of research in western Iran, and especially in the Zagros area. But only one site has been published in detail, and few quantitative data are presented in the preliminary reports that have appeared. Virtually all this research has been carried out by non-residents and foreigners; research by Iranian archaeologists in the Palaeolithic of their country has not been a priority in official circles.[1] Finally, it may be worth pointing out that there has been remarkably little communication or collaboration between the foreigners working in Iran, who have not even attempted to devise a system of Palaeolithic taxonomy or nomenclature to standardize their published descriptions.

What this means is that in spite of the activity of the last few decades, the Palaeolithic range of Iranian prehistory still rests on an insubstantial foundation. There has yet to develop a tradition of sustained research, of the type taken for granted elsewhere in the Old World (including the Levant area of Western Asia) whereby a respectable corpus of data is regularly produced and then discussed and debated by an active, even competing group of scholars. Perhaps this is one of the reasons the Iranian Palaeolithic— like its counterparts in Iraq, Afghanistan, and Turkey—has remained nearly unknown on the international level and has contributed so little to our understanding of human prehistory, either factually or methodologically. Although books and articles of synthesis on Near Eastern prehistory dutifully mention the Iranian data, the investigations have had far less impact on our thinking than the Palaeolithic research that has been done in recent years in the Levant or even in Egypt.

1. No Iranian prehistorian has ever, to my knowledge, specialized in Palaeolithic studies or has even produced a published report in this area. Very few, if any, seem to have participated in Palaeolithic investigations in the field apart from those representatives of the Archaeological Service assigned to foreign expeditions. This lack of official interest in the Palaeolithic is perhaps not surprising, since the Neolithic is almost as completely ignored by Iranian archaeologists who tend to emphasize the Bronze and Iron Ages and the historic periods of their country's past. This situation prevails in most countries of the Near East, though not always to the same degree.

III

The Natural Background: Present and Past

As hunters and gatherers, Palaeolithic groups were intimately involved with their natural environment and governed by the opportunities and restrictions it imposed on their lives; perhaps more so, indeed, than any human beings since. Hence, a knowledge of the environment and the available resources is a necessity in trying to understand the inert residues they have left behind which, taken alone, reveal so little about the activities of these vanished peoples.

Modern Iran covers an area of 1,648,000 square kilometers. Within this vast extent there is a great deal of diversity created by landforms, water resources, latitude and altitude, and the proximity of the seas. As one botanist pointed out, "there are few countries in Eurasia which have temperate or even cool-temperate forests at their northern limits and tropical savanna at their southern fringes, and all this within a latitudinal belt of some eleven degrees" (Zohary 1963:5).

In its simplest terms the country consists of a complex of mountain chains that enclose a series of basins lying at altitudes of some 300 to 1,200 meters above sea level (Fisher 1968:3). Half of these basins have no outlet, and depend on evaporation to remove internal drainage; from the others water flows to the Caspian, the Persian Gulf, and a few lakes. Since the Iranian Plateau lies across the great desert belt of the Old World, it is exposed to a variety of climatic influences, both at its edges (e.g., the westerly conditions in the northwest, and the monsoons in the south), and in its whole interior (e.g., the continental anticyclonic regime of Central Asia and Siberia, cf. Bobek 1968). Except for the Caspian area, Iran today has a dry continental-type climate, with meager precipitation between September and May, and this was probably true in general for most of prehistory. It has long been a tectonically and seismically active zone as well, and these movements have created many of the landforms existing today, although water and wind erosion have been mainly responsible for the evolution of relief since Pliocene times.

The number of physiographic units or natural regions into which Iran can be divided depends to some degree on the criteria selected and the purposes of the classifier. A reasonably precise and useful scheme for the purposes of this essay consists of five regions (Fig. 1). These might of course be further subdivided, and indeed for later periods of prehistoric and for historic times they no doubt should be; but for a discussion of the Palaeolithic as we know it today a simpler scheme seems adequate.[2]

1. The Zagros Highlands extend from Azerbaijan in the northwest along the western border about 1,600 km. to the Persian Gulf and the Straits of Hormuz. One can further subdivide this natural region into the northwest, central, southwest and southern Zagros to accommodate its local conditions. These mountains resulted from tectonic forces in the Red Sea rift system when crustal spreading created folding and faulting. Today they display long, parallel limestone ridges up to 4000 m. above sea level in some places, and deep intermontane valleys which are drained principally by the Khabur, Saimarreh, Karkheh, Karun, Dez, Greater Zab, Lesser Zab, and Diyala rivers in Iran and Iraq. The climatic regime here was more extreme than in the Mediterranean zone of the Near East, particularly in cooler phases, and the natural environment and food resources must have reflected this difference. Within this huge area there is today, as there probably was in the Pleistocene, considerable climatic and ecological diversity; thus the western side of the chain receives more precipitation than the eastern which is in a precipitation

---

2. The basic subdivisions used are those of Fisher (1968, fig.3), and much of the text description of each is based on this source. I have added a fifth subdivision, the Khuzistan Lowlands, at the suggestion of Dr. T. C. Young, Jr.

shadow with cooler winters. Individual valleys create a mosaic of environments. Snowfall is often heavy, and its melting has important effects. The predominant natural vegetation (varying according to altitude) is oak, pistachio, almond and other deciduous trees. Wild wheat and barley, as well as wild goat, sheep, boar, deer, and gazelle still survive. This area today contains about a third of the country geographically as well as the largest concentration of its population and many of its largest cities. Most of the known Palaeolithic sites are also found in the Zagros; so its cultural importance in relation to the rest of the country may be a very ancient feature. This essay will supplement the purely Iranian evidence by frequent reference to archaeological sites on the Iraqi side of the Zagros.

2. The Khuzistan Lowlands, which are really extensions of the Mesopotamian alluvial plain, were also formed by tectonic forces as a trough was downwarped and then deeply filled with alluvium transported from nearby and distant uplands. It is today relatively flat and low-lying; it extends from the Zagros foothills to the head of the Persian Gulf and is watered by five large permanent streams (the Karkheh, Karun, Dez, Jarrahi, and Zohreh). Some of it is marshland, but most is semiarid steppe with many microenvironments. Winters are milder than in the Zagros and summers much hotter. The vegetation includes steppe and desert types, with rich grasslands in winter. Gazelle, cattle, fallow deer and boar seem to have been the prehistoric fauna, with goat in the nearby hills, while fish, aquatic birds and turtle were found in the streams and marshes.

3. The Northern Highlands comprise the Elburz massif and the Talish Hills, including its southern flanks and the small valleys and steep gorges within the mountains, and the coastal plain of the Caspian Sea (although strictly speaking the latter might be considered apart). Geographically this area extends in a shallow arc some 960 km. long from the Soviet frontier at Astara in the west to Jajarm in the east. These mountains include Iran's highest peak, Mount Damavand near Tehran, a dormant volcano. Small icefields survive today, but during the Pleistocene the region was more extensively glaciated than the Zagros. Because of the height of the range, winter moisture from the north is largely barred; the northern side is thus much wetter than the inner side. Several large rivers, such as the Sefid Rud, flow into the Caspian. Winter temperatures in the mountains are low, though higher than in the Zagros. In the lowlands mild and humid conditions prevail most of the year, producing a modern average annual precipitation (ca. 2,000 mm.) five times the Iranian average. The natural vegetation seems to be the Hyrcanian forest with very large numbers of trees and shrubs, mainly broad-leafed deciduous types: ash, linden, elm, walnut, maple, beech and hornbeam. Besides goat and sheep, there were several distinctive faunal elements in this zone—including the Caspian seal and a tiger, the latter now probably extinct.

4. The Eastern Highlands and the Seistan Basin extend from Khorasan to Baluchistan, the Makran and the Gulf of Oman. They consist of a number of upland massifs separated by plains and basins, the basins all at least 900 meters above sea level. There are high peaks, wide valleys and drainage swamps and lakes fed by rivers rising in Afghanistan, such as the Helmand. The climate varies from moderately humid to arid with hot summers and cold winters. The modern vegetation includes semihumid oak forest, dry juniper forest, some humid forest, and pistachio and almond. The modern fauna includes wild sheep and goat, boar, gazelle and onager, and these were very likely among the important game animals exploited by Palaeolithic hunters as well. The Pleistocene fauna is poorly known, however, particularly in Baluchistan.

5. The Central Plateau (or Interior Desert Basins) covers about one half of the area of the country, or some 780,000 km.[2] It can be imagined as an enormous saucer rimmed on all sides by highlands, with no outward drainage to the sea, and containing two great inland basins: the Dasht-i Kavir to the north, consisting of viscous mud under a saline crust, and the Dasht-i Lut to the south, composed for the most part of gravel but containing a large area of sand in the southeast. (There are, however, no enormous sand seas on the scale of Arabia.) There are several smaller basins as well, with silt deposits, and some salt lakes, together with some mountain chains. Rainfall is low; in the heart of the plateau it is less than 100 mm. annually. Summer temperatures are extremely high, while the winters are cold. The vegetation is composed mainly of desert-steppe shrubs. Gazelle and onager were probably the most important indigenous game animals.

As already mentioned, the modern climate of Iran (apart from the Caspian zone) is marked by continentality with hot, dry summers and cold, moist winters. Two other features are important as well: the great contrasts in rainfall, with considerable precipitation in the north and the northwest and little or none in the rest of the country; and the frequency of high winds which intensify the effects of the extreme temperatures. The high mountain ranges largely exclude the moisture borne from the Mediterranean, the Persian Gulf and the Caspian Sea from the interior of the country, while the interior similarly receives no benefit from the dried-out summer monsoonal airstream flowing from India and Pakistan. In winter the Siberian anticyclone imposes low temperatures on most of the region. The result of these features and of the topography is that a Mediterranean climate prevails in northwestern Iran (the Zagros and Elburz mountains); a subtropical steppe climate exists in the rain-shadow zone just east of the Zagros and south of the Elburz; and there is a subtropical desert climate in the drier interior plateau. "In addition, we find considerable altitudinal zonation in the country, such as the lowlands and foothills in the semitropical south, the cool upland valleys and plateaus, and the alpine country above any forests or cultivated land" (Fisher 1968:284). Movement up and down these zones according to season is one means by which recent Iranians have adapted to the rather rigorous relief and climate of their land. Whether such transhumance was significant in the Palaeolithic period is one of the most interesting and important questions facing the prehistorian.

How closely do the present climatic zones correspond to those existing in the distant past? This is not an easy question to answer even for the recent phases of the Pleistocene Epoch. It is certain that the basic climatic gradient of increasing aridity from west to east and from northwest to southeast existed during the Pleistocene, so we might expect the existing vegetation zones (insofar as they are natural zones in which the flora is not apparently degraded or altered by recent human activities) to have had analogues in the Palaeolithic (Zohary 1963). Probably the present regional patterns of climate were present, although climatic extremes were at times accentuated. Unfortunately, as already mentioned, the state of research into the palaeoclimatology of Iran does not allow us to be precise about details, especially in the older time ranges. There are four kinds of evidence used to reconstruct past climates: traces of glacial fluctuations in the mountain areas, fluvial geomorphology, animal and plant remains found in archaeological sites, and lacustral evidence obtained by pollen-coring in lakes and swamps. The last method is the newest and by far the most promising of the three; in the last few decades it has been employed at a number of places in the Zagros (e.g., at lakes Zeribar and Nilofar and at Lalabad Springs by H. E. Wright, Jr. and W. van Zeist), and has thrown a great deal of essential light on the natural background to human activities. These detailed data will be presented later on in this essay, but much of what follows in the present general section is based on their studies. Up to now it has been possible to obtain this palynological information only from deposits of the last 40,000 years; beyond that we can say very little except what is drawn from the scanty and coarse data provided by glacial action

(which are difficult to date), and the even more imprecise evidence from stream terraces, coastal beaches, some rare aeolian (loess) deposits, and playa kavir formations in the deserts. The study of soils and pollen in cave sediments has been of great value for charting environmental fluctuations, especially local, short-term ones, in other parts of the world including the Levant. This has unfortunately never been intensively undertaken for any Palaeolithic cave site in Iran, although some pollen studies were made by Leroi-Gourhan (1981) at Humian in Luristan. As for the faunal remains, the study of these has not so far been of great value for environmental purposes in Iran.

The Near East, in contrast to Europe and some other parts of Asia, was much less strongly affected by the alternating cold and warm fluctuations (the "glacial" and "interglacial" phases) that characterize the Pleistocene Epoch in the temperate and sub-Arctic zones of the planet. There were some small glaciers in the Zagros mountains when the snow line descended between 1,200–1,800 m. below modern snow lines (Wright 1980) during cold spells, but no great ice sheets such as occurred in Europe and North America were formed. In the Elburz, too, there were some mountain glaciers, perhaps more important ones than in the Zagros. Thus the overall "glacial" climate in Iran was cooler than at present, although there is no consensus on how much cooler. Estimates of temperature depression have varied, in the Zagros, from as little as $3°–4°$ C. to as much as ca. $11°$ C. (Wright 1980), while others (Krinsley 1970; van Zeist and Bottema 1977) prefer intermediate figures of ca. $5°–8°$ C. lower. The latter estimate is adopted here. It is very likely (although this is a controversial topic) that conditions were no moister than today, and probably were considerably drier as a rule.[3] During the warm phases the situation was probably fairly similar to that of today. Certainly we cannot speak of either true glacial or pluvial periods in Iran, but rather of a generally semiarid regime that was periodically modified by somewhat lower temperatures and lower evaporation rates. The cooler phases, however, did not necessarily lead to

3. The climatic reconstruction presented here, particularly of the Zagros, is derived from the interpretations of van Zeist and Bottema (see especially their 1977 paper). It is only fair to point out, however, that there are competing views about the significance of the absence of trees in "last glacial" times. While I have here interpreted this as reflecting cold, dry conditions, others favor the view that cold but more humid conditions prevailed in glacial maxima, as suggested perhaps by the high lake levels in Iran and eastern Turkey, and the glaciers on Iranian mountains (Farrand 1981, and personal communication). In this view it was the cold, not the aridity, that prevented tree growth. Another opinion is that excessive snow, rather than aridity, may account for the treeless conditions in Iran.

richer vegetation and more abundant animal life with more hospitable conditions for these hunting and gathering groups, nor were the warmer periods necessarily more severe. The situation was probably a highly complex one, and it would be dangerous to generalize in our present primitive state of knowledge. In the mountains at least the summers were probably mild, but the winters would have been extremely cold with longer snow seasons (Wright 1976). Lake levels were at least seasonally higher in cool periods because of decreased evaporation and meltwater, while in warm phases many depressions may have dried up.

In Europe and elsewhere the traditional four-glaciation classification of the "glacial" phases based on the old Alpine sequence and terminology has long been discarded as too simple, and it is now accepted that the shifts in temperature and the resulting glacial advances and retreats were much more numerous than previously thought. Gradually, thanks to studies in marine and terrestrial deposits and to more accurate methods of dating, many parts of the world are yielding data that prehistorians can use with some confidence in establishing the backgrounds of their cultural units. Iranian prehistorians can share in little of this new information, however, and at the moment must content themselves with working against a relatively impoverished background. Only the local equivalent of the last European glacial period (the "Würm"), which began perhaps ca. 80,000 years ago, is even moderately well known in Iran and Iraq and its fluctuations and shifts beyond ca. 40,000 years ago remain almost undocumented (see van Zeist and Bottema 1977, 1982; Brookes 1982).

Even less is known about climatic and environmental conditions in other parts of Iran beyond the Zagros. The interior basin which makes up nearly half the country contains dune fields, playas (flat depressions with fine sediments) and broad alluvial fans. Many of the playas were formerly shallow lakes, fed in places near the Zagros and Elburz mountains by runoff from the mountain snow fields, as, for example, near Qom and Damghan. Several perennial streams from the Elburz fed the Great Kavir basin. The currently stable dunes in eastern and central Iran were probably formed during the last cold period by sand blown under arid conditions from the Great Kavir (Krinsley 1970). Contrary to former belief, there were no large Pleistocene "seas" in central Iran, but there were lakes of various sizes and depths. Since the end of the Pleistocene most of these have dried up or have been reduced in size though some, such as lakes Shiraz and Neiriz in Fars, persist at least perennially. The Helmand lake in Seistan was much larger and deeper in Pleistocene times, fed by meltwater from the Hindu Kush and maintained by the lower evaporation rate. Thus during the cooler phases at least there was much more surface water present than today in the interior basins of Iran, and one supposes somewhat more favorable living conditions for hunters, gatherers and perhaps fishermen. The more extreme seasonal changes probably imposed considerable mobility on the inhabitants. Probably the low temperature and aridity in the last "glacial" period sustained few trees. Very few Palaeolithic materials are known in this interior zone, although surface artifacts are found but usually without precise chronological context or any organic remains. While the area was unquestionably frequented by humans during the Pleistocene it is difficult to say how intensive the occupations were or just what resources were being exploited. At a rough guess we might suppose that much of the area was at least as favorable for hunters and gatherers as the interior desert of Australia today, a region that has permitted sparse populations to survive in spite of harsh conditions.

Attempts to evaluate the southern coastal regions of Iran meet with similar difficulties. It is certain that the coastlines of the Persian Gulf and the Arabian Sea were often different from their present states as the world's oceans rose and fell according to the melting and expansion of the great ice sheets in the northern and southern hemispheres. Thus during the last glacial period the Persian Gulf was much smaller than it is today and during the colder intervals was mainly dry land bisected by a river flowing from Mesopotamia down to the Straits of Hormuz; presumably passage from Arabia to southern Iran was feasible at times for man and animals as the water level of the depression dropped by over a hundred meters (Kassler 1973). Probably the same was true in earlier glacial periods as well. In interglacial periods, on the other hand, the Gulf may have extended further north than today into the Mesopotamian plains.

Along the Gulf of Oman in glacial times the coastline probably extended further out on the continental shelf than is the case today. Whether this now-submerged coastal belt was inhabited by Palaeolithic groups and (as sometimes suggested) served as a migration route towards the Indian subcontinent, is unknown; very little Palaeolithic archaeology has been attempted in that area of the country. Further work in Baluchistan might be rewarding, however, especially in the Sarhadd Plateau near the Pakistan border, since the altitude (ca. 2,000 m.) may have permitted somewhat more favorable conditions for plants, animals and man even in the cool, semiarid phases. Here, too, there is some possibility of finding sealed occupation sites in caves and rock shelters (see Field 1956). The Makran region, with its marginal monsoonal climate, may have been another favored environmental zone, permitting somewhat more varied vegetation and more abundant game, despite its aridity. The marine terraces in this part of Iran might profitably be studied for artifacts and possibly they can be dated by the associated marine shells (Hume 1976:277).

The Pleistocene conditions in the northern highlands are also not well known in detail. Precipitation then, as now, was probably higher than elsewhere in Iran, at least on the northern face of the Elburz, and a mesic (i.e., neither dry nor excessively humid) vegetation pattern may have prevailed. Some glaciers exist even today, and no doubt were more widespread in the colder periods. Whether humans lived in the Elburz at that time, as they certainly did in the Zagros, is not certain; to my knowledge no Palaeolithic sites have been reported there, but it is difficult to believe that such a promising hunting-gathering territory would have been unexploited during at least the warmer seasons.

The Caspian zone was of course as unique in climatic and environmental terms in the past as it is today. The surface of the sea is at present below mean modern ocean level by some twenty-eight meters and at times in the past it was both higher (ca. sixteen meters) and lower (ca. thirty to forty meters) than ocean level. The Caspian is a shallow and unstable body which is dependent in extent and depth on the state of its water balance—the influx from rivers versus evaporation and outflow—and it fluctuated a good deal in Pleistocene times. A number of beaches considerably higher (up to 90 m.) than the modern one have been identified, and tentatively correlated by Soviet and other geologists with European glacial events. There has been controversy over just how the high and low Caspian sea levels are to be correlated with those events. The most acceptable explanation today is that during glacial periods the Caspian, which unlike the Oceans is a closed sea, was higher than at present: part of the water now flowing into the Baltic and White seas was diverted to the Volga and so to the Caspian, while the evaporation rate was less because of lower temperatures (Butzer 1970). A rather schematic representation of this model as reconstructed by Soviet researchers is shown in Fig. 2 (see Dolukhanov 1977); conversely, during warmer periods sea levels dropped considerably, to the point where the Caspian may have contracted to two small lakes. In Holocene times (i.e., since the end of the Pleistocene) the sea has risen and fallen several times though possibly never attaining its former extreme high and low levels. Perhaps tectonic factors (uplift and subsidence) altering the form and capacity of the Caspian basin are also involved (Gerasimov 1978). The real history of Caspian behavior is probably more complex than any of the current models sug-

gests, but for the moment the prehistorian faces a very unclear picture as he tries to understand the background to the cultural events in this region. Certainly all Middle and Upper Pleistocene archaeological sites then located near the present coastline would now either be drowned or destroyed or buried deep beneath the modern plain. During Middle and Upper Palaeolithic times (except perhaps during warmer interstadial phases) the present coast would have been inaccessible to people, but of course the northern flanks of the Elburz mountains above high-water level would have been habitable. It is very likely there was (except in more arid Gorgan) a continuous mesic forest vegetation in the Caspian area of Iran where a warmer and more humid climate stood in distinct contrast to the treeless regions of most of Iran where cold, dry climate prevailed (van Zeist and Bottema 1977). The decreased temperatures brought increased snowfall to the Caspian Basin in "glacial" times (Krinsley 1970). The study of loesses in Gorgan and of moraines and terraces in the Elburz range as they are correlated with the Caspian beaches should illuminate this problem. With the higher temperatures at the end of the Pleistocene the sea level dropped, the Caspian shrank in area, the coastal plain was expanded, caves in the limestone escarpment at the foot of the Elburz hitherto drowned were available for human occupation, and eventually the modern floral and faunal patterns came into being.

The animals that must have formed a major part of the diet of the Palaeolithic peoples in Iran were probably for the most part "modern," although we cannot be certain of the fauna in the earlier periods of human occupation. We are on firm ground only for the last cold period, and even then most of our information comes from the Zagros area and its archaeological sites. We can be sure that there were no very "cold" or "Arctic" fauna present such as reindeer, or woolly mammoth, and perhaps few "tropical" species. The Indian elephant may have been present at one time (it occurs in the Zagros site of Barda Balka, Iraq, dating perhaps to the time of the late last interglacial); a rhinoceros was also found at Barda Balka, and apparently, in the last glacial period at the site of Ké-Aram I in Mazandaran. But for the most part the food animals were such familiar Palaearctic types as cattle, sheep, goat, pig, onager, deer, and gazelle. Snails and molluscs were being eaten towards the end of the Pleistocene and in the early Holocene, as were some fish and birds. Along the Caspian, seals seem to have been actively hunted in early post-Pleistocene times, together with terrestrial fauna. The most common carnivores were bear, wolf and fox, and their skins may have served for clothing at times. We know virtually nothing directly of the plant resources (nuts, fruits, seeds, tubers, roots) prevalent during the Pleistocene or the extent to which they were used by the human groups. Zohary's (1963) description of the modern flora of Iran may be used with caution in extrapolating to prehistoric times.

At a very rough guess, under present conditions perhaps about one-third of the land area of Iran would be suitable for hunting and gathering (Flannery 1969:94); the rest, marginal or uninhabitable zones, would probably be little exploited by humans. However, environmental conditions must have fluctuated considerably during the Palaeolithic period and our estimate must be highly elastic. To estimate the number of people living in Iran at a given time is almost impossible, even in very approximate terms. Certainly the number must have varied through time, with very likely a gradual build-up from the Lower to the Upper Palaeolithic. At the beginning of the sequence the human groups were probably sparse and organized in small, fluid bands, while at the end of the Pleistocene, shortly before food-producing transformed them, they were probably larger and more densely distributed. Some writers even speak of a population crisis at this time. But of course there was neither uniformity of growth through time, nor uniformity of numbers spatially. In climatically unfavorable periods the population probably decreased. Such favored regions as the Zagros almost certainly had larger populations than the interior basins except perhaps in the coldest phases.

Some mention must be made now of the subdivisions of the Pleistocene Epoch, in order to clarify some of the discussion that follows. Geologists conventionally subdivide it into three (or sometimes four) major stages (Fig. 15). The Lower Pleistocene, which for some authors includes a Basal Pleistocene, was a very long period beginning nearly two million years ago when glacial activities had not yet become important, a generally warmer climate prevailed, and many now-extinct species of animals existed. This was also the time when the evidence for the earliest tool-making hominids becomes indisputable on the African continent, although there are some traces of such behavior even earlier; these hominids gradually developed culturally and biologically while spreading through Europe and Asia. The Middle Pleistocene began at least 700,000 years ago and was a shorter period with considerable glacial activity as well as important faunal changes; it also saw the proliferation of industries characterized especially by hand axes (although these had appeared late in the Lower Pleistocene), as well as other industries emphasizing tools made on flakes and nodules but generally lacking in hand axes. The Upper Pleistocene began not later than 125,000 years ago with further faunal changes and more advanced forms of man; types generally classed as Neanderthals replaced the earlier *Homo erectus* forms, and in turn anatomically modern *Homo sapiens* (who may have developed as early as 100,000 years ago in Africa) replaced the Neanderthals in the last part of the Upper Pleistocene. There were also increasingly complex cultural manifestations that gradually diffused into nearly all parts of the inhabitable world. These three subdivisions of the Pleistocene are essentially geological and climatic concepts, of course, but they provide a useful framework into which prehistorians can fit their regional cultural variants and attempt to make interregional correlations. It is unfortunate that firm documentation for this broad framework for subdividing the Pleistocene is lacking in Iran at the present time, because of the paucity of research there. Only the Upper Pleistocene is reasonably well known in Iran, and only the latter part of that, during the colder period corresponding to the last or "Würm" glacial; the preceding "interglacial" period, which apparently ended ca. 80,000–100,000 years ago, is very poorly known in Iran, although there is some reason to believe the territory was inhabited by human groups.

IV

The Lower Palaeolithic

When did the first humans come to Iran, and from where? We do not know. Since it is highly improbable that Iran or any other part of the Near East was the (or a) "cradle of mankind," we must assume that its first human inhabitants were immigrants from some other continent. Unfortunately we cannot yet be sure of the direction from which they came or the cultural and biological levels they had attained when they arrived. This is because up to the present time no certain Lower Palaeolithic occupation site has been found in a sealed and dated deposit in Iran, although such sites are known in the Levant, particularly at Ubeidiyah in the Jordan Valley of Israel. It is reasonable to suppose that sometime in the late Lower Pleistocene—say, about a million years ago or a little earlier—hominids with identifiable stone tools slowly moved out of Africa, the ancestral continent, into the adjoining regions of Europe, Southwest Asia, the Levant and, possibly southern Arabia, and thence gradually diffused eastward and northward into Mesopotamia and ultimately Iran. These migration routes are still mere conjecture, however. It is not inconceivable, for example, that the earliest inhabitants of Iran were derived from the north, from Central Asia or across the Caucasus; it now appears that the southern parts of the Soviet Union were occupied at least a quarter million years ago in the Lower Palaeolithic, that is, sometime in the Middle Pleistocene (Ranov and Davis 1979). Or the direction of diffusion may have been from east to west, from the Indian subcontinent where the earliest archaeological traces probably date to the Middle Pleistocene somewhere between a half million and a million years ago (although it still remains to be demonstrated that southern Asia was an independent early center for hominid origins or for tool making). But as yet we cannot answer this question of origins. Indeed, one of the most puzzling things about the Palaeolithic of Iran (and Iraq) is the paucity of evidence for its earlier stages. Whether this reflects a real scarcity of ar-

chaeological sites or is merely due to insufficient research is impossible to say at the moment.

It should be mentioned here that in some parts of the Old World (Africa, and possibly the Levant, Western Europe and the Indian sub-continent) there are two broad phases of the Lower Palaeolithic. In the earlier the stone tools were typically made on cobbles, pebbles or heavy flakes and this grouping is often (although not altogether accurately) called the pebble-tool tradition. The later phase—allowing for some overlapping—is presumably derived from the earlier one and is characterized by such bifacial tools as hand axes and cleavers. The first phase, which lasted well over a million years, is generally called the Oldowan in Africa; the second, which ended perhaps between one and two hundred thousand years ago, is universally termed the Acheulian. The makers of the earlier type were, if not the early hominids called Australopithecines, at least very early forms of *Homo*; the second type is apparently associated with the more advanced *Homo erectus* who may also, however, have been responsible for some of the "pebble tool" industries. In some parts of the Old World, however, such as the Far East and eastern Europe, the hand axe/cleaver industries are poorly represented or are absent, their place being taken by industries made on pebbles, nodules, and flakes and featuring rather heavy implements called choppers and chopping-tools. In still other regions there is some reason to suspect that the two main traditions were broadly contemporaneous, as with the Acheulian and Clactonian in England, or the Acheulian and flake-tool industries claimed by some prehistorians to exist in the Levant.

Whether such a multiplicity of Lower Palaeolithic traditions existed in Iran is unknown. Indeed, another puzzling aspect is the virtual or perhaps total absence of Acheulian hand axes in the country. There are a few hand axes known, it is true, but only as surface finds and they may in reality belong to

Middle Palaeolithic assemblages or conceivably in some cases even to the Neolithic period. Yet hand axes are common in the Levant, where many good occupation sites are known, and they occur also in Arabia and eastward to about the Euphrates in Mesopotamia, where they become rare. Were there environmental reasons making hand axes less functional in the east, as has been suggested (McBurney 1950:178)? It is hard to see what such reasons could be. Or did the hand axe users simply fail to penetrate into Iraq and Iran? Or did they penetrate in such feeble numbers that their traces are not archaeologically recognizable or have not survived? Here another problem is raised. In the Indian subcontinent classic Acheulian assemblages are well known, particularly in the south, and the hand axes and cleavers are virtually indistinguishable from those in Africa, Europe and the Levant. In China and Southeast Asia they are again rare. So it is reasonable to surmise that, unless the Indian Acheulian evolved locally from a preceding pebble-tool tradition (and there is no good evidence that this happened), the hand axes and cleavers were introduced there from somewhere to the west. If so, Iran would be one logical diffusion route. But so far we have not found the evidence. Is this due only to the rudimentary level of exploration in the country? Or has the evidence been destroyed or deeply buried beneath later sediments, or by submersion of the coastal shelf along the Persian Gulf and the Gulf of Oman? Were the putative migrants composed of such small and quickly moving groups that they left few traces? None of these speculations is very satisfying, for it is hard to accept the idea that Acheulian peoples, who were quite successful in adapting to varied environments from South Africa to England and India, would not have spread broadly across the interior of Iran and Iraq—by no means an inhospitable region, after all—if they had once entered it rather than limiting themselves to now conveniently submerged or buried areas. The origins of the Indian Acheulian remain an unsolved problem and the Iranian data contribute very little to its solution.

At the present time all the evidence for the Lower Palaeolithic in Iran comes from open-air occurrences, for no cave or rock shelter sites are known in this period (Fig. 3). This is fairly consistent with the situation in Africa and the Levant as well as the Indian subcontinent, where caves were little utilized apparently until the end of the Lower Palaeolithic. Whether this was due to environmental factors such as generally mild climates which reduced the need for such natural shelters, or to the reluctance of people to live in places frequented by dangerous carnivores, or because very early cave deposits have not been preserved, is not clear.

Perhaps the most important and earliest Lower Palaeolithic locality reported from Iran is one in Khorasan, investigated in 1974 and 1975 (Ariai and Thibault 1975–77). Some sixty stone artifacts were found at several locations on the surface and in the alluvial deposits of the Kashafrud Basin some forty to one hundred kilometers east of Mashhad. A vast, shallow lake had existed here in late Pliocene times and was gradually filled in later. Presumably, human groups lived around the contracting lake and were responsible for the artifacts (both finished tools and waste flakes) found. The industry is basically composed of choppers and chopping tools made on quartzite and andesite cobbles whose ends had been intentionally chipped, but there are also smaller tools on flakes, including scrapers of several kinds, notched pieces, and a sort of knife (Fig. 4). It shows general resemblances to other "pebble-tool" industries found in the sub-Himalayan zone of India and Pakistan as well as to some in Soviet Central Asia, Africa and the Levant. No faunal or floral remains were found associated and this prevents us from saying anything about the subsistence of the people or the general nature of the environmental conditions. It is unfortunate that we cannot be more certain of the age of these Khorasan artifacts. The investigators tentatively placed the industry in the Lower Pleistocene, largely, one gathers, because the tools appear "archaic," and believed it is pre-Acheulian and at least 800,000 years old, perhaps contemporary with the late Oldowan in Africa. But there is an obvious danger of circular reasoning in using stone tools in this way to provide a chronology. While these claims may eventually be justified, at the moment we should maintain a reasonable skepticism and hope that better evidence—preferably in the form of a sealed site with preserved organic materials and a geologically datable context—will one day be discovered in the region.

Similar criticisms and hopes might be expressed about an industry described in recent years from inland Baluchistan and baptized the "Ladizian" (Hume 1976). These stone tools are found in open-air sites on two river systems, the Ladiz Rud and the Mashkid, on the Sarhadd plateau near the Pakistani frontier between Seistan and Makran. The sites allegedly represent workshops where raw materials were transformed into tools, and camps where the people lived; the scatters are claimed to be basically *in situ* on a series of ancient river terraces. On geological grounds, Hume has dated the Ladizian to a period beginning no later than the time of the penultimate European glaciation, the "Riss" in classical terminology, and ending during the equivalent of the last or "Würm" glaciation; that is, from the late Middle well into the Upper Pleistocene, a duration of at least

100,000 years. Later derivatives of the "Ladizian," suggests the author, would have survived even longer, into the Middle Palaeolithic of the region. The industry is described as part of the "Asian chopper-chopping tool complex" which is found widespread from Pakistan eastward. Quartzite was the preferred raw material, though chert and jasper were also used, and from the nodules the makers manufactured chopping tools, scrapers, knives, notched and pointed pieces, but no hand axes or cleavers (Fig. 5). No traces of faunal or floral remains were found, and the climatic and environmental backgrounds are completely unknown, but the investigator has suggested that it was basically a foraging economy emphasizing plant foods though some game such as onager, gazelle and ibex were taken by hunters who lived in a semi-arid environment somewhat moister than today and camped around natural springs. More recently similar artifacts have been reported in the Khash valley of the Sarhadd plateau (Marucheck 1976).

At the moment, just as with the Khorasan materials described above, it is difficult to evaluate the Ladizian. Unfortunately, Hume's attempt at a chronological framework based on the dating of local river terraces which were then correlated with glacial events in Europe is unacceptable, being founded on an outmoded idea of the European glacial sequence. The internal or relative chronology claimed for the development of the Ladizian through time must similarly be regarded with skepticism until more reassuring geological and geomorphological studies have been made of the fluvial system in the Sarhadd plateau. But the suggestion that the Ladizian represents a non-hand axe industry, very possibly of lower Palaeolithic age and related to the Soanian of Pakistan and India (to be discussed later), should not be dismissed out of hand. It is not out of the question, however, that many of the lithic pieces are merely natural products or of post-Palaeolithic age. The poor quality of the published illustrations adds to the uncertainty.

In the rest of Iran the Lower Palaeolithic evidence is scanty, is found mainly in the Zagros region, and is even more difficult to evaluate. Indeed the best evidence of all comes from just beyond the Iranian frontier at the site of Barda Balka in Iraqi Kurdistan, and the occurrences in western Iran might best be seen against the background of this site. Located in the Chemchemal valley on the western slopes of the Zagros, at an altitude of ca. 700 m., it was tested in 1951 but never extensively excavated (Wright and Howe 1951; Braidwood and Howe 1960). Apparently a spring had existed there in Pleistocene times. The artifacts are found in a formation of Upper Pleistocene river gravels between two silt layers, and seem

to be basically undisturbed apart from those eroded out on the surface. The industry includes choppers on limestone pebbles, many tools on flint flakes, nuclei from which the flakes were detached and, very interestingly, a small number of Acheulian-like hand axes of various types; some of the hand axes are miniatures. There are also remains of the animals that presumably were hunted and consumed by the people who made the stone tools, including elephant, rhinoceros, deer, sheep or goat, and especially an equid (onager). Judging by the presence of land snails, the climate at the time may not have been unlike the present one. Unfortunately for our understanding of this site, it is, like all the Lower Palaeolithic ones in the region, plagued by uncertainty about its age. It probably belongs, as the investigators believed, to the equivalent of the final phases of the last interglacial or to the beginning of the last glacial period that is, to somewhere around 100,000–70,000 years ago, but this is only a tentative correlation in the absence of further field work at the site.

Whatever its real age, what is interesting here is the apparent association of hand axes and pebble tools; further east, in Iran, this combination is rare or absent. Barda Balka thus lends some support, if the association is genuine, to the argument that the so-called chopper-chopping tool and hand axe industries are not always separate entities but perhaps variants (at times functional variants) of each other. Whether we should call the Barda Balka assemblages a late or "evolving" Lower Palaeolithic, or an early Middle Palaeolithic, or a regional hybrid created at the geographical boundary where the otherwise separate hand axe and pebble/flake tool traditions of the Lower Palaeolithic overlapped, is a problem that remains unresolved. There may be similar sites in the Caucasus mountains and Transcaucasia (Georgia, Azerbaijan, Armenia and South Ossetia), and traces elsewhere in Iraq. Perhaps the site of Pal Barik in the Hulailan valley of Luristan, where several small hand axes occur on the surface with chopping tools and flake tools (Fig.6), also belongs to this still undated tradition (Mortensen 1975), as may a surface find of an Acheulian-like hand axe near Kermanshah at Tepe Gakia (Braidwood 1960), and another hand axe in Azerbaijan (Singer and Wymer 1978). A study of the still undated stream terraces in eastern Azerbaijan east of lake Urmia, however, has yielded only artifacts of the general chopper/flake tool type without hand axes (Sadek-Kooros 1976), perhaps belonging to the category of tools described earlier in Khorasan and Baluchistan. One has the impression that if there were Acheulian peoples on the western, lower slopes of the Zagros, they penetrated only rarely into the higher zones or beyond and left few traces. To my knowledge, no artifacts that might be Lower Palaeolithic in age have yet been reported from the Caspian Lowlands (but see Note 8 for a possible occurrence at Hotu Cave), the Elburz range, the central deserts or the southern coast.

Thus the real nature of the Lower Palaeolithic of Iran eludes us. For the most part we can do little more than draw inferences about it based on the situation in better known regions of the Old World, and on what we suppose to have been the environmental circumstances in Iran at the time. We cannot make any firm statements about the time of arrival of the earliest inhabitants, the region or regions from which they came, or the biological types of hominids involved. The manners in which they exploited the physical environments and the nature of their settlement patterns are largely unknown. How much variability there was through time and space during the possibly long period of time represented, and how many lithic traditions were present, are other problems awaiting solution.

These are the kinds of problems, however, that should be addressed by prehistorians in the future if we are to have any sort of adequate understanding of the role of Iran in the global scheme of Lower Palaeolithic archaeology, particularly that of the Asian continent. To locate the desired sites, which preferably should be living sites sealed by later deposits and with preserved organic materials, in dateable contexts (and it must be mentioned that such *in situ* sites are rare throughout Asia), there should be more determined searches in zones in which filled-in basins with fine lacustrine or alluvial deposits occur. It is in these contexts, in some parts of Africa as well as the Levant, that the most informative sites have been found. Caves and rock shelters are also promising localities, especially for establishing stratigraphic details; and it is perhaps in such closed sites that the best likelihood exists for finding the skeletal remains of the Lower Palaeolithic populations, even though evidence from other parts of the world, suggests it is unlikely that any intentional human burials will be found at this early date.

V

The Middle Palaeolithic

With the second phase of the Iranian Palaeolithic we are on somewhat firmer ground. We now have a fair number of intact or sealed occupation sites in caves and rock-shelters, as well as open-air finds in the form of surface scatters and workshops on hilltops. The materials are better preserved, especially animal and in a few cases plant remains; and for the first time there is a human fossil as well. The chronology is more secure since this stage falls partially into the range of conventional radiocarbon dating. Stratified sites are known so that, in principle at least, the relative chronological relationship of assemblages to each other can be understood. We can even speak with slightly more authority about regional or functional variations in the stone industries. This period seems to represent the first intensive occupation of the Zagros region; whether this was true for the rest of the country remains to be seen.

Some twenty Middle Palaeolithic sites have been reported for Iran, exclusive of a number of isolated finds (Fig. 7). Most of them occur in the Zagros mountains, but some are known in other zones as well. However, the most important Middle Palaeolithic site for this region occurs not in Iran but just across the border in Iraqi Kurdistan; this, it will be recalled, is true also for the Lower Palaeolithic of the Zagros. The site of Shanidar Cave, in northern Iraq near the Turkish border on the Greater Zab river (a tributary of the Tigris), is the richest and most informative so far found and has yielded the only complete Middle Palaeolithic human skeletons known from Iraq or Iran. Although this site has not yet been published in full (see Solecki 1955, 1963, 1971), its wealth of data makes it an essential reference point for the examination of the Iranian sites in both the Middle and Upper Palaeolithic periods. While sites as rich are probably present in Iran also (e.g., perhaps Ghar-i-Khar at Bisitun, briefly tested by the writer in 1965), none has yet been excavated so extensively or has yielded such useful information as Shanidar.

The Iranian (like the Iraqi) sites occur in the form of sealed deposits in limestone caves and rock shelters, and as surface scatters on hilltops or in gravels. In the former group faunal remains are well preserved in the calcareous earth and for the first time we can speak with some confidence about the subsistence patterns; for the final phase of this period at least we can even reconstruct the general climate and physical environment in the Zagros with the aid of palaeobotany. Finally we can now be reasonably sure of the anatomical subspecies of man present in the Middle Palaeolithic: it was Neanderthal man. Indeed, there is even some suggestive evidence about his social and perhaps his spiritual life and ritual behavior, as will be discussed later.

We cannot say with precision when the Middle Palaeolithic began in Iran but, extrapolating from regions where the chronology is better established, we can place it sometime around 80,000–100,000 years ago. This was approximately when in higher latitudes, the last interglacial conditions were changing to cooler, damper ones. It is not clear what environmental changes occurred at this time in Iran, though we can suppose that temperatures dropped, arid or semiarid conditions prevailed in most of the land, the snowline descended, lakes expanded, the level of the Persian Gulf fell as did the sea level on the southern coast, and the forest cover was reduced except perhaps in refuge areas such as the Caspian zone. There were several fluctuations during this cold phase when "interstadial" pauses allowed somewhat more humid conditions and more forest cover, e.g., between ca. ?80,000–62,000 and 56,000–42,000 years ago (Farrand 1981). These pauses are not, however, well documented in Iran, or indeed anywhere in the Near East, in contrast to the well-known fluctuations in Europe during the last glacial period. At Shanidar Cave some attempts have been made at identifying these fluctuations from pollen and trace-element studies (Solecki and Leroi-Gourhan 1961) but the results are inconclusive. Only towards the close of the Middle Palaeolithic do we have specific information. The pollen in the cores obtained from Lake Zeribar in western Iran ca. 40,000 years ago (see Fig. 11) indicates colder and drier conditions than prevail today; a steppe or desert-steppe environment in the Zagros; the existence of a few oak, pistachio and maple trees; and few grasses but much steppe vegetation, such as *Artemisia* or wormwood shrub, dry grasses, etc. (van Zeist and Bottema 1977).

The fauna in this period seems, in the Zagros at least, to have been completely modern in type: goat, sheep, deer, onager, cattle, pig, and various carnivores. Elephants had apparently vanished, perhaps from the whole country, while rhinoceros are found only in a site in northeastern Iran. Perhaps few plant foods, at least tree and grass products, were available most of the time except in the warmer phases. The precise nature of subsistence strategies, particularly the seasonal adaptations; how these changed through time in adjusting to shifting environmental circumstances; and how much geographic variability there was in the subsistence patterns, are problems that remain for future research. There is now good evidence for the use of fire although we do not know how it was made or the precise functions it served—in the form of hearths in some of the caves; quite possibly it was known to some of the Lower Palaeolithic people as well but the archaeological evidence for this is still lacking in Iran, although well documented in other parts of the Old World.

Most but not all of the Middle Palaeolithic stone industries throughout the Near East can be classed as Mousterian. This is a broad and by no means uniform grouping of stone industries found from western Europe and northern Africa through the Near East, and extending at least some way into Central Asia and South Asia. In general—there are numerous variants—there is an emphasis on tools made on flakes, and the large implements such as hand axes, cleavers and pebble tools of earlier times have nearly disappeared. Scrapers, notched pieces, borers and some burins are the typical artifacts in the tool-kits. The Levallois method of special core preparation is frequently important, as it often was in the Acheulian tradition.[4] In Iran all known assemblages can probably be placed in this Mousterian category, and they resemble most closely what is called Typical Mousterian in Europe. Some variations can be noted, however; there may be significant differences between assemblages found in caves and those in open-air sites, though whether these differences are due to variations in the activities practiced in the two types of sites (possibly according to the season of occupation and the resources being exploited), to the kinds of lithic raw materials available, to the traditions of

distinct ethnic groupings, or to slow changes in the basic lithic technology accumulating through time, remains an open question as far as the Iranian Mousterian is concerned. Again, compared to the Levant region there is in the Middle Palaeolithic of Iran a markedly low emphasis on the Levallois method (which is similarly neglected, apparently, in the local Lower Palaeolithic). It is present but rare in the Zagros cave sites, but may be more frequent in open-air sites in Khuzistan and southern Iraq.[5] Whether the discrepancies in its frequency are governed simply by technological opportunism (the Levallois method is generally more popular when large nodules of stone are present), or whether the explanation lies in the realm of cultural preferences, remains to be seen. This question, and the question of typological variability in the Mousterian as a whole, have been much discussed in recent years by prehistorians working in Europe and the Levant area, with several very distinct attempts at explanation emerging. There is no room to discuss this subject in the present essay, except to mention that so far the Iranian archaeological materials have been too scanty and too superficially studied to contribute to the eventual solution of the problem.

It is not known whether there was direct local continuity from the Lower to the Middle Palaeolithic, whether the Mousterian was introduced from outside the Iran-Iraq region, or whether a combination of both mechanisms was at work. (In this respect, of course, prehistorians of Iran are not much worse off than those on other continents where much the same ambiguity exists.) The presence of a few small hand axes in occasional Middle Palaeolithic sites of the Zagros, such as Hazer Merd in Iraq, might be used as evidence of local evolution from some earlier industrial tradition where hand axes occur with flake tools, as Barda Balka allegedly illustrates—unless, of

---

4. The Levallois method (or, more accurately, methods) of stone-working involves the careful removal of pieces from the core with the purpose of sculpting a blank (flake, blade, or point) of predetermined form which can then be detached with its basic shape and size already designed and requiring little or no modification. Generally only one or a few such blanks are removed from a single core. This method appears in the Lower Palaeolithic (Acheulian), and continues in the Middle Palaeolithic, but tends to be rare or absent thereafter. It is common in Europe, Africa and the Levant, but is less frequent further east, in Mesopotamia, Iran, and the Indian subcontinent, while it is virtually unknown in the Far East. It is not clear if it was present in Iran in the Lower Palaeolithic.

5. Judging by published accounts and personal inspection, the Levallois method is present with certainty in only six Iranian sites (Gar Kobeh, Hunter's Cave at Bisitun, Ghar Villa, Humian, Jahrom, and an unnamed site on the Deh Luran Plain in Khuzistan), and may be present in three more (Warwasi, Site 16 near Harsin, and D. G. 9 in upland Khuzistan).

course, Barda Balka is itself an early form of Middle Palaeolithic. But the possibility of diffusion of techniques and even people from some outside region—from the Syro-Palestine area, from the Caucasus region (which is rather similar to the Zagros in topography, climate and resources, factors that may have favored infiltration), or from Central Asia (Turkmenistan, Uzbekistan, Kazakhstan, Tadjikistan)—cannot be excluded. One argument that might be advanced in favor of a basically indigenous development in the Zagros region turns on the infrequency of the Levallois method of stone-working in both the Lower and Middle Palaeolithic, in contrast to the situation in most of the Levant; that is, a long-lasting regional technological tradition perhaps existed in this area and possibly in the entire Iran-Iraq sector of the Near East, indicating a high degree of continuity and relatively weak external contacts or stimulation from the west. Whether this suggestion has any merit can only be determined by future field work.

Nor can we speak with much greater confidence about the age of the earliest Mousterian in Iran or its subsequent patterns of development. It has been claimed on climatic grounds (McBurney 1964) that the site of Ké-Aram I in Mazandaran dates to the last interglacial or to an early last-glacial interstadial (the presence of a fauna suggesting forest conditions and climate much like the present one), while the base of the Mousterian at Shanidar Cave in Iraq has been estimated at ca. 100,000 years (Solecki 1963). In truth these are only guesses, though not altogether improbable ones; by analogy with Europe and the Levant area the earliest Mousterian is considerably beyond the range of the traditional radiocarbon dating method and it has not been linked to any datable geological deposits in Iran or Iraq.

The internal development within the Mousterian tradition also remains unclear since, until the end of the sequence at least, it is impossible to arrange the sites studied in any meaningful order; and few sites with multiple levels are known. (This difficulty in finding trends in the Mousterian is, however, a common problem elsewhere in Eurasia.) Thus we cannot say whether, as several authors have speculated, the earliest Mousterian was a "generalized" and relatively crude industry represented perhaps by surface scatters found in the Zagros ranges and predating the technically more "advanced" industries found in the caves and rock-shelters of the same area; or whether in fact the two types are contemporaneous and perhaps only functional variants (see Braidwood and Howe 1960:60–61). At the other end we cannot really be sure just when the Mousterian terminated; it seems to disappear about or shortly after 40,000 B. C., in the Zagros at least. Whether it lingered on elsewhere in Iran is unknown.[6] Thus a duration of

some 50,000 or 60,000 years would be a reasonable estimate, and within that respectable span of time much may have happened in the way of trends and tendencies that our present one-dimensional view of the materials prevents us from observing and understanding.

On the whole there is considerable uniformity among the artifacts throughout the Zagros and the rest of Iran. As mentioned earlier, hand axes are rare and small and the Levallois method only sporadically present. There is strong emphasis on points (possibly used in some cases as tips for stabbing or throwing spears) and side scrapers (perhaps employed in preparing animal hides at times), though there is not a very wide range of types represented. Various kinds of perforators, notched and denticulated pieces, and a few burins also occur. One distinct feature is the technological tendency to produce small, thick, narrow implements rather than the large, thin, wide ones frequent in the Levant and there associated with the Levallois method of flaking. All in all the Mousterian industry of Iran and Iraq seems to be a distinct regional variant within western Asia. Tools made on bone or antler are rare, being limited to bone "compressors" presumably used in flaking stone.

The sites described are widely and very unevenly distributed. Most of those known occur in the Zagros mountains from Azerbaijan to Fars and perhaps northeastern Khuzistan, with the densest concentrations found in Luristan and Kurdistan. Only one is reported in Mazandaran, one in Khorasan, and a few in Khuzistan. In the interior of the country there is a possibly Mousterian piece reported from the Tehran Plain, and another from Kerman. No Mousterian is yet described from Baluchistan, the homeland of the "Ladizian." In reality it is difficult to say just how many genuine sites we are talking about; there are at least sixteen cave or rock-shelter sites, and perhaps four open-air scatters that may represent living and factory sites, while the rest are isolated pieces found on the surface where they may have been dropped by the original users or transported by water action from elsewhere.

Probably the cluster of sites near Khoramabad in Luristan is the best documented and most informative. Some seventeen small caves and rock-shelters with Mousterian and Upper Palaeolithic occupations are found in a small valley just below 1,200 m. elevation, with abundant springs of water nearby. Some

---

6. It has been argued that Neanderthal man survived later in the isolated fastnesses of the Zagros mountains than in the Levant region of western Asia or in Europe. Thus Coon (1957:126) suggested in his usual colorful way that the Hunter's Cave at Bisitun, which he had excavated, was a "rustic refuge inhabited by already outmoded types of humanity." This is not impossible, but it is a question best left open at present.

of these were investigated in 1963 and 1965 (Hole and Flannery 1967). The three tested are Kunji Cave (later re-excavated by Speth—see Speth 1971—and found to be much disturbed); Gar Arjeneh rock-shelter; and Ghamari Cave. The Mousterian here may be a late variant; the authors tentatively place it between 50,000 and 38,000 B. C. Several radiocarbon determinations from Kunji Cave gave dates "older than 40,000 years before the present." The stone industry is composed mainly of flake tools featuring side scrapers, unifacial triangular points, a few burins and borers, and no Levallois method. Not much is known about the subsistence patterns practiced, since faunal remains are poorly preserved, but onagers were hunted by the inhabitants of Kunji Cave at least, and we might expect that goat, sheep, red deer, cattle, and pig were also being exploited in what seems to have been a well-endowed environment. To what extent these occupations were seasonal is unknown as yet. However, in another Mousterian site in Luristan, in the Kuh-i Dasht area near Sarsahun mountain, there is some evidence of seasonal activities. A rock-shelter called Humian was investigated in 1969 (McBurney 1970; Bewley 1984). It is located at ca. 2,000 m. above sea level and is thus among the highest Palaeolithic sites in the Near East. The Mousterian here may represent a specialized montane type of Mousterian in an environment in which only summer occupation was possible; today the shelter is filled with snow in winter, and in the late Pleistocene winter conditions were probably even more severe. It is likely the site was frequented in summer to hunt ibex or goat and sheep that migrated up from the plains; possibly the inhabitants were related in some way to those at Khorramabad and at another cluster of Luristan sites in the Hulailan valley, on the Saimarreh river. Here, at an altitude of ca. 930 m., Mortensen located at least seven Mousterian sites near the Acheulian site of Pal Barik already mentioned. Two of the Mousterian sites are rock-shelters (Ghar Villa, Ghar Huchi) while the other five are surface scatters of worked flints. The stone tools resemble those at Khorramabad but the Levallois method is present (Fig. 8). Possibly—though this is not clear—the Hulailan sites represent seasonal occupations by hunting parties (Mortensen 1974a:15; 1974b; 1975).

About seventy to eighty kilometers northward and at a higher altitude than the Hulailan valley (ca. 1,300–1,400 m.) is another group of Middle Palaeolithic sites on the edge of the Kermanshah plain and near Bisitun and Harsin. The best known is the Warwasi rock-shelter just outside Kermanshah in the Tang-i Kenesht, which has Mousterian stratified beneath several Upper Palaeolithic horizons. It was partially excavated in 1959–60 by B. Howe as part of R. J. Braidwood's research programme in this area

(Braidwood 1960). The stone industry seems to be the orthodox Zagros Mousterian. The faunal remains have been carefully studied and they suggest that the main game animal was the onager, but that red deer, cattle, goat and sheep also were killed. There is some evidence that the shelter, which is a small one, served more as an overnight camp site for hunters tracking onagers than as a base camp or butchering site, and that this was true in Upper Palaeolithic times as well (Turnbull 1975). Less is known about the other Mousterian sites in the area (Gar Kobeh near Kermanshah and Kal-i-Daoud in the Sar-i-Pol valley), but the industry is apparently the same. About thirty-five kilometers away is the first Mousterian site excavated in Iran, the Hunter's Cave at Bisitun overlooking the famous spring and very near Darius' inscription. It was completely excavated by Coon in 1949, and is the only excavated Palaeolithic site in Iran that has been published in detail in a monograph (Coon 1951). The industry here is much like that at Warwasi, being well made with some Levallois element present. Judging by the faunal remains, red deer were the principal game, followed by an equid (probably an onager) and some gazelle, but oddly enough, no sheep or goat. Perhaps it was less a living site (there are no hearths and the site is small, really a rock-shelter rather than a true cave) than a place to butcher game that came to drink at the spring gushing from the base of Bisitun rock; however, Coon suggested, rather improbably, that it may also have served the Mousterian people as a kind of shrine where they cached their finer artifacts. From here, too, came a fragment of a human arm bone described by Coon as "Neanderthaloid." Perhaps the nearby site of Ghar-i-Khar, tested by the writer in 1965 (Young and Smith 1966) was a true living place for the Mousterian inhabitants of the Bisitun area. It is a long and deep cave in the cliff high above the valley floor, and the Mousterian level—barely touched in the narrow test pit dug—is surmounted by about two meters of Upper Palaeolithic deposits; the industry features thick blades and flakes with scrapers. No Levallois element was found, possibly because the sample was small. In 1977 the writer and P. Mortensen discovered near Harsin a very large open-air site (no. 16 in our survey) on a hillside adjacent to chert and flint outcrops; it may well have been a quarry site where tools were roughed out during many prehistoric periods. Some pieces collected at random here look Mousterian-like although an earlier age cannot be excluded. Not far away, in a cavity (called site 17) in a cliff near Harsin we collected a small number of flint implements on the surface including a characteristic Mousterian side-scraper. Finally, in a gravel deposit a meter beneath the early Neolithic site of Ganj Dareh, we found flint artifacts that may be Middle Palaeolithic (Smith 1975).

In the northern and southern Zagros evidence for Middle Palaeolithic occupations is rather sparse. In Fars in 1969 Sumner discovered at Jahrom, southeast of Shiraz near the Persian Gulf, a huge surface site that seems to be a quarry or factory site, with scrapers, burins, notched pieces and denticulated pieces, but no points. It is possibly a Middle Palaeolithic variant that differs in some respects from the Mousterian in the Central Zagros (Piperno 1972), although Hume (1976:250) suggests it may be related to the Ladizian. A few other surface finds in Fars near Shiraz (Field 1939) and in the Kur river basin (Sumner 1980) are less informative. Several Mousterian-like pieces are also reported at Tal-i Iblis in Kerman (Caldwell 1967). Isolated surface finds have been made in northeastern Khuzistan in the Dasht-e-Gol, at Iveh, and on the Izeh plain (Wright 1979). There are Middle Palaeolithic surface sites in lowland Khuzistan in both Iraq and Iran, apparently, but little is known about the kinds of occupation they represent or the artifacts they contain; one such site near the Deh Luran plain has Levallois cores (Hole and Flannery 1967).

At the northern end of the Zagros Coon in 1949 explored a cave called Tamtama in Azerbaijan, near Urmiyeh (formerly Rezaiyeh). The few artifacts are amorphous typologically, but may be Mousterian. At an altitude of ca. 1,500 m., it was probably uninhabitable in winter, so it was probably a warm weather site used by people who hunted red deer and other game (Coon 1951).

The rest of northern Iran is nearly blank as far as any recognizably Middle Palaeolithic is concerned. A few "Mousterian-type" implements are reported from the alluvium on the Tehran plain (Rieben 1955), but to my knowledge only one site is known from the Elburz mountains and nothing from the central basins north of Kerman. However, the large cave in Mazandaran called Ké-Aram I, at the eastern end of the Elburz near the Soviet frontier, contains an industry featuring diminutive tools said to be essentially similar to the Mousterian ones of the Zagros (McBurney 1964). The animals hunted here—cattle, red deer, even rhinoceros— allegedly reflect forest conditions and so a modern-type of climate, perhaps dating to the last interglacial period or to a warm phase of the last glacial, according to the excavator. However, this claim should be regarded with some reserve until it can be confirmed by means other than faunal remains alone. Finally, at Khunik Cave in Khorasan at Birjand, near the Afghan frontier, Coon in 1949 found Mousterian artifacts in a disturbed context (Coon 1957). Nothing has yet been reported from inland Baluchistan, although Hume (1976) argues that derivatives of his "Ladizian" survived late in this region. Middle Palaeolithic sites are known in

Afghanistan, however. On the Makran coast some surface finds of possibly Middle Palaeolithic pieces including Levallois flakes and cores, chopping tools and perhaps denticulated pieces have been reported at several localities, but little more than this can be said (Vita-Finzi and Copeland 1980).

The Middle Palaeolithic human skeletal material from Iran, limited as it is to a single arm bone fragment from Hunter's Cave at Bisitun, does not permit us to say much about the biological side of the inhabitants.[7] Fortunately, however, we have from another source a very good idea of the physical type responsible for part if not all of the Mousterian occurrences in the Zagros. This is because the earliest occupation (Level D) at Shanidar Cave in northern Iraq has yielded nine complete or partial skeletons, all of Neanderthal type, and ranging in age from about one to fifty years. So far, no more advanced anatomical type has been found with the Middle Palaeolithic of Iran or Iraq, although there seems to have been a more developed form, generally considered a robust variant of modern man, *Homo sapiens*, associated with the Mousterian in some Levant sites such as Jebel Qafzeh and Skhul in Israel. The Shanidar evidence suggests that the population was essentially "classic" Neanderthal in type, with large cranial capacities, massive faces with fairly large brow ridges, receding chins and heavy bodies (Trinkaus 1983). Even more interesting is the behavioral evidence (Solecki 1971). Not only were the dead intentionally buried, but in one case (Shanidar skeleton 4) the body was apparently ritually covered with summer flowers whose pollen is preserved in the earth around the burial. In another case (Shanidar 1), a male whose right arm had been amputated below the elbow in youth following paralysis survived until about forty years of age—a remarkable feat for a member of a hunting-gathering group living in a severe environment, and perhaps the reflection of a close-knit community spirit that compensated for his infirmity. It is also claimed that artificial cranial deformation was practiced. Finally, healed fractures and lesions occurring on most of the adult skeletons, and in one case signs of a stab wound between the ribs, suggest a certain amount of physical violence in the community (Trinkus 1983). Whether some of the traumas were incurred in hunting accidents and falls, or whether they reflect interpersonal or intergroup conflict, is unsettled. Clearly, however, like their contempor-

---

7. A recent re-examination of the "Neanderthaloid" upper incisor from Hunter's Cave at Bisitun reveals that it is from a bovid, while the femur from Tamtama Cave belongs to a deer. The Hunter's Cave radius is human but it is not possible to say whether it is Neanderthal or modern *Homo sapiens*. (Information from Nancy Minugh-Purvis, University of Pennsylvania)

aries in Europe, the Shanidar people lived rough, even dangerous lives.

It is very likely that the same biological and behavioral patterns characterized the Middle Palaeolithic population in Iran, at least in the Zagros—indeed, we should remember that the Zagros populations probably flowed through the mountains fairly freely. It is uncertain whether these Neanderthals evolved locally from a preceding and more archaic population or migrated to the region; this question remains unresolved for the Levant area as well. Similarly, we cannot say whether these Neanderthals survived unchanged to the close of the Middle Palaeolithic and even later, or had already been replaced by (or developed into) a fully modern form of *Homo sapiens* before the Mousterian ended. The latest skeleton dated by radiocarbon at Shanidar Cave is placed at ca. 44,000 B. C.; after that and until the beginning of Holocene times after ca. 9,000 B. C. we face a nearly complete blank in Iran and Iraq as far as human skeletons are concerned. This gap is one of the most important to be closed by future field work, or to be explained if it persists in the archaeological record.

VI

The Upper Palaeolithic and "Epipalaeolithic"

We might expect a remarkable improvement in our archaeological knowledge of Iran as we approach recent times; but this is not so. Later Palaeolithic sites are more numerous but once again are mainly found in the Zagros (Figs. 9, 10). In addition, as just mentioned, in at least one respect much less is known than for the Middle Palaeolithic in the Zagros region, for human skeletal materials are less abundant; this is true in the Levant as well

We do, however, at least have a good view for the first time of the climate and environmental conditions in western Iran thanks to the work of palynologists (van Zeist and Bottema 1977, 1982), and their interpretations can, with the appropriate caution, be extended to areas further away (see Fig.11). At about 40,000 years ago the climate was cool and dry, probably somewhat more so than in late Mousterian times judging by the decreasing number of trees, and certainly colder and much drier than at present. This situation grew even more severe after ca. 30,000 B. C. and lasted until ca. 12,000 B. C., when the upland zones were treeless and only tamarisk and willow (but no oak or pistachio) were found in the sheltered valleys. Then, at about 12,000 B C., a shift occurred to considerably higher temperatures and perhaps more precipitation, though the increasing warmth meant that environmental conditions remained arid. Temperatures reached their maximum between ca. 10,000; and 9,000 B. C. (the equivalent of the Allerod warm phase in Europe) and later decreased somewhat. Trees began spreading in the final phase of the Pleistocene, about 9,000 B. C.—mainly pistachio, with little oak— and *Artemisia* decreased. It is at about this time, in the early Holocene, that we see the last recognizable traces of true hunters and gatherers in the archaeological record in the Zagros, although they probably continued along the Caspian foreshore and very possibly in the eastern half of Iran until considerably later. Archaeologically recognizable evidence for attempts at food production also appears at this time, as a forest-steppe environment replaced

the desert-steppe one of the late Pleistocene. In other words, we should envisage the Upper Palaeolithic/ Epipalaeolithic climate and physical background as even more severe, except at the very end, than in at least some parts of the Middle Palaeolithic. The same is true, of course, for much of the Upper Palaeolithic elsewhere, including Europe. Whether some of the new features present in the cultural remains represent adaptations to these austere conditions we cannot say; indeed, far from proposing a Toynbeean "response" to challenging circumstances, we are by no means sure that life in general was then more difficult than before, particularly as far as the hunting of game animals was concerned. This again is a problem to be attacked by future prehistorians and their colleagues in the natural sciences. Up to now we cannot point with any confidence to either techno-typological changes in the stone tools or to shifts in settlement patterns and resource exploitation methods that might reflect human adaptations to the new situations throughout the approximately thirty thousand years of the Upper Palaeolithic and Epipalaeolithic in Iran.

To date we find no traces in Iran or Iraq of an older lithic tradition emphasizing blades and "advanced" tool types that long preceded the true Upper Palaeolithic and that was perhaps ancestral to it. In the Levant area there is a somewhat ambiguous industry variously called "Pre-Aurignacian or "Amudian" that occurs in a late Lower or early Middle Palaeolithic context, probably considerably before 50,000 B. C., and even perhaps as old as 100,000 years ago. It features a modern-looking tool kit including burins and end scrapers made on somewhat robust blades (Garrod and Kirkbride 1961; Bordes 1977). For some prehistorians this reflects a cultural intrusion into the Middle Palaeolithic and particularly the Mousterian world of the Levant from somewhere outside; others, however, prefer to see it as some kind of functional or technological variant of local industries, of purely indigenous origin. Whichever explanation is preferred, it remains a fact that further east we have no suggestion of such a phenomenon. Whether this discrepancy is an accident of field research, or genuinely reflects a situation of less technological diversity and a different developmental process in the Lower and Middle Palaeolithic of Iran and Iraq, remains to be seen. If the later is true, then there are some interesting questions to be asked about the reasons for this difference between the western and eastern zones of Southwest Asia.

Nor can we say whether the local Mousterian of Iran and Iraq evolved directly into the local Upper Palaeolithic, since no genuine cases of transition from one to the other have been found. (Such "transitions" are claimed in the Levant and Europe, perhaps correctly.) In some sites, such as Gar Arjeneh near Khorramabad, Warwasi near Kermanshah and Ghar-i-Khar at Bisitun, there are no stratigraphic hiatuses between the Middle and Upper Palaeolithic occupations, and this strengthens the argument for a gradual transition between Mousterian and Baradostian. There is, it might be mentioned, an argument based on negative evidence supporting some degree of continuity in the lithic tradition from the Middle to the Upper Palaeolithic in the Zagros. As already mentioned, the Levallois method of stone working is very feebly represented in the Middle Palaeolithic here and seems completely absent in the Upper Palaeolithic. On the other hand, in the Levant where the Levallois method is important in the Middle Palaeolithic it is also apparently present well into the local Upper Palaeolithic sequence (unless artifical mixing of deposits is responsible). One might, therefore, argue that in both regions of Southwest Asia there was a certain degree of technological continuity between the two stages, and that this suggests some degree of continuity in other aspects of the cultural traditions. But whether this postulated continuity in the Zagros reflects the momentum of an ancestral lithic tradition functioning in a somewhat isolated region without important external influences, or represents a persistent cultural adaptation to the peculiarities of life in this region across the "stages" created by the archaeologist, or is a combination of both, is a topic that awaits more serious investigation.

At any rate, the old hypothesis that the Upper Palaeolithic cultures of Eurasia were born in some remote Shangri-la on the Iranian plateau—as suggested by Garrod (1938) and later pursued by McBurney (1964)—has not yet found any empirical support. (This archaeological perspective, incidentally, seems to have had its counterpart among some students of human biological evolution; thus the geographer Huntington [1938:435] argued ingeniously that it was on the Iranian plateau, and more specifically in Baluchistan and southern Iran, that *Homo sapiens sapiens* developed between 30,000 and 60,000 years ago because climatic conditions then were more humid and hence more suitable for man than in any other part of Asia.) McBurney concluded after his fruitless search for an ancestral Upper Palaeolithic industry that Iran is "more likely to have been an area of passage than the ultimate homeland of the earliest Upper Palaeolithic" (1964:398)—a conclusion that Coon also had reached some years earlier (Coon 1957:127). If so, then we might expect that Iran would throw considerable light on the origins of the Upper Palaeolithic industries now known in Central Asia, Afghanistan, and the Indian subcontinent. How far these expectations are justifiable will be discussed later. For the moment we shall examine and try to understand the Iranian Upper Palaeolithic within its own context.

One of the characteristics of the later Palaeolithic as a general prehistoric stage of all Eurasia is that in a much shorter period of time (about 30,000 years probably), it appears to present much more diversity than does the Middle Palaeolithic. The more pronounced degree of cultural change and differentiation now evident suggests a greater capacity, or tolerance, for innovation than in earlier times. Prehistorians find it easier to identify many more Upper Palaeolithic/Epipalaeolithic "cultures" because the great number of artifactual innovations and variability seem to cluster more neatly and predictably. In other words, strong patterning is evident in the archaeological record. This may be connected to another typical feature, regionalism: although a great deal more of the habitable world was occupied in Upper Palaeolithic and Epipalaeolithic times than in the Middle Palaeolithic, there seems to be by and large a decrease in the geological range of the individual cultures as compared with the Middle Palaeolithic. Local groups are now more specialized and distinct from each other for reasons which are no doubt in part rooted in ecological and economic factors, but probably have other causes as well. The diversity may be to some degree linked to conscious or subconscious inclinations to maintain ethnic idenities in a world where neighbors were more numerous than before and where groups impinged on each other more frequently and intensively. At any rate, for the first time we can now subdivide one of the three major Palaeolithic stages in Iran into at least two distinct artifactual groupings which have temporal if not spatial distinctiveness. The first of these is called the Baradostian, and the second the Zarzian. They are found only in the Zagros, to our knowledge, more particularly in the northern and central Zagros. The situation in other parts of Iran is far less clear.

Even in the Zagros, the only part of the country where the Upper Palaeolithic and Epipalaeolithic are found in any quantity, we know relatively little about it. Still unsettled are the problems of the internal chronologies of the Baradostian and the Zarzian, how the two industries were related to each other in a broad developmental scheme, and their relationships to phenomena in other areas. They are known almost entirely from cave and rock-shelter sites, apart from a few surface scatters in the open, so we cannot say much about the different types of settlements that may have been present at any one time. Elsewhere in the Old World by this time fairly large open-air sites with huts are known, sometimes as seasonal supplements to rock-shelter or cave sites. Nothing of this kind is yet reported from the Zagros or other parts of Iran. Were the Upper Palaeolithic peoples more successful than their predecessors at surviving in the cold and snowy mountains during winter when most high caves were uninhabitable, by erecting artificial shelters, with more efficient heating methods, and using more cold-resistant clothing? Was there a pattern of seasonal movement to and from the more habitable lowlands? We do not know, nor can we say anything definite about any improvements there may have been in their subsistence techniques and technology. As for possible changes in the nature of the social organization, some prehistorians suggest that the Upper Palaeolithic groupings tended to be larger and both more sedentary and more far-ranging in their tactics of exploitation of resources, with a higher level of collaboration and specialized work teams. There may well have been some such shifts in organization, but the Iranian evidence is mute on this point. For ritual or religious behavior there is nearly a complete blank. Extrapolating from what has been observed among modern hunter-gatherers, and from what is deduced for other Upper Palaeolithic societies elsewhere, we might expect that the Iranian representatives sometimes assembled, perhaps seasonally, in larger aggregates for social and ritual purposes. It is not easy, however, to recognize such meeting places archaeologically. So far we know of no instances of art in the Zagros such as paintings, engravings, or sculptures on rock walls or in stone, bone or antler, and the closest thing may be the occasional drilled or polished pebbles coated with ochre in the late Baradostian, and a painted pebble in the Caspian Epipalaeolithic. Beads, pendants, and other objects of personal adornment are rare, as they are for that matter in all Near Eastern sites.

One of the possibilities we must face is that the terms Baradostian and Zarzian are too inclusive and general, and so mask too much diversity. They have never been clearly defined in the literature, and there is a temptation to drop each newly-discovered lithic assemblage into one or the other of these categories without adequate consideration, often on the basis of

a few "typical" artifacts. In other parts of the Old World, and even elsewhere in the Near East, prehistorians are learning how much more complex the Upper Palaeolithic is than we used to think. In the Levant, for instance, it is now recognized that such categories as "Aurignacian" or "Kebaran" are too broad and disguise important chronological and regional variants to which some investigators, indeed, now prefer to ascribe independent taxonomic status. It may very well be that the late Palaeolithic of the Zagros will turn out to be equally complex and varible, and that further study will show the Baradostian-Zarzian dichotomy to be an oversimplified and inadequate description. Until then, however, we must work within the established framework which appears, superficially at least, to reflect considerably less cultural volatility than existed elsewhere.

The Baradostian was christened by Solecki after his investigations at Shanidar Cave, in the Baradost mountains of northern Iraq. There is some evidence that this industry is one of the earliest Upper Palaeolithic manifestations known anywhere. If the radiocarbon determinations from level C at Shanidar Cave and from Yafteh Cave near Khorramabad are correct, then it was in existence in these sites by 33,000 B. C. and 36,000 B. C. respectively, and perhaps even before 38,000 B. C. This would make its appearance in the Zagros about contemporaneous with the earliest Upper Palaeolithic of the Levant as known in Lebanon and the Negev desert. So far the Baradostian is securely known from only six sites—five in Iran and one in Iraq. It was first defined in 1955 at Shanidar Cave where it succeeds the Mousterian (Solecki 1955,1963). It is, parenthetically, an interesting thought that had Coon dug Ghar-i-Khar, near Bisitun, in 1949 as he originally planned, instead of the nearby Hunter's Cave (Coon 1957:91–2), this industry might today be known as the "Bisitunian" or bear some other Iranian designation. So far there have been only two formal attempts to apply Iranian names to Palaeolithic industries—the "Ladizian" and the "Mazandaranian"; but the latter term, coined to describe a stone industry on the Caspian shore (Dupree 1952) has not caught on.

The Baradostian is essentially an industry made on blades, including some microblades (Fig. 12). Typologically it is rather simple and restricted; it is dominated by burins of various types and scrapers on flakes including some carinated (keel-shaped) ones, many notched blades, and a delicate elongated piece called the Arjeneh or Font-Yves point which is perhaps a substitute for the Mousterian point of earlier times. There is apparently no use of the Levallois method. There are also heavier implements such as picks, choppers and grinding stones, and some very small retouched bladelets. Bone tools are rare and simple, limited to a few points or awls. No doubt this general assemblage changed qualitatively and quantitatively through what seems to have been a duration of many thousands of years, but so far it has not been possible to subdivide it chronologically with certainty. On the basis of the Khorramabad evidence Hole and Flannery (1967) saw two phases: an early Baradostian (38,000 B. C.–30,000 B. C.), and a late Baradostian (30,000 B. C.–20,000 B. C.), with a progressive reduction in size of the implements and an increase in the microlithic element. This requires confirmation at other sites.

If we are reasonably sure of the beginning of the Baradostian, we are far less so about its end. There are at least twenty-two radiocarbon determinations available, all from Shanidar and Yafteh Caves, which range from ca. 38,000 B. C. or older to ca. 19,000 B. C. (although no dates after ca. 25,000 B. C. are considered reliable). Thus we cannot really say how late the Baradostian survived in the Zagros, or whether it lasted later in some areas, e.g., the lowlands, than elsewhere. It is possible that some sites such as Shanidar Cave were abandoned between ca. 26,000 B. C. and 12,000 B. C. when, it will be recalled, the climate in the Zagros was at its coldest and driest, but of course occupations may have persisted in other Zagros sites; much depended on local conditions. As before, we do not know how much seasonal movement there may have been between altitudinal zones.

Apparently the same food animals were being hunted as in the Mousterian (goat, sheep, red deer, cattle, onager), and it would be interesting to know whether the proportions of species were the same as before, whether the stalking and killing techniques were unchanged, and whether the hunting technology had now improved with the introduction of such aids as spear-throwers, or even bows and arrows as the smaller stone points and bladelets may indicate. These would certainly be advantageous in hunting ferocious animals, such as wild boar and cattle. Again, were plant foods very important in the diet? Cereals, even if present in some very sheltered zones, were probably insignificant, but some vegetable products such as roots, bulbs and sprouts may have been used. However, the occasional grinding stones were more likely to have been used for pounding ochre than for serious food preparation, and a single flint blade with "sickle sheen" on its edge found in the Baradostian of Ghar-i-Khar may have no connection with subsistence. Perhaps as has been suggested (Hole and Flannery 1967) the basic settlement pattern involved occupying a large base camp for some length of time, with hunters working out from it to secure game and establishing temporary butchering or transit sites which would of course leave comparatively fewer ar-

chaeological remains; and shifting the base camp periodically as game became scarce in proportion to the effort required to forage for it. But, again, this simple settlement model needs far more study and testing before it can be accepted literally.

The northernmost Baradostian sites found in Iran are located in Kermanshah District. Ghar-i-Khar at Bisitun has about one meter of Baradostian deposits sandwiched between deposits containing Mousterian and Zarzian artifacts (Young and Smith 1966). Just outside the city of Kermanshah at Warwasi rockshelter the Baradostian occurs in the same stratigraphic sequence as at Ghar-i-Khar and Shanidar Cave, and just as in the Mousterian the faunal materials suggest it was a lookout spot to which hunters of onager and, to a lesser extent, of goat, sheep, and cattle made brief, sporadic visits (Turnbull 1975). There may be some Baradostian in the Hulailan valley of Luristan among the fifteen "Upper Palaeolithic" sites surveyed, but this is not certain (P. Mortensen, personal communication 3.23.1981). A statement that at the high cave of Bardé Spid I in Luristan near Sarahun an "undiagnosed blade industry" occurs between the Mousterian and the Neolithic (McBurney 1970) has now been withdrawn (Bewley 1984). We are on firmer ground with the sites around Khorramabad—Yafteh Cave, Gar Arjeneh, Pa Sangar—where the stone industry is described as similar to that at Shanidar and Warwasi (Hole and Flannery 1967). At Yafteh Cave a series of radiocarbon determinations was obtained ranging from ca. 38,000–33,000 B. C. to at least 29,000 B. C., and perhaps as late as ca. 25,000 B. C. Wild goat seems to have been the principal game. Ochre was used fairly often, perhaps for body decoration, and some pebbles were drilled and polished for (it is presumed) personal ornaments. At nearby Pa Sangar two large salt-water scallop shells suggest distant contacts, whether by exchange or physical migration. Some fragments of human bone covered with ochre were found apparently at one of the sites (Hole and Flannery 1967).

Further south, in Fars, evidence for the Baradostian becomes amorphous. It probably occurs at the cave of Shekaft-i Ghād-i Barmi-i Shur, on Lake Maharlu near Shiraz, judging by surface collections (Piperno 1974). It may be present too on the shore of Lake Tashk, also in Fars (Krinsley 1970:224). There is some kind of Upper Palaeolithic, not yet defined, at Eshkaft-i Gavi Cave near the Kur river (Sumner 1980). While it is by no means unlikely that these occurrences are Baradostian, we need more information, particularly from excavations, before a definite determination can be made. To my knowledge no Baradostian site has yet been reported from Khuzistan, although Wright (1979) reports six possibly

"Upper Palaeolithic" sites on the Izeh plain in the Zagros zones of Iraq; nor has a Baradostian site been reported in Iran east of the Zagros. In the non-mountainous regions settlements would have been in the open with, at least in the colder months, the need for some kind of artificial shelter such as tents or huts. Nothing of this kind is yet known.

Before leaving the Baradostian, something might be added about its geographical distribution in Iran (and Iraq), and its possible significance in terms of human adaptation. In both countries we are faced with a somewhat anomalous situation. The Mousterian, as already mentioned, is fairly widespread, especially in Iran, where it is found from the central Zagros to, albeit sparsely, the Caspian shore and the Afghan border. The early Upper Palaeolithic that immediately follows it—the Baradostian—seems to have a much more restricted distribution in Iran, having been found so far only in the western part of the country. Yet the Upper Palaeolithic, as a cultural stage, is traditionally seen as the product of people with greater adaptive powers, who were more expansive geographically with a tendency to fill all zones suitable for hunters and gatherers and to exploit the available resources more intensively and efficiently than did those of the Middle Palaeolithic. On present evidence this was not the case in Iran. We can offer various attempts at explanation. Environmental factors outside the Zagros and its slopes may now have hindered settlement. The Baradostian and its contemporaries (if there were any) may have been less adaptable to life on the Iranian plateau than were the Middle Palaeolithic groups, particularly if the climatic conditions were more severe. Or—and this is probably the best answer—the Baradostian and equivalent sites beyond the Zagros are still to be found and identified as such. But in the present inadequate state of knowledge about Iranian prehistory it is impossible to choose with any confidence among these explanations.

The Zarzian, named by Garrod in 1930 after a small site she excavated in Iraq in 1928, is frequently described as an Epipalaeolithic industry. As we noted, the term "Epipalaeolithic" is a general one used by some prehistorians to embrace the cultures of hunters, gatherers and fishermen found in Europe, North Africa and Southwest Asia after roughly 16,000 B. C. (or somewhat earlier for some authors), and lasting until the appearance of "Neolithic" food producers in the early Holocene. The stone tools of this grouping usually have a distinct microlithic quality, including at times geometric elements such as triangles, crescents, and trapezoids; sites are often numerous; and some archaeologists see a tendency towards new patterns of subsistence including trends that may herald food production. In Iran (and Iraq)

the Zarzian is the best known of the Epipalaeolithic groups, though much remains to be learned about it and its possible contemporaries in the region.

To begin with, we do not know precisely when the Zarzian began nor what its origins were. It was certainly present by about 13,000 B. C., and lasted until at least 11,000–10,000 B. C. judging from three radiocarbon determinations from Shanidar and Palegawra caves in Iraq. Whether it goes back much further than 13,000 B. C. is uncertain, although it quite likely does. It may have even coexisted to some extent with the later Baradostian; or, as Hole (1970) has suggested, it may have developed directly out of the Baradostian ca. 20,000 B. C. This latter claim is based on typological and technological continuities said to be present at Pa Sangar in Luristan between the late Baradostian and the Zarzian, such as retouched rods, polyhedric burins, and retouched bladelets (Hole and Flannery 1967), as well as a basic similarity in techniques of manufacture (Hole 1970). The lack of firm radiocarbon determinations in the Zagros between ca. 25,000 B. C. and 13,000 B. C. forces us to suspend judgement on this hypothesis for now. One explanation is that most sites of this time are deeply buried or eroded away. On the other hand, it is not impossible that there *is* a real gap of ten thousand years or more between the latest Baradostian and the earliest Zarzian in much if not all of the Zagros. As mentioned earlier, Shanidar Cave appears to have been vacated after this time, perhaps for environmental reasons. A similar hiatus seems to occur in northern Afghanistan between ca. 30,000 B. C. and 14,000 B. C., while in Soviet Central Asia only one site is known between 27,000 B. C. and 12,000 B. C. (Davis 1980). Possibly the cool and very arid climate with its treeless landscape and long, harsh winters inhibited human occupation of the highland zones of Iran and adjoining regions at this time, or permitted only sporadic visits whose traces are hardly visible archaeologically. In this case, perhaps the "missing" earlier Zarzian sites are to be found in the warmer lowland zones of Iran and Iraq. Indeed, they may already have been found even if they have not yet been identified as such; these lowland sites need not be represented by stone tools identical in all respects to those characterizing the Zarzian as defined in the central or northern Zagros mountains, since different needs and activities may have required somewhat different tools. More research should be directed to this particular problem in the southern Zagros on the lower flanks of the mountains, in Khuzistan, along the Persian Gulf and Indian Ocean, in Baluchistan, and on the central plateau, particularly around the former lakes. At the moment, however, my own feeling is that the case is stronger for discontinuity than for continuity between the Baradostian and the Zarzian.

It might of course be asked why, perhaps for ten or twelve thousand years, these late Upper Palaeolithic groups, with their presumably more advanced technology and organization, would have found it so difficult to survive in the Zagros, which their Mousterian predecessors had not abandoned. This question has been discussed earlier in asking why the Baradostian failed, apparently, to diffuse as widely in Iran as did the Mousterian, but here it has a somewhat different slant. One response is that we do not know that the Mousterian occupation of the Zagros *was* continuous and unbroken. Possibly in the Mousterian sequence too there were considerable gaps which we cannot yet identify archaeologically in the absence of a finer and more reliable chronology. Another response is that environmental conditions were possibly more unfavorable to hunters and gatherers in the later phases of the last glacial than they were earlier. Van Zeist and Bottema (1977) seem to suggest that the final Mousterian climate was milder with more trees than the period beginning 40,000 years ago. The cold, dry conditions that followed, with consequent scanty vegetation, may have drastically reduced the herbivore population on which the hunters depended, as well as those plant foods which had been exploited in less severe periods.

The Zarzian as it is currently understood seems to continue the upland zone adaptation already present in the Baradostian. The known Zarzian sites are now more numerous, however (ten in Iran, seven in Iraq, plus a half dozen or so sites whose status is less certain). Open-air settlements are documented as well as those in caves and rock-shelters. While most are found at high elevations in the Zagros, above ca. 800 meters, at least one occurs in southwestern Iran at only 480 m. above sea level. Inevitably we must wonder if seasonal movements were involved as the hunters followed the main game animals on their migratory cycles.

There is a fair amount of information to help us reconstruct the climatic and environmental context of the Zarzian sites in the Zagros (Fig. 11). Before 12,000 B. C., that is presumably in the hypothetical earlier phase of the Zarzian, the cold, dry conditions had become even more pronounced, and the uplands were treeless; although some tamarisk and willow grew in the sheltered valleys there was virtually no pistachio or oak. But about 12,000 B. C. this Pleniglacial (Full Glacial) stage ended, and in spite of several short-term fluctuations a climatic regime with generally higher temperatures and perhaps greater precipitation set in. Trees, especially pistachio (but little oak) began spreading by, probably, 9,000 B. C.–8,000 B, C., and the cool steppe-type grasses diminished in these closing moments of the Pleistocene (van Zeist and Bottema 1977). The presence of wood charcoal of tamarisk, poplar, oak and conifer at Palegawra is consistent with this general picture for the earlier phase of the Zarzian as currently known, and perhaps the proliferation of snails is a result of the warmer conditions that set in a little later. At some point, still not clearly fixed chronologically, wild cereals must have begun to spread and proliferate, although this may have occurred only at the close of Zarzian times.

In general, the Zarzian chipped stone artifacts are smaller than the Baradostian ones (Fig. 13). Blades are frequent and there are also some microliths including geometrics (especially scalene triangles), and microburins. Burins are less common than before but there are many end scrapers, particularly the small "thumb-nail" type, as well as backed blades and bladelets, perforators or drills, notched and denticulated blades and flakes, and occasional single-shouldered points that may have served as projectile tips. One commonly accepted explanation for microlithic industries is that they reflect a stronger emphasis on composite tools in which small stone implements were inserted in wooden, bone or antler hafts as barbs, arrow points, knives, etc. For the Zarzian we have no direct confirmation as yet for this quite plausible explanation. In addition, bone tools such as awls are fairly common; there are some grinding or rubbing stones; and occasional stone and shell beads and pendants, and possibly even seashells, served as personal ornaments. Generally, as before, the local Zagros chert and flint is used, but a little obsidian brought apparently from eastern Anatolia is reported present at three sites in northern Iraq (Zarzi, Palegawra, and Shanidar Cave)—unless, that is, they are intrusions from later levels of these sites.

The subsistence patterns in the Zarzian in the main are similar to those in the Baradostian, but with some differences that may be significant in evolutionary and adaptive terms. Most sites seem to specialize in one or a few principal animals, e.g., onager at Warwasi and Palegawra, sheep and goat at Shanidar, gazelle and goat/sheep at Zarzi, depending of course on the game available in the vicinity. A few interesting innovations now appear, however. Land snails (*Helix salomonica*) are found in abundance in some sites like Shanidar and Zarzi. At other sites there are freshwater crabs, clams, turtles and (at Zarzi, for the first time in the Zagros), fish. The dog, apparently domesticated from the wolf, is claimed to be present at least at Palegawra at ca. 12,000 B. C. (Turnbull and Reed 1974), although this identification has been questioned by other zoologists (Heere and Röhrs 1977). Various birds (rock partridge, duck, stork, eagle, kestrel, sheldrake) also occur. To what extent plant foods were now becoming significant is not clear; although some grinding stones are present, and at Ghar-i-Khar there is a flint blade with "sickle sheen" on one edge, we have no direct evidence of cereals being utilized even if they were present in the Zarzian habitat at this time. Pistachio nuts may have been consumed, however. Several seeds of buckthorn were found recently in new excavations at the type-site of Zarzi (Wahida 1981) but, being poisonous, they would not have been eaten; perhaps they were collected for medicinal purposes or as dyes.

This apparently new emphasis on non-traditional foods has suggested to some authors that an important directional shift in subsistence was taking place at this time towards a "broad spectrum" subsistence pattern, in contrast to the more narrowly based one of earlier times that depended heavily on large ungulate game animals. Associated with this trend, which has even been termed a "revolution" (Flannery 1969), were technological developments such as grinding and pounding stones to process (plant?) foods, possibly storage pits at Shanidar Cave, and perhaps changes in the pattern of settlement and the division of labor (Hole and Flannery 1967). Some see these new elements as indicative of efforts by at least some Zarzian groups towards developing a closer cultural control of certain plants and animals. Just why this new emphasis came about—if it really did occur at the magnitude suggested—has not yet been explained satisfactorily; the roles of such factors as environmental changes, or increasing human population pressing on natural resources, or even influences from other regions such as the Levant affecting the local cultural attitudes, have been suggested by various authors. Nor is it universally accepted that this shift, if it did take place, was a stage-setter for the thrust towards formal food production that developed in Iran and elsewhere in the early Holocene. But the possibility is worth keeping in mind.

Whatever its duration, and whether one opts for a short or a long chronology, a few clues suggest that the Zarzian was not an unchanging unit through time as far as its lithic remains are concerned. As early as 1928 Garrod had remarked at the Zarzi type-site that there might be a subdivision with geometrics, especially scalene triangles, occurring only in the upper part of the deposits (Garrod 1930), and recent new excavations at Zarzi tend to confirm this (Wahida 1981). The same subdivision seems to occur at Palegawra (Braidwood and Howe 1960:155) and Ghar-i-Khar (Young and Smith 1966). The absolute dating of this change—which of course need not have been a rapid one— has not been established, however, nor is it yet known what, if any, other shifts are associated with it in the rest of the stone tool kit, let alone in the realm of subsistence or other behavior.

There were of course probably variations in space and according to site-functions as well as changes through time; indeed, it remains to be seen whether the simple non-geometric/geometric chronological dichotomy mentioned above will accommodate the data that new and better field research should bring us.

The Zarzian sites in Iran occupy roughly the same geographical areas as the Baradostian ones. The northernmost sites yet known are Ghar-i-Khar at Bisitun and Warwasi near Kermanshah. Only one site (Pa Sangar) was excavated in the Khorramabad valley. In the Hulailan valley of Luristan, however, they are more abundant with at least four cave sites represented: Mar Ruz, Mar Gurgalan Sarab, Dar Mar, and Ghar-i Gogel. There are in addition at least three open-air Zarzian sites in the valley which may represent brief waiting stations, and about six other late sites which cannot be definitely attributed to the Zarzian (Mortensen 1974a,1974b,1975). No radiocarbon determinations were obtained from these Hulailan sites, but the emphasis on geometric microliths suggests (if the dichotomy mentioned above is correct) the later phase of the Zarzian. Three of the cave sites in the Hulailan valley probably functioned as base camps situated near running water with a fine view over the plain for hunters watching for game, while the small scatters of tools, etc., in the open-air sites located along the Saimarreh river may mark the temporary locations of fishermen, or of hunters waiting for game to come to drink (Mortensen 1979).

In contrast to the Baradostian, there seems to be a large number of "Epipalaeolithic" sites in southwestern Iran (Fars and Khuzistan; Fig. 10). How many of these are truly Zarzian, as that term has been used in the central Zagros, is uncertain. They have cautiously been called Epipalaeolithic by their discoverers, largely because they contain microliths and geometric forms, though here a risk of circular reasoning is apparent. Conceivably some might be Baradostian, others early Neolithic; or we may be dealing with an Epipalaeolithic variant peculiar to this subregion. Unfortunately, we know little more about these sites than their stone tools, and the sampling of these is not very satisfactory. Their absolute ages are unknown. They represent both rock-shelter and open-air localities. Two are in rock-shelters on the shore of Lake Maharlu near Shiraz, where "Palaeolithic-type microliths" were located in 1935 (Field 1939:445–5). More lithic artifacts including blades and thumbnail scrapers were gathered on the surface of a beach strand of intermittent Lake Tashk called Neiriz Playa, ca. 150 km. southeast of Shiraz; apparently the pieces were left by hunting parties which encamped beside a freshwater lake that may have reached its maximum height ca. 20,000 B. C. and then dropped gradually. It is unclear, however, whether the artifacts at this locality are "Late Baradostian," Zarzian, or some other kind of Epipalaeolithic (Krinsley 1970:244 and Fig. 145).

Surface collections of flints, including bladelets and blades, from two small caves at Tang-i-Tikoe near Kazerun may also be Epipalaeolithic, although bifacial "arrowheads" suggesting a later date are also present. In the Kur river basin of the Marv Dasht valley some nineteen cave, rock-shelter and open-air sites seem to represent some kind of Epipalaeolithic with geometric microliths; but they are known only from surface finds, not excavations, and their ages are unknown. Some of them may represent early Holocene occupation, and their localities seem to be associated with springs, forests and marshes; no tools suggestive of plant food exploitation (sickle blades, pestles, mortars, etc.) are found, so the dietary emphasis may have been on animals (Rosenberg 1980).

On the outer slopes of the Zagros in northeastern Khuzistan a number of Epipalaeolithic sites have recently been reported: three at Dasht-e Gol, two in the Iveh area, and perhaps eighteen near the Izeh plain (Wright 1979). How many of these are Zarzian or Zarzian-related is unclear. The best represented is Reza Qoli Abod Sangi (also called D. G. 5) in the Dasht-e Gol area at ca. 500 m. elevation on a high terrace of the Karun river east of Dezful. It is a very small site at the foot of cliffs and may represent numerous winter occupations which accumulated, over an unknown period, more than six meters of deposits. Sheep and goat bones (some burnt, perhaps for fuel) are found, as are land snails and grinding stones. The flint industry has end scrapers, burins and notched pieces, and is said to resemble the Zarzian of Luristan; no geometric microliths occur, although there are microblades. This site was only sounded and, regrettably, is now flooded and unavailable for further excavation; it would almost certainly have been a very rewarding site for a better understanding of the final Palaeolithic of this part of Iran. Two other sites (D. G. 7, D. G. 9) seem to contain similar industries. Two surface sites on hills and terraces near the Iveh plain at ca. 500 m. elevation have also been termed Epipalaeolithic on typological grounds. At a somewhat higher altitude (ca. 750 m.) the Izeh plain is a relatively high valley of the outer Zagros with several lakes between rugged mountains; it may have been an ideal habitat for hunters of wild sheep, goat and pig, and collectors of wild cereals if these resources were present. The nine sites occur as rock-shelters, the larger ones, offering protection from the prevailing winter winds, perhaps serving as winter and spring camps, and the smaller ones perhaps serving as summer or autumn camps. In addition there are surface sites, so that a total of at least eighteen "Epipalaeolithic" occurrences are reported, all apparently lacking geometrics and distinguished from six "Upper Palaeolithic" sites by the large blade tools of the latter.

Certainly these mountainous zones of northeastern Khuzistan, like those already discussed in Fars, deserve much more serious attention from Palaeolithic archaeologists than they have hitherto received. The existence of rock-shelters with sealed and perhaps stratified deposits containing faunal and possibly floral remains and charcoal for radiocarbon dating; the presence of former lakes from which good pollen sequences may possibly be obtained; the numerous sites of several kinds with their implications for discovering functional interpretations of the settlement patterns; the suggestions of some kind of continuity into Holocene times of hunting and gathering populations—all these promise eventually to illuminate the nature of the Epipalaeolithic in the Zagros region.

The evidence for Epipalaeolithic occupation of the rest of the Iranian plateau is meager. A few surface finds of bladelets, microliths, etc. on the Makran coast are difficult to evaluate (Vita-Finzi and Copeland 1980). The microlithic assemblage with geometrics reported from Kuhbanan in Kerman in lake and peat deposits claimed to be "last glacial" in age (Huckriede 1961) falls into the same uncertain category; it may be much later, perhaps Neolithic of some kind. Yet it is difficult to accept the notion that all of the plateau outside the Zagros was unexploited and uninhabited at this time when, in the Zagros at least, the human population may have been expanding both geographically and numerically. We are left with the lame but necessary plea for more fieldwork. In central eastern Iran future research may well reveal some industry resembling the one termed "Kuprukian" in Afghanistan which may be roughly contemporary with the Zarzian in the Zagros (Dupree 1952; Davis 1978).

How long after the close of the Pleistocene did "pure" Epipalaeolithic hunters and gatherers continue, and how much coexistence was there with their presumed kinsmen, those foragers who during the early Holocene were supposedly making the transformations that by about 7,000 B. C. had brought an archaeologically recognizable food-producing way of life into existence? We do not know, just as we do not know which particular Epipalaeolithic groups made the first successful transitions to food production. Perhaps by the 9th millennium B. C. sheep were already coming under increasing cultural control (if we accept the somewhat ambiguous evidence from the site of Zawi Chemi in the Shanidar valley in northern Iraq (Perkins 1964; Solecki 1981), and goats and some wild cereals may simultaneously have been undergoing the same human interference. Certainly more permanent forms of settlement and architecture, such as huts partially built of mud or stone, seem to be used at this time by Epipalaeolithic groups in the Levant, indicating an increasingly sedentary life, and similar trends may have been developing in

Iran. It is also possible that while some Epipalaeolithic groups became more sedentary with an emphasis on the use of plant foods including cereals, others remained more mobile with a stronger reliance on foraging and on herding goats and sheep, a way of life that is analogous to later pastoral nomadism. Whether pastoral nomadism as an institution evolved out of such a context, or instead developed considerably later as an offshoot of settled village economies, is a debated question today. It is interesting and probably significant that at the eighth millennium site of Ganj Dareh in Kermanshah district (Smith 1978), barley was being cultivated *before* any signs of animal domestication appear in the sequence. The same precedence of cultivated cereals over domesticated animals occurs at the roughly contemporaneous site of Çayönü in southeastern Anatolia (Braidwood et al. 1981).

However late the "pure" hunters and gatherers lasted in Iran, or elsewhere in the Near East for that matter, they had all apparently vanished by historic times; at least, they are not mentioned in the early texts. It is possible, however, that in some parts of the region hunters survived late in prehistoric times by providing animal protein and other wild products to cultivators in exchange for cereals and other carbohydrate-rich foods. As yet, however, such situations have not been identified archaeologically, and in the Zagros at least the apparently early development of goat and sheep rearing may argue against such a hypothesis.

The best evidence for a late survival of non-food producing cultures may eventually come from the Caspian shores. Here, on the edge of the Mazandaran plain between the Elburz foothills and the sea, there are several sites that illustrate a different variety of Epipalaeolithic life, one apparently adapted to the peculiar environmental conditions and particularly to the abundant food resources of the foreshore already described here. Somewhat similar occupations based largely on hunting and fishing occur further north near the Soviet shores of the eastern Caspian, especially in the cave sites of Dam Dam Chesme I–II, Djebel, Kailia and Hadja-Su I, situated inland from the present shoreline in western Turkmenistan (Masson and Sarianidi 1972).

Very few earlier Palaeolithic traces have been found in the Caspian region although it was very probably frequented by foraging groups. We might expect that even in the coldest Pleistocene intervals this zone would have been milder and more humid than surrounding zones at higher elevations. The ancient land surfaces and any archaeological remains deposited since the Lower Pleistocene are now deeply buried beneath the modern alluvial plain.[8] Perhaps the best place to look for Palaeolithic remains is in

the slope colluviums of Mazandaran or in the loess deposits of arid Gorgan to the east. At Pa'in Zarandin near Behshahr stone tools have been found beneath the colluvium but little is yet known about them apart from a summary description: they are denticulated and notched pieces for the most part whose age is not indicated (Keraudren and Thibault 1973). Some caves high on the northern slopes of the Elburz, above the maximum Pleistocene sea level, might also be informative. Coon had suggested (1952:236) that Hazer Jerif, a valley drained by the Nika river, might be a promising place to look for such sites; to my knowledge no one has made such a search. It is difficult to believe that the Caspian borders would not have been frequented by at least Middle and Upper Palaeolithic peoples, even if only seasonally or in the coldest intervals.

At the present time, however, the earliest human occupation sites known in this zone are three limestone caves in the Elburz escarpment. They are all of Epipalaeolithic age (although Coon, the excavator of two of the sites, preferred the term Mesolithic), and the period of occupation begins about 10,500 B. C. in the final phase of the Pleistocene. They are Belt Cave (also known as Ghar-i Kamarband) and Hotu Cave, excavated by Coon in 1949 and 1951 (Coon 1951, 1952, 1957), and Ali Tappeh I nearby, investigated in 1962 and 1964 (McBurney 1968). These caves are situated near Beh hahr in Mazandaran, between eight and thirteen kilometers from the present shoreline. The first indication of human presence occurs ca. 10,500 B. C. at Ali Tappeh I when warmer conditions were underway and the Caspian level was dropping (Fig.2). Shortly afterwards (perhaps ca. 10,000 B. C., during the temperature maximum corresponding to the Allerod in northern Europe), Belt and Hotu caves nearer the sea became habitable. The Epipalaeolithic groups exploited a number of local resources in the two principal adjacent but contrasting ecological zones: the mountains with dense deciduous and coniferous forests and alpine meadows, where were probably found deer, sheep, and goats, as well as various plant foods such as acorns, nuts, roots, leaves, and grasses; and the coastal plain with its mixed landscape of dry grassland, swamps, meandering streams and the brackish sea itself, which provided such foods as cattle, gazelle, antelope, pig, equids, Caspian seal, waterfowl, fish,

---

8. At one time Coon believed he had discovered Lower Palaeolithic artifacts, and a human skull, from the "last interglacial" period at Hotu Cave. The skull is now known to be "Mesolithic" in age. The stone objects, one of which resembles a hand axe, the other a cleaver, may belong to the so-called Mazandaranian industry, and thus be of similar age; or they may be genuine Lower Palaeolithic pieces picked up elsewhere by the Epipalaeolithic occupants and brought to Hotu (see Coon 1957:196,206).

snails, as well as wild plants (McBurney 1968). It is by no means unlikely that watercraft were used. While the various occupations of the three sites are not yet precisely correlated with each other or with the several climatic and lacustrine fluctuations that occur in the approximately two thousand years involved, it would seem that the first occupants at Ali Tappeh I exploited gazelle and a few seals. After ca. 9,800 B. C., when Belt and Hotu were also occupied under rather warmer conditions, seals were intensively consumed for a while together with some gazelle, sheep and goat. Voles (small burrowing herbivores) were apparently eaten at times at Hotu Cave, as were thrushes—unless, that is, the presence of their bones in this site has some other explanation. The fluctuations in importance of game, which need not be discussed in detail here, may be related to Holocene climatic shifts with alternating arid and moist or cool phases encouraging steppe versus forest or aquatic fauna. By about 9,000 B. C. Ali Teppeh I was abandoned, though it may be that the other two sites were occupied by hunters and gatherers until the mid-eighth or even the seventh millennium when, apparently, the sea level had dropped abruptly and the coastal plain was much wider than before.

The stone industry in Belt and Ali Teppeh I sites is microlithic in type and has a general similarity to the Zarzian of the Zagros; but it is premature to affix a specific cultural label to it until we have a more detailed comparative analysis. It features many geometric microliths including triangles and perhaps trapezes, with backed bladelets and blades, but also many heavier tools on flakes and blades (see Fig. 14). There are also grinding stones (rubbers and querns), but their functions are not known. The worked bone tools include eyed needles (presumbly for sewing), possible netting hooks, and spear or dart heads. A painted pebble from Ali Tappeh I is the only surviving evidence of art or ritual. On the other hand, the "Mesolithic" industry at Hotu has no microliths and is essentially made up of amorphous flake and pebble tools (Fig. 14) for which the name "Mazandaranian" was coined (Dupree 1952); as already mentioned, this term is rarely used today. Why there should be two such different lithic assemblages represented in such a short span of time, and in such a restricted area, is an interesting question: to what extent do they reflect different cultural traditions on the one hand and different subsistence and processing activities or lithic material available on the other? So far we have no answer.

A half-dozen skeletons were found at Belt and Hotu Caves dated to between ca. 7,200–6,600 B. C., and they provide the only view we have of the physical anthropology of Epipalaeolithic groups in Iran—indeed, one of the best views of any population in the Iran-Iraq region since Middle Palaeolithic times. They show a fully modern population but not a homogenous one; some of the individuals were tall and muscular, in reasonably good health, who lived to nearly forty years (Coon 1951; Angel, in Coon 1952). Unfortunately, we can say nothing about their ancestry, nor whether they contributed to the gene pool of later Iranian peoples. Both primary and secondary burials occur, at times sprinkled with red ochre; these are among the earliest deliberate burials so far found on Iranian territory, although they may overlap in time with some of the "early Neolithic" burials in the Zagros.

Just how intensively the Epipalaeolithic inhabitants of this part of Iran exploited certain animals and plants which later were domesticated is an interesting question bearing on the problem of agricultural origins. One author (McBurney 1968) has suggested that there may have been an "incipient domestication" of goats or sheep and perhaps of wheats and other local grains.[9] Whether, if this incipient pattern existed, it was a purely indigenous development or was influenced by processes already going on elsewhere, especially in the Zagros, remains to be established. There were later occupations in these sites, variously labelled Sub-Neolithic, Preceramic Neolithic and Ceramic Neolithic, but it is not clear when they began or how important food production was for the societies concerned. It may be that in the Caspian area, with its rich and diverse food resources, the economy remained basically a hunting-gathering-fishing one until quite late in the Holocene. New elements such as simple pottery and polished stone artifacts were perhaps adopted from contemporaries in other parts of Iran who were already well advanced in food production and sedentary village life. Some of the last surviving Epipalaeolithic groups in Iran may have flourished on the Caspian shores, side by side with agriculturalists, until at a still unknown date they were eventually submerged or displaced by farmers or even converted into farmers themselves. This should be a worthwhile proposition to test in future research here.

At any rate, it is very likely that at some time during those murky millennia before about 5,000 B. C. the immensely long Palaeolithic tradition of Iran came to an end and new forms of human society replaced it. The "Neolithic" phenomenon based on various kinds of food production need not concern us here except

9. Coon's suggestion that an early form of Neolithic culture may have developed on the southern Caspian foreshore, and have been the source from which at least some of the European Neolithic was derived (1957:172), is not viewed seriously today. Nonetheless, further research on the Epipalaeolithic and early food producing cultures of the Caspian area of Iran is urgently needed. A most interesting situation probably existed there in the early and middle Holocene.

insofar as it illustrates continuities with its predecessor and one supposes, its ancestor, the Epipalaeolithic grouping.

Is there any evidence suggestive of increasing human population and its frequent concomitant, demographic pressure on natural resources, in the Iranian Epipalaeolithic immediately before the development of formal food production? This is an important and controversial question today (Smith and Young 1983) and opinion varies considerably about the extent to which such population pressure, if it existed, may have played a significant or even determining role in the appearance of the new economy. Quite obviously it is impossible to test this hypothesis (and unfair to deny its relevance) in areas where few sites are known because of inadequate or insufficient field surveys; it is risky to argue from negative evidence. At the moment the central and southern Zagros mountains are the only zones of Iran where any considerable number of Epipalaeolithic sites is known, and even there the lack of chronological controls makes it difficult to say how many of these immediately precede the development of agriculture. Nevertheless, it is interesting to note that the number of apparently Epipalaeolithic sites known in this region has increased markedly in recent years. It is true that a larger number of sites is not always proof of a growing regional population, and a growing population does not necessarily exert sufficient stress on available resources to produce a fundamental change in the subsistence economy. More sites may, for instance, simply reflect shorter occupation periods by a group using a larger number of places during the course of an annual cycle, or a more widespread range of activities at specialized stations than in the immediate past. But even when these provisos are made, and a proper degree of prudence called into play in view of the small sample of sites available, there does remain the possibility that the larger number of known Epipalaeolithic sites in the Zagros indicates a larger population than was the case, for say, the Baradostian in that area; and that this increase had certain consequences in terms of more intensive cultural control over some plants and animals, of somewhat more sedentary life, of perhaps less

egalitarian and more hierarchically organized societies, and of some technological developments such as food-processing and food-storage techniques— that is, of the elements that went to make up what is often called the Neolithic revolution. This is no more than a plausible affirmation at the moment as far as the Zagros Epipalaeolithic and Neolithic are concerned, but it is a topic that deserves serious study when research in the area is resumed. The prelude to food production is poorly known in Iran. It is not until the eighth millennium B. C. that we can speak with some confidence of food producing groups whose subsistence economies were becoming reliant on goat and sheep raising and (perhaps to a lesser extent) on cereal cultivation, and who were building permanent structures in mud and brick and making simple pottery vessels. These occurrences are first known, in Iran, in southern Kurdistan, Luristan and Khuzistan, against a background of a generally warm, dry climate and gradually expanding forest cover. There is no reason to believe that any major impetus for these innovations (except possibly for some of the domesticated cereals) came from outside this region, and we may take it as highly likely that its origins are to be sought principally in the local foraging populations of the final Pleistocene and early Holocene. The Zarzian is one, but not necessarily the only, candidate for the role of "ancestor" of the earliest food producers in Iran.

Up to now we cannot, in the Iran-Iraq area, point to a well-defined cultural unit or complex similar to the Natufian of the Levant zone which may illustrate the immediate context in which food producing developed. The Natufian (ca. 10,000-8,500 B.C.) is characterized by small village-like communities with some permanent architectural forms in mud, stone, plaster and wood, an economic emphasis on intensive exploitation of wild cereals extending perhaps to rudimentary cultivation, perhaps increasing control over some game animals, and very likely a fairly sedentary form of settlement. If such a development occurred in the final stages of the Epipalaeolithic of our area, it has not yet been unequivocally identified in the archaeological record. Perhaps we have not been looking in the right places.

VII

Iran in the Palaeolithic World

Few parts of the Old World were entirely isolated or autonomous for long once the earliest tool-making hominids had spread beyond their putative homelands in Africa. The small Palaeolithic aggregates were mobile only within certain narrow limits; but over the many millennia we are dealing with here there seems to have been a slow seepage across natural frontiers so that—particularly in the earlier phases—it is very difficult to define neat cultural entities or cultural areas. This makes it all the more difficult to speak of zones of origin or directions of flow for the industries we have described. Yet in spite of the lessened interest in such topics in the last few decades, it is not a problem prehistorians can conscientiously ignore; diffusion of ideas, movements of peoples and the changes they produce are integral mechanisms of the evolutionary process. So although the many gaps in our knowledge at present make a serious attempt at tracing diffusion and movements difficult, we must still make the effort, if only to emphasize how little we know, and to point in the direction future research should take.

The Palaeolithic archaeologist working in Iran today is obliged, perhaps more so than those involved in other parts of the Old World, to look about him in all directions for affinities. It is traditional to maintain that Southwest Asia represents, today and in the past, a great isthmus or crossroad linking Europe, Africa, Central Asia and Southern Asia. Within this supposed crossroad Iran itself might be seen as a node or meeting point. To the north it opens both to the Caucasus, with its links to eastern Europe, and to Central Asia; to the east and southeast it fronts on Afghanistan and the Indo-Pakistani zone; to the south it faces Arabia, and to the west, Anatolia, Mesopotamia and the Levant, with Africa impinging on the first and last of these zones. Any effort at understanding the distant past of Iran, therefore, requires some attention to this larger cultural and geographical setting. In a very broad sense Iran functioned as

one part of a much larger network or cultural macrocosm composed of the other parts of Southwest Asia and adjoining regions. While a great many regions of the world, except the more isolated ones, can in some sense be viewed as "crossroads" or intermediate zones, this characterization seems particularly appropriate for Iran.[10]

It is reasonable, therefore, to suppose that in the Palaeolithic period, as in historic and late prehistoric times, Iran was a zone where cultural influences from all these regions met and even "blended," and that it was also one that sent forth its indigenous features in several directions. Unfortunately, at the moment this is no more than an attractive assertion, well worth examining but requiring careful handling. The Palaeolithic world was vastly different in many ways from the one that succeeded it, and a different set of mechanisms and processes was in effect. We are not sure how useful it is to think in terms such as migrations, colonization, "influences," etc., at this level of cultural development. Palaeolithic groups, like many modern hunting-gathering peoples, certainly must have moved about, but the extent and rate of movement were probably different from those of post-Pleistocene times, when in many areas there were food-producers present to modify part of the behavior of the foragers. In addition, the fact that our comparisons are based almost entirely on stone tools for most of the time—a field in which resemblances arising from convergent developments, basic technical methods, and the physical properties of various

---

10. It is tempting to suggest an analogy—although it should not be pressed too far—with the unique geobotanical position Iran occupies among Near Eastern countries. It serves as a bridge between four major plant geographical regions: the Irano-Turanian, the Euro-Siberian, the Saharo-Arabian, and the Sudanian (Zohary 1963), and this situation is apparently of considerable antiquity. Interestingly enough, the Mediterranean floral elements are very unimportant in Iran, their spread having perhaps been arrested by the Zagros mountain barrier.

kinds of stone, often create the illusion of historical relationships—forces us to be prudent, even skeptical in evaluating claims of cultural affinities or direction of "influence." Indeed, since we still know so little about the purposes and functions of the majority of the stone tools used in the Palaeolithic, it is almost impertinent to attempt to diagnose the processes through which changes in the industries and tool-sets occurred as consequences of contacts, exchanges through social networks, and displacements among these small and scattered groups of hunters and gatherers of the Pleistocene.

Having made this gloomy prognostication, we are obliged nonetheless to look beyond the present borders of Iran to see whether and to what extent the Palaeolithic inhabitants of that land did at times share the traditions found in neighboring regions. This is indeed part of the theme stated at the beginning of this monograph: to attempt to understand the place of Iran in the Palaeolithic world in the broadest anthropogeographical perspective. Earlier in this essay, in the discussion of the various industries and periods, references were occasionally made to possible analogues outside Iran. In the following section the procedure adopted is to study each adjoining region in turn and to try to define the extent to which we can distinguish linkages or resemblances to the Iranian materials throughout the Palaeolithic.

When we examine the regions to the west and to the south we find little that seems particularly relevant to the Iranian materials. The Palaeolithic of the Arabian peninsula is too poorly known to offer useful parallels, and the the same is true for Anatolia, particularly the eastern parts. In the Mesopotamian lowlands the same situation reigns. In the Levant region adjoining the Mediterranean and extending a few hundred kilometers inland a far richer body of data is of course available from a large number of sites, some of which have been well excavated and are chronologically fairly firmly established. But it is difficult to see any very specific parallels between the materials of this region and those of Iran. There are of course some general parallels in the sense that each region has a fairly well defined Lower, Middle and Upper Palaeolithic/Epipalaeolithic, and some of the industries within these categories share certain broad features. Thus, the Iranian Mousterian has a general resemblance to that of the Levant in spite of certain technological and stylistic differences; the Baradostian contains some steep scrapers that resemble somewhat those found in the "Aurignacian-like" (Antelian and Atlitian, to use the classic terminology) assemblages of Palestine, and the Arjenah points resemble somewhat the El Wad points of the "Antelian"; while the Zarzian and some other Epipalaeolithic assemblages with an emphasis on microlithicism is reminis-

cent of the Kebaran of the Levant. But, having said this, it is virtually impossible to define closer or more specific links that might denote either contacts or common ancestry. The absence in both areas of Upper Palaeolithic art and the weak emphasis placed on tools made of bone and horn are probably too generalized traits to be significant in seeking linkages of the kind we are discussing here.

The situation is somewhat more promising, at least for certain periods, when we look to the regions north and east of Iran, and more specifically to the adjoining Soviet territories.

It should not surprise us if, as several writers have pointed out (Garrod 1938; Hole 1970; Solecki 1963; McBurney 1964), there seem to be some rather interesting affinities or resemblances between the Palaeolithic of the Zagros and that of the Caucasus and Transcaucasia further north (Georgia, Armenia, Azerbaijan, Ossetia). The factors generally associated with mountain ecosystems (rugged terrain, lower temperatures, high weather variability, frequently high precipitation rates), with the accompanying reduction in the growing season and considerable snow cover, mean that severe conditions are often imposed on most of the animal and plant species and consequently, on the people who exploit them. Throughout the Palaeolithic sequence the same basic forms of life, with marked vertical seasonal movements of game animals and a strong emphasis on wild sheep and goat as the principal species hunted, seem to have prevailed from the Caucasus mountains to the Zagros. This stands in some contrast to the adjoining steppe or desert zones where quite different conditions existed.

In the Caucasus and Transcaucasia it is difficult, just as it is in the Zagros, to speak with certainty of the Lower Palaeolithic. No pre-Acheulian "pebble-tool" phase is known. Soviet prehistorians claim evidence for the Acheulian in a number of cave sites containing hand axes (Azykh Cave in Azerbaijan, Kudaro and Bub in Georgia) and at surface sites (e.g., Satani-Dar in Armenia). Some skepticism has been expressed about their true nature and age (see Klein 1966) just as there is some uncertainty about Barda Balka in Iraq and Pal Barik in Iran. This consistency in ambiguity is what might be expected if the essential unity of the mountain zone is accepted, of course, but on the whole there seems better evidence for an independent hand axe tradition in the Caucasus and Transcaucasia than in Iran. Some of the hand axes in Transcaucasia are made of obsidian; there is no evidence, however, that this volcanic glass was physically transported south into the Zagros during the Lower Palaeolithic.

The Middle Palaeolithic is well represented in the Caucasus and Transcaucasia where, just as in the Zagros, it seems to constitute the first intensive occupation. Some of the cave sites are located at high altitudes and, as in Iran, may represent summer habitations. A number of Mousterian variants have been identified (Lyubin 1971). There are some resemblances among stone tools to those in the Zagros, particularly in the production of narrow scrapers and points. The Levallois element is said to be more important in the Soviet sites than in the Zagros, however, for reasons that are unclear; possibly a different definition of the technique is used than among western prehistorians. Certain parallels seem to exist with the Upper Palaeolithic as well. Some Baradostian-like elements may be present in such Georgian sites as Taro Klde, Virchow's Cave and Kerguli Klde, which contain some scrapers, laterally retouched blades and multifaceted burins (see Field and Prostov 1936, figs. 1–2). The Zarzian of the Zagros also seems to have parallels further north, e.g., at Devis-Khureli in Georgia, which contains backed blades and bladelets and even a single-shouldered point (Golomshtok 1938, fig. 33), and at Gvardzhilas-Klde with its microliths, including geometrics, backed blades, multifaceted burins and notched pieces (Field and Prostov 1936, fig.2b). These are termed the Imeretie and Shan-koba cultures by Soviet prehistorians (Kozlowski 1979), and there may also be typological links with the Epipalaeolithic industries of the Caspian shore of Iran. If actual movements of people were involved it is not possible to be sure of the directions but it is not out of the question that the Zarzian and Baradostian were intrusive into the Zagros from the north, from Transcaucasia and eventually even from the Black Sea region.

A number of parallels have also been seen between the industries of eastern Iran and those of Soviet Central Asia, especially in Turkmenistan, Uzbekistan and Tadjikistan. It is of course difficult to compare the supposedly very earliest Iranian materials (the Lower Palaeolithic chopper and flake tools exemplified by the "Ladizian" and the artifacts from the Kashafrud basin in Khorasan) with similar assemblages elsewhere because these are highly generalized and non-diagnostic. The level of patterning is so low that comparisons may be largely useless. Whether more detailed analyses, both qualitative and quantitative, will improve this situation is hard to say. At present there is too much scope for judgements that are largely intuitive and that tend to respond easily to the preconceptions or biases of the observer. Nonetheless, these Iranian assemblages, poorly defined and dated though they are, do resemble fairly closely the Lower Palaeolithic of Central Asia. Here, similarly, the Acheulian seems rare or absent, particularly in the mountainous regions, and recent research in Tajikistan suggests that a long-lived tradition of chop-

pers and flake tools began as early, perhaps, as 250,000 years ago (Ranov and Davis 1979). The broad Kashafrud valley, it has been suggested (Ariai and Thibault 1975–1977:6), might have been a favorable migration route between the Iranian plateau and the southern plains of Turkmenistan. One might even claim that the western limit of the celebrated East Asiatic flake and chopper tradition is situated in eastern or central Iran.

In the Middle Palaeolithic the links may have been maintained; thus McBurney (1964:393) believed that the Mousterian at Ké-Aram I has its closest analogue with the industry found at Teshik-Tash in Uzbekistan. The emphasis on pebble tools in the Central Asian Mousterian does, however, mark it off considerably from the industries in Iran and the rest of Western Asia; how far available raw materials may have determined this feature is an intriguing question. The same is true to some extent for the Upper Palaeolithic and the Epipalaeolithic, and the fact that the prismatic core technique for removing parallel-sided blades appears in Central Asia only towards the very end of the Palaeolithic sequence reinforces the view that there are few links with the Baradostian. Again, nothing is yet known in Iran comparable to what seems a very early Upper Palaeolithic industry found at Kara Kamar in northern Afghanistan, which features steep and keeled scrapers and is older, apparently, than 30,000 years (Coon 1957:217–54; Davis 1978). For the Epipalaeolithic and "Mesolithic" there are general resemblances between Iran and Central Asia (including Afghanistan north of the Hindu Kush), and it is even suggested that the industries in Central Asia with geometric microliths and backed blades stemmed from the arrival of populations out of the Iranian plateau after ca. 11,000 B. C. (Ranov and Davis 1979:259–60). Certainly, as already mentioned, the "Mesolithic" of the southern Caspian shore has its closest parallels in sites of western Turkmenistan, especially the caves of Dzhebel and Dam-Dam-Chesme just east of the sea.

Finally, what resemblances or parallels can we see between Iran and the Indo-Pakistan area that might indicate relationships of some kind in the Palaeolithic?[11] If there are any it is logical to look to Pakistan and northwest India for them. Probably during arid phases the desert regions of northwestern India and of Pakistan formed a barrier to some extent to movements between western Asia and the subcontinent; and conversely, during humid phases the desert more readily facilitated diffusion between the two areas.

---

11. A useful summary of the present status of Palaeolithic research in India and Pakistan is given by Jacobson (1979). The most detailed and informative source is Sankalia (1974), although not all Indian prehistorians agree with certain of his interpretations and assumptions.

For the Lower Palaeolithic we can only repeat the hesitation expressed earlier concerning Central Asia: there seem to be general resemblances between the "Ladizian" of eastern Iran and the Kashafrud Basin materials of northeastern Iran, on the one hand, and the chopper-chopping tool industry called the Soanian in the sub-Himalayas of India and Pakistan on the other. The Soanian does seem to be distinct geographically and perhaps ecologically from the Acheulian in the zones where the two occur, although the Acheulian seems to be much less frequent and to begin later than the Soanian. There is a widely held view that the Soanian is merely a facies of the hand axe tradition, perhaps a functional variant, and this opinion should not be easily dismissed; nevertheless, the evidence from eastern Iran as it is currently understood tends to support the opposing interpretation that the two are separate: since no hand axes are yet known in central or eastern Iran where the pebble-tool assemblages are found, it is difficult to believe that they are merely "variants" of a local Acheulian. For the time being we might therefore, consider eastern Iran as an area represented during the Lower Palaeolithic (which might here go back no further than the Upper Pleistocene) by the same broad pebble-tool tradition that occurs in Pakistan and northwestern India. How long the Iranian tradition and the Soanian persisted remains to be demonstrated; late versions may have continued until nearly the close of the Pleistocene. Whether the Indian Acheulian is of indigenous orgin, as some Indian prehistorians claim and others vehemently deny, is a problem that need not be discussed here; as I have remarked earlier, the Iranian evidence throws no light on the issue of whether, or how, the Acheulian diffused to the subcontinent from the west.

A kind of Middle Palaeolithic is recognized in India which seems to pre-date ca. 25,000 B. C. and with its points, scrapers and occasional use of the Levallois technique does have a vague Mousterian appearance. Its analogies with the Mousterian of the Zagros or with that of Ké-Aram I in northeastern Iran, however, seem rather indistinct and tenuous.

In recent years a true Upper Palaeolithic has been shown to exist in the subcontinent from at least ca. 25,000 B. C., with blade tools of several types represented as well as, in some sites, many bone artifacts. There are few specific resemblances with the Baradostian, however, and most sites seem to be in central and southern India, with few well-defined ones in the northwestern areas where we might expect them if a simple model of diffusion from Iran is entertained. The presence of art in the Indian Upper Palaeolithic in the form of sculptures, incised ostrich eggshells and, possibly, even wall paintings is another difference between India and Iran at this time. It is not

impossible that there are somewhat closer links in the Epipalaeolithic or "Mesolithic" when many assemblages in the subcontinent are microlithic (including some geometric specimens) and recall the Zarzian and the Caspian assemblages; but again, it is difficult to be more precise until we know what was happening at this time in southeastern Iran (Baluchistan) and Pakistan. A possibly more important feature is that recent research in Pakistani Baluchistan has revealed a fairly early form of food production based on cereals and domestic animals at the site of Mehrgarh that goes back to perhaps about 6,000 B. C. (Jarrige and Meadow 1980). It is not yet clear to what extent this food producing economy is an extension of that already present in western Iran, and to what degree purely indigenous processes were involved. There is some reason to suspect that the cultivated barley and wheat were introduced into the area from the west across the Iranian plateau, but the goats and sheep might well have been domesticated from local stock. At any rate, the Mehrgarh evidence raises the possibility that similar sites may yet be discovered in Iranian Baluchistan, with the implication that the final Palaeolithic and Epipalaeolithic groups in southeastern Iran were also involved to some extent in the developments that culminated in food production.

The rather unsatisfying conclusion we reach after this panoramic survey of the events in Iran's neighbors is that at several points in both space and time the peripheral regions of Iran share stronger links with adjoining areas than they do with each other. This is not surprising when we consider that Palaeolithic Iran resembles, in our present state of knowledge, a doughnut in which an archaeologically empty sector—most of the interior of the plateau—is surrounded by various parts of the circumference where considerably more is known. One conclusion that seems justified, however, is that while in the Lower Palaeolithic, Iran seems to fit most comfortably into a Central and South Asian framework, this is less true in the Middle Palaeolithic, and even less so in the Upper Palaeolithic, when its strongest links seem to be with the cultures of the Caucasus and Transcaucasia and, possibly, the northern Black Sea areas.

This in turn is a reflection of the fact that with the passage of time there was, in Iran as in many other regions, a tendency for the stone tool to become more highly "patterned," that is, more easily recognizable as "types," and this trend reaches its ultimate level of patterning or distinctiveness in the Upper Palaeolithic and Epipalaeolithic. At first glance this might seem a banal observation, but it is worth pointing out that this trend is by no means the rule in all parts of the Old World. In this respect Iran, and other parts of Southwestern Asia, closely parallel Europe and North Africa, but differ significantly from much of

Southeast Asia and perhaps Central Asia where weaker patterns of differentiation seem (at least on the basis of our current knowledge) to have been the rule throughout the Palaeolithic sequence. Just what these differences in modes of patterning and development mean is a problem on which prehistorians are not agreed, but they probably signify broad and deep cultural and technological traditions which may have multiple roots. One rather obvious explanation is that the differences may be related to the kinds of subsistence adaptations to the natural environments that had evolved. Another factor may be the degree to which the stone artifacts functioned as *primary* instruments (for hunting, processing, etc.) and thus may have required a high level of specificity in form, as contrasted with contexts where the stone tools were mainly used to manufacture other implements in perishable materials, and thus demanded less specificity. In addition to these factors, however, the momentum of cultural tradition may also have played a role in maintaining the continuity of a local way of doing things where there was no particular pressure for change.

To summarize, and even to oversimplify somewhat a complex situation, it appears fair to say that throughout the Palaeolithic, Iran was on the whole more closely integrated with the territories to the northwest (Transcaucasia, the Caucasus, and perhaps the northern Black Sea coast including the Crimea), to the northeast (Central Asia), and even to some extent northwestern India and Pakistan, than it was with the Mediterranean and lowland Mesopotamian spheres of the Near East. This suggests that diffusion across what is now the Syrian Desert and Mesopotamia was not very significant during the Pleistocene and, probably, the early Holocene. The reasons for this are quite unknown. The parallel with the botanical situation (see Note 10) where the Mediterranean floral elements are rare, is, however, rather striking.

VIII

Conclusion

At the end of this survey of the Palaeolithic of Iran it would be appropriate, or at least seemly, to summarize our results and interpretations and to offer some capsuled wisdom about the meanings of the events we have traced. Obviously, in the face of such scanty primary evidence and such ambiguity in the data now available, we risk producing merely a litany of ignorance and an inventory of the lacunae in our basic information. We are still a long way from being able to speak with any confidence about processes, patterns and regularities—which many authors see as the ultimate aim of archaeological research—in the Iranian Palaeolithic. We are still very much in the pioneering stage of inquiry, but unfortunately it is one that has been too long drawn out and threatens even further stagnation.

Many of the weaknesses in our basic data have already been enumerated and need not be repeated here. The need for a more accurate chronology for the Palaeolithic cannot, however, be overstressed. Since we do not know how early humans occupied the land, or how long the various cultural periods lasted, or how much continuity there was between them, it is not possible to say whether a short or long chronological framework is appropriate. We need more regional lithostratigraphic and climatostratigraphic studies throughout Iran, and efforts to place the archaeological materials within these contexts, if we are to come closer to understanding what happened there during the Palaeolithic. A tentative synthesis of what we know of the Iranian Palaeolithic is offered in Fig. 15, but its provisional nature must be emphasized.

Similarly, more intensive surveys are required throughout the country to fill in many of the gaps in our knowledge of the distribution and density of occupation in the various geographical zones and cultural periods. Even in the areas which have been reasonably well explored, it should be mentioned, there are inexplicable blank spots. During a survey made

in 1965 by the writer in the Zagros in Kurdistan and Azerbaijan, one of the most striking features was the large number of caves and rock-shelters, apparently offering excellent protection and situated in areas that seemed promising from the viewpoint of foraging populations, that contained no Palaeolithic deposits. Whether this is because the sites did not exist in the Pleistocene, or if they did were never occupied by Palaeolithic peoples, or because the early deposits have been removed by human or natural agencies, is not known. Surveys in western Azerbaijan north of Lake Urmiyeh have revealed the same absence of Palaeolithic occupation sites (apart from the ambiguous Tamtama Cave) although today this area is the best watered and most fertile in Iran and would, one supposes, have been an excellent habitat for game animals and plant foods during the Palaeolithic. Whether the area was for climatic or other reasons inhospitable during most or all of the Palaeolithic (Solecki 1969) is impossible to say; but it is the kind of problem that needs to be investigated in many parts of Iran in the course of future research. Further pollen core sampling in these areas might help resolve this puzzle as far as local climatic conditions are concerned.

A study of great importance from the viewpoint of human adaptation would be the analysis of archaeological faunal materials within a single region through the various prehistoric periods. This would establish several factors: 1) whether or not there were significant changes in the type and frequency of major prey species exploited through time, 2) what age and sex classes were culled within a species, and 3) how they were butchered and the skeletal residues disposed of. These investigations would be particularly valuable for understanding the Middle to Upper Palaeolithic change when (supposedly) innovations in technology and social organization led to greater hunting efficiency and an emphasis on certain game animals. But it is important also for the evaluation of any possible changes in hunting strategy and consumption as revealed between the several "cultures" of the Upper Palaeolithic. There may well have been more continuity than discontinuity in this respect between the Baradostian and the Zarzian, but this remains to be demonstrated.

Another weak point in the study of the Iranian Palaeolithic occurs in the analyses of the stone artifacts. Relatively little effort has been invested in detailed stylistic, typological, and technological analysis that might enable the prehistorian to identify sensitive horizon markers which serve to build up local archaeological sequences. The investigators of the Khorramabad sites in Luristan did attempt this (Hole and Flannery 1967), but their sample was rather small and the stratigraphic contexts of the deposits not always reliable. The identification of zonal styles, which might reflect regional specializations if not genuine ethnic groupings, has similarly been neglected. Again, the problem of the extent to which the local raw materials influence the typology and technology, particularly in the Lower and Middle Palaeolithic, has been little discussed in Iran, although it is a matter to which archaeologists in many other parts of the world are increasingly sensitive. One explanation that has been offered for the relative insignificance of the Levallois method in the Zagros is that good raw materials are rare here, in contrast to the Levant where the occurrence of large nodules of good quality flint facilitates this technique. I doubt that this is the true answer—good flint and chert are by no means rare in the Zagros—but obviously the problem requires much more careful study than it has received hitherto. Finally, the study of use-wear on stone tools for the purpose of understanding their functions is virtually ignored up to now.

In spite of the present unsatisfactory state of our knowledge about the Palaeolithic of Iran, it may not be premature to suggest that we can glimpse at least four patterns of adaptation and environmental utilization. Whether some patterns began earlier than others it is not yet possible to say, but all four were probably in existence by the close of the Palaeolithic.

1. The only pattern that is reasonably well documented and that extends over a considerable period of time (from late Lower Palaeolithic to Epipalaeolithic) is the highland one, as exemplified in the Zagros. Its presence during the Palaeolithic in the Elburz and the Eastern Highlands (except for Khunik Cave) is not yet documented, but it seems unlikely that these areas were not being exploited to some extent from at least the Middle Palaeolithic onward.

2. At the close of the Pleistocene and lasting some time into the Holocene a mixed aquatic and terrestrial pattern existed on the Caspian foreshore; its antiquity is unknown, however, and while similar patterns may have been present on the southern coasts of Iran we have so far only vague hints of their existence. In the Persian Gulf and along the Makran Coast dolphins, porpoises, whales and fish may have contributed to the diet even in (late?) Palaeolithic times.

3. A third broad pattern which we might think of as a desert adaptation in eastern (and central?) Iran is also virtually unknown from the viewpoint of the resources exploited; but, if the "Ladizian" has been correctly interpreted, it may have been a very long and well-established pattern from the Lower Palaeolithic onward.

4. There are a few hints of what may have been an independent pattern in the Mesopotamian lowlands (Khuzistan) linked to riverine, marshland, and dryland exploitation. Unfortunately the reliable finds, both here and in neighboring Iraq, are so rare that we can do little more than indulge in speculation at the present time. It is possible that this pattern, if it existed, was in part linked to the adjoining highlands (the southern Zagros) in a framework of seasonal transhumance.

Most of the foregoing discussion has centered on the specific archaeological problems and gaps which must be filled in, together with a highly tentative picture of human adaptation in the Palaeolithic that may serve as a guide or a target in future work. The final point in this essay deals with the future prospects for Palaeolithic archaeology in Iran.

Until now, it must be admitted, the Iranian Palaeolithic has not been particularly well served by its practitioners. Although the quality of a few excavations has been acceptable, the level of research on the whole still remains in an underdeveloped state. In a world-wide perspective it is a poor relation, receiving far more information and concepts than it contributes. Like neighboring Turkey, Iraq and Afghanistan, Iran is in the world of Palaeolithic studies a depressed area situated between regions where there are now continuous and dynamic programs of inquiry and research: in the Levant, the Caucasus and Central Asia, and on the Indian subcontinent. In Iran field research has been sporadic, small scale, and insufficiently documented; one has the impression that few very important questions are being asked. This is one of the trademarks of an immature discipline. In the latter regions, on the contrary, especially in the past decade, the pioneering phase characterized by a let's-see-what's-there outlook has been, or is being, replaced by a more planned and comprehensive approach oriented frequently to the solution of certain specific problems. While there are no doubt very good political, cultural and economic reasons for these contrasting attitudes, the net result is the unsatisfactory situation in which Palaeolithic research in Iran finds itself today.

A problem that threatens to aggravate this situation is the destruction of sites in Iran. This is still an unknown quantity as far as the severity and extent of loss are concerned. Clandestine excavations by amateurs or antique dealers probably are rare, fortunately. The destruction of sites or parts of sites by agricultural and other operations seems to be more of a menace; certainly hydroelectric projects have drowned some Palaeolithic sites in recent years. Quarrying in the mountains north of Tehran for building stone is a potential danger to any Palaeolithic caves or rock-shelters that may exist there, and the same seems true on the Caspian foreshore where, for example, Hotu Cave had been dynamited before Coon's discovery of the site, and a nearby cave was destroyed (Coon 1957:162). In 1977 the small valley near Kermanshah in which Warwasi shelter is located was closed off and being used as an artillery firing range; the fate of Warwasi is unknown. In general the destruction of Palaeolithic sites seems to receive much less attention than that of sites of later periods of Iranian prehistory, but the loss is no less serious.

Perhaps a fitting way of concluding this survey is to quote the geographer W. B. Fisher (1968:740):

> If we seek to define Iran's function as a state and as a human grouping in terms of a 'personality,' then the country can be said to generate, to receive and transmogrify, and to retransmit.

Whether the land of Iran played that role in Palaeolithic times is still unknown; certainly Iranian Palaeolithic archaeology as a discipline has not done so. For a better understanding of what Iran's function and special character or "personality" was in the Pleistocene, when it formed one piece in the mosaic of widely varying hunting and gathering cultures throughout Asia, there can be no substitute for enlarged and—we must hope—better programs of field work in the country. As much as is practicable of this work should be the responsibility of Iranian scholars themselves. The development of an indigenous professionalism in Iran may, however, have to await a greater popular appreciation of prehistory in general, and of Palaeolithic archaeology in particular, than has existed up to now in that country.

Bibliography

Ariai, A. and C. Thibault
1975–77 Nouvelles précisions à propos de l'outillage paléolithique ancien sur galets du Khorassan (Iran). Paléorient 3:101–08.

Bewley, R. H.
1984 The Cambridge University Archaeological Expedition to Iran 1969. Excavations in the Zagros Mountains: Houmian, Mir Malas, Barde Spid. Iran 22:1–38.

Bobek, H.
1968 Vegetation. In The Cambridge History of Iran, Vol. I. The Land of Iran. W. B. Fisher, ed. pp. 280–93. Cambridge: University Press.

Bordes, François
1977 Que sont le Pré-Aurignacien et le Jabroudien? Eretz-Israel 13:49–55.

Braidwood, R. J.
1960 Seeking the World's First Farmers in Persian Kurdistan. Illustrated London News 237: 695–97.

Braidwood, R. J., H. Çambel and W. Schirmer
1981 Beginnings of Village-Farming Communities in Southeastern Turkey. Journal of Field Archaeology 8:249–58.

Braidwood, R. J. and B. Howe
1960 Prehistoric Investigations in Iraqi Kurdistan. In Studies in Ancient Oriental Civilization, Vol. 31. Chicago: University of Chicago Press.

Brookes, I. A.
1982 Geomorphological Evidence for Climatic Change in Iran During the Last 20,000 Years. In Palaeoclimates, Palaeoenvironments and Human Communities in the Eastern Mediterranean Region in Later Prehistory. J. L. Bintliff and Willem van Zeist, eds. pp. 191–228. Oxford: British Archaeological Reports, International Series 133.

Butzer, K. W.
1970 Physical Conditions in Eastern Europe, Western Asia and Egypt Before the Period of Agricultural and Urban Settlement. In Cambridge Ancient History, Vol. I. Prolegomena and Prehistory. I. E. S. Edwards, C. J. Gadd and N. G. L. Hammond, eds. pp. 35–69. Cambridge: University Press.

Caldwell, J. R., ed.
1967 Investigations at Tal-i-Iblis. Illinois State Museum Preliminary Reports No. 9. Springfield.

Coon, C. S.
1951 Cave Explorations in Iran 1949. Museum Monographs, The University Museum. Philadelphia: University of Pennsylvania.

1952 Excavations in Hotu Cave, Iran, 1951. A Preliminary Report (with Sections on the Artifacts by L. B. Dupree and the Human Skeletal Remains by J. L. Angel). Proceedings of the American Philosophical Society 96:231–69.

1957 The Seven Caves. Archaeological Explorations in the Middle East. New York: Alfred A. Knopf.

Davis, R. S.
1978 The Palaeolithic. In The Archaeology of Afghanistan. F. R. Allchin and N. Hammond, eds. pp. 37–70. London: Academic Press.

1980 Pleistocene Archaeology in the Southern Afghan-Tajik Depression. In Granitsa Neogena i Chetvertichnoy Sistemy. K. V. Nikiforova and A. E. Dodonov, eds. pp. 32–42. Moscow: Nauka.

de Morgan, J.
1907 Le plateau iranien pendant l'époque Pléistocène. Revue de l' Ecole d'Anthropologie de Paris 17:213–16.

Dolukhanov, P. M.
1977 Evolution of Eco-Social Systems in Central Asia and in Iran in the Course of Upper Pleistocene and Holocene. *In* Le Plateau Iranien et l'Asie Centrale des Origines à la Conquête Islamique. J. Deshayes, ed. pp. 13–22. Paris: Colloques Internationaux du C.N.R.S. No. 567.

Dupree, L. B.
1952 The Pleistocene Artifacts of Hotu Cave, Iran. Proceedings of the American Philosophical Society 96:250–57.

Farrand, W. R.
1981 Pluvial Climates and Frost Action During the Last Glacial Cycle in the Eastern Mediterranean—Evidence from Archaeological Sites. *In* Quaternary Paleoclimate. W. C. Mahaney, ed. pp. 393–409. Norwich: GeoAbstracts Ltd.

Field, H.
1939 Contributions to the Anthropology of Iran. Field Museum of Natural History, Anthropological Series, Vol. 29, No. 2 (2 vols.). Chicago.

1951 Reconnaissance in Southwestern Asia. Southwestern Journal of Anthropology 7:86–102.

1956 Ancient and Modern Man in Southwestern Asia. Coral Gables: University of Miami Press.

Field, H. and Eugene Prostov
1936 Recent Archaeological Investigations in the Soviet Union. American Anthropologist 38:260–90.

Fisher, W. B., ed.
1968 The Cambridge History of Iran, Vol. I. The Land of Iran. Cambridge: University Press.

Flannery, K. V.
1969 Origins and Ecological Effects of Early Domestication in Iran and the Near East. *In* The Domestication and Exploitation of Plants and Animals. P. J. Ucko and G. W. Dimbleby, eds. pp. 73–100. Chicago: Aldine.

Garrod, D. A. E.
1930 The Palaeolithic of Southern Kurdistan: Excavations in the Caves of Zarzi and Hazar Merd. Bulletin of the American School of Prehistoric Research 6:8–43.

1938 The Upper Palaeolithic in the Light of Recent Discovery. Proceedings of the Prehistoric Society, n.s. 4-1:1–26.

Garrod, D. A. E. and Diana Kirkbride
1961 Excavation of the Abri Zumoffen, a Paleolithic Rock-Shelter near Adlun, South Lebanon, 1958. Bulletin du Musée de Beyrouth 16:7–45.

Gerasimov, I. P.
1978 The Past and Future of the Aral and Caspian Seas. *In* The Environmental History of the Near East and Middle East since the Last Ice Age. W. C. Brice ed. pp. 335–49. London: Academic Press.

Golomshtok, E. A.
1938 The Old Stone Age in European Russia. Transactions of the American Philosophical Society, n.s. 29, Pt. 2. Art. 3:189–468.

Herre, W. and M. Röhrs
1977 Zoological Considerations on the Orgins of Farming and Domestication. *In* Origins of Agriculture. C. A. Reed, ed. pp. 245–79. The Hague: Mouton.

Hole, F.
1970 The Palaeolithic Culture Sequence in Western Iran. Actes du VII Congrès International des Sciences Préhistoriques et Protohistoriques (Prague 1966), I. pp. 286–92. Prague.

Hole, F. and K. V. Flannery
1967 The Prehistory of Southwestern Iran: A Preliminary Report. Proceedings of the Prehistoric Society 33:147–206.

Huckriede, R.
1962 Jung-Quartär und End-Mesolithikum in der Provinz Kerman (Iran). Eiszeitalter und Gegenwart 12:25–42.

Hume, G. W.
1976 The Ladizian: An Industry of the Asian Chopper-Chopping Tool Complex in Iranian Baluchistan. Philadelphia: Dorrance and Co.

Huntington, E.
1938 Season of Birth. Its Relation to Human Abilities. New York: Wiley and Sons.

Jacobson, J.
1979 Recent Developments in South Asian Prehistory and Protohistory. Annual Review of Anthropology 8:467–502.

Jarrige, J. F. and R. H. Meadow
1980   The Antecedents of Civilization in the Indus Valley. Scientific American 243:122–33.

Kassler, P.
1973   The Structural and Geomorphic Evolution of the Persian Gulf. *In* The Persian Gulf. B. H. Purser, ed. pp. 11–32. New York: Springer-Verlag.

Keraudren, B. and C. Thibault
1973   Sur les formations Plio-Pleistocènes du littoral Iranien de la Mer Caspienne. Paléorient 1:141–49.

Klein, R. G.
1966   Chellean and Acheulean on the Territory of the Soviet Union; a Critical Review of the Evidence as Presented in the Literature. American Anthropologist 68-2, Pt. 2:1–45.

Kozlowski, S. K.
1979   Le Paléolithique final entre les Carpates et l'Oural. *In* La Fin des Temps Glaciares en Europe. D. de Sonneville-Bordes, ed. Vol. 2, pp. 837–45. Paris: Colloques Internationaux du C.N.R.S. No. 271.

Krinsley, D. B.
1970   A Geomorphological and Paleoclimatological Study of the Playas of Iran. Parts 1 and 2. U.S. Geological Survey, Interagency Report IR—Military—1. Final Scientific Report Prepared for Air Force Cambridge Research Laboratories. Washington.

Leroi-Gourhan, A.
1981   La végétation et la datation de l'abri moustérien de Houmian (Iran). Paléorient 7:75–79.

Lyubin, V. P.
1971   Mousterian Cultures of the Caucasus (in Russian). Leningrad: Academy of Science.

Marucheck, J. T.
1976   A Survey of Seasonal Occupation Sites in Northern Balučestān. *In* Proceedings of the IVth Annual Symposium on Archaeological Research in Iran, Tehran 1975. F. Bagherzadeh, ed. pp. 272–83. Tehran: Iranian Centre for Archaeological Research.

Masson, V. M. and V. I. Sarianidi
1972   Central Asia. Turkmenia Before the Achaemenids. London: Thames and Hudson.

McBurney, C. B. M.
1950   The Geographical Study of the Older Palaeolithic Stages in Europe. Proceedings of the Prehistoric Society, n.s. 16:163–83.

1964   Preliminary Report on Stone Age Reconnaissance in North-Eastern Iran. Proceedings of the Prehistoric Society, n.s. 30:382–99.

1968   The Cave of Ali Tappeh and the Epi-Palaeolithic in N.E. Iran. Proceedings of the Prehistoric Society, n.s. 34:385–413.

1969   Report on Further Excavations in the Caves of the Kuh-i Dasht Area, during August 1969. Bastan Chenassi va Honar-e Iran 3:8–9.

1970   Palaeolithic Excavations in the Zagros Area. Iran 8:185–86.

Mortensen, P.
1974a   A Survey of Prehistoric Settlements in Northern Luristan. Acta Archaeologica 45:1–47.

1974b   A Survey of Early Prehistoric Sites in the Holailān Valley in Lorestān. *In* Proceedings of the IInd Annual Symposium on Archaeological Research in Iran, Tehran 1973. F. Bagherzadeh, ed. pp. 34–52. Tehran: Iranian Centre for Archaeological Research.

1975   Survey and Soundings in the Holailān Valley 1974. *In* Proceedings of the IIIrd Annual Symposium on Archaeological Research in Iran, Tehran, 1974. F. Bagherzadeh, ed. pp. 1–12. Tehran: Iranian Centre for Archaeological Research.

1979   The Hulailan Survey: A Note on the Relationship between Aims and Method. *In* Akten des VII Internationalen Kongresses für Iranische Kunst und Archäologie, München 1976. Berlin: Dietrich Reimer Verlag, pp. 3–8.

Negahban, E. O.
1981–82   Problems of Archaeology of Iran. *In* Iranian Studies Seminar, University of Pennsylvania, Annual Proceedings, pp. 17–21.

Perkins, D., Jr.
1964   Prehistoric Fauna From Shanidar, Iraq. Science 144:1565–66.

Piperno, M.
1972   Jahrom, a Middle Palaeolithic Site in Fars, Iran. East and West, n.s. 22:183–97.

1974   Upper Palaeolithic Caves in Southern Iran. Preliminary Report. East and West, n.s. 24:9–13.

Ranov, V. A. and R. S. Davis
   1979   Toward a New Outline of the Soviet Central
   Asian Paleolithic. Current Anthropology
   20:249–70.

Redman, C. L.
   1978   The Rise of Civilization. From Early
   Farmers to Urban Society in the Ancient Near
   East. San Francisco: W. H. Freeman.

Rieben, H.
   1955 The Geology of the Teheran Plain. American Journal of Science 253:617–39.

Rosenberg, M.
   1980   Paleolithic and Early Neolithic Settlement in
   the Marv Dasht, Iran. Ms., Malayan Symposium,
   Society for American Archaeology Meeting. Philadelphia.

Sadek-Kooros, H.
   1974   Palaeolithic Cultures in Iran. In Proceedings
   of the IInd Annual Symposium on Archaeological Research in Iran, Tehran 1973. F. Bagherzadeh, ed. pp. 53–65. Tehran: Iranian Centre
   for Archaeological Research.

   1976   Early Hominid Traces in East Azerbaijan.
   In Proceedings of the IVth Annual Symposium
   on Archaeological Research in Iran, Tehran
   1975. F. Bagherzadeh, ed. pp. 1–10. Tehran:
   Iranian Centre for Archaeological Research.

Sankalia, H. D.
   1974 The Prehistory and Protohistory of India
   and Pakistan (2nd ed.). Poona: Deccan College.

Singer, R. and J. J. Wymer
   1978   A Hand-ax from Northwest Iran: the Question of Human Movement between Africa and
   Asia in the Lower Palaeolithic Periods. In Views
   of the Past. L. G. Freeman, ed. pp. 13–27. The
   Hague: Mouton.

Smith, P. E. L.
   1971   The Palaeolithic of Iran. In Mélanges de
   Préhistoire, d' Archéocivilisation et d'Ethnologie
   offerts à André Varagnac. pp. 681–95. Paris:
   Ecole Pratique des Hautes Etudes, VIe Section.
   Centre de Recherches Historiques.

   1975   Ganj Dareh Tepe. Iran 13:178–80.

   1978   An Interim Report on Ganj Dareh Tepe,
   Iran. American Journal of Archaeology 82:
   538–40.

Smith, P. E. L. and T. C. Young, Jr.
   1983   The Force of Numbers: Population Pressure in the Central Western Zagros 12,000—
   4500 B.C. In The Hilly Flanks and Beyond: Es-
   says on the Prehistory of South Western Asia Presented to Robert J. Braidwood November 15,
   1982. T. C. Young, Jr., P. E. L. Smith and P.
   Mortensen, eds. pp. 141–61. Studies in Ancient
   Oriental Civilization, Vol. 36. Chicago: University of Chicago Press.

Solecki, R. S.
   1955   Shanidar Cave, a Paleolithic Site in
   Northern Iraq. Smithsonian Report for 1954.
   pp. 389–425. Washington: Smithsonian Institution.

   1963   Prehistory in Shanidar Valley, Northern
   Iraq. Science 139:179–93.

   1969   Survey in Western Azerbaijan. Iran 7:
   189–90.

   1971 Shanidar; The First Flower People. New
   York: Alfred A. Knopf.

Solecki, R. S. and A. Leroi-Gourhan
   1961   Palaeoclimatology and Archaeology in the
   Near East. In Solar Variations, Climatic Change
   and Related Geophysical Problems. R. W. Fair-
   bridge, ed. pp. 729–39. Annals of the New York
   Academy of Sciences 95.

Solecki, R. L.
   1981   An Early Village Site at Zawi Chemi Shanidar. Bibliotheca Mesopotamica 13. Malibu: Un-
   dena Pubs.

Speth, J.
   1971   Kunji Cave. Iran 9:172–73.

Sumner, W. M.
   1980   Problems of Large Scale, Multi-disciplinary
   Regional Archaeological Research: the Malyan
   Project. Ms., Malyan Symposium, Society for
   American Archaeology Meeting. Philadelphia.

Sunderland, E.
   1968   Early Man in Iran. In The Cambridge History of Iran, Vol. I. The Land of Iran. W. B.
   Fisher, ed. pp. 395–408. Cambridge: University
   Press.

Trinkaus, E.
   1983   The Shanidar Neanderthals. New York: Academic Press.

Turnbull, P. F.
  1975   The Mammalian Fauna of Warwasi Rock
  Shelter, West-central Iran. Fieldiana: Geology
  33:141–55. Chicago: Field Museum of Natural
  History.

Turnbull, P. F. and C. A. Reed
  1974   The Fauna from the Terminal Pleistocene
  of Palegawra Cave, a Zarzian Occupation Site in
  Northeastern Iraq. Fieldiana: Anthropology
  63:81–146. Chicago: Field Museum of Natural
  History.

van Zeist, W. and S. Bottema
  1977   Palynological Investigations in Western
  Iran. Palaeohistoria 19:19–85.

  1982   Vegetational History of the Eastern Mediterranean and the Near East during the Last
  20,000 Years. In Palaeoclimates, Palaeoenvironments and Human Communities in the Eastern
  Mediterranean Region in Later Prehistory. J. L.
  Bintliff and W. van Zeist, eds. pp. 277–321. Oxford: British Archaeological Reports, International Series 133.

Vita-Finzi, C. and L. Copeland
  1980   Surface Finds from Iranian Makran. Iran
  18:149–55.

Wahida, G.
  1981   The Re-excavation of Zarzi, 1971. Proceedings of the Prehistoric Society, n.s. 47:19–40.

Wright, H. T., ed.
  1979   Archaeological Investigations in Northeastern Xuzestan, 1976. Research Reports in Archaeology; Contribution 5, Technical Report 10.
  Museum of Anthropology, The University of
  Michigan. Ann Arbor.

Wright, H. E., Jr.
  1976   The Environmental Setting for Plant Domestication in the Near East. Science 194:
  385–89.

  1980   Climatic Change and Plant Domestication in
  the Zagros Mountains. Iran 18:145–48.

Wright, H. E., Jr. and B. Howe
  1951   Preliminary Report on Soundings at Barda
  Balka. Sumer 7:107–117.

Young, T. C., Jr. and P. E. L. Smith
  1966   Research in the Prehistory of Central
  Western Iran. Science 153:386–91.

Zohary, M.
  1963   On the Geobotanical Structure of Iran. Bulletin of the Research Council of Israel, Section D
  (Botany), 11D, Suppl.

Figures

Descriptions and Proveniences of Illustrated Artifacts

Figure 4. Lower Palaeolithic artifacts from the Kashafrud Basin, Khorasan (from Ariai and Thibault 1975–77). 1; chopping tool; 2: naturally backed knife; 3: flake; 4: nucleus.

Figure 5. Lower Palaeolithic ("Ladizian") artifacts from the Sarhadd Plateau, Baluchistan (from Hume 1976). 1: steep core-scraper; 2–7: flake scrapers.

Figure 6. Lower Palaeolithic (Acheulian) artifacts from Pal Barik site, Hulailan Valley, Luristan (from Mortensen 1975). 1: hand-axe; 2–3: chopping tools.

Figure 8. Middle Palaeolithic (Mousterian) artifacts from Ghar-i-Khar, Hulailan valley sites and Khorramabad sites. 1–3: side scrapers, Ghar-i-Khar; 4: Levallois point, Ghar Villa; 5: end scraper, Garacherach; 6: Mousterian point, Ghar Villa; 7–9: Mousterian points, Khorramabad sites. (1–3 from Smith, unpublished; 4–6 from Mortensen 1975; 7–9 from Hole and Flannery 1967).

Figure 9. Baradostian artifacts from Ghar-i-Khar and Khorramabad sites. 1–4: burins; 5–7: Arjeneh points; 8: backed blade. 9, 14–16: retouched bladelets; 10: Baradostian bladelet; 11–21: side scrapers; 12: retouched blade; 17–18, 20: end scrapers; 19: blade; (1 and 5 from Ghar-i-Khar, Smith unpublished; others from Khorramabad sites, Hole and Flannery 1967).

Figure 13. Zarzian artifacts from Khorramabad sites, Hulailan Valley site and Ghar-i-Khar. 1–2, 22, 26, 29–32: geometric microliths; 3–4, 14, 27–28: retouched bladelets; 5–6, 21, 23, 36–38, 41: backed bladelets; 7, 10–11: plain blades; 8, 12: retouched blades; 9, 20: notched blades; 13, 16–17, 25, 33–35: end scrapers; 15: microburin; 18–19: burins; 39: backed blade; 40: perforator. (1–20 from Khorramabad sites, Hole and Flannery 1967; 21–38 from Mar Gurgalan Sarab, Mortensen 1975; 39–41 from Ghar-i-Khar, Smith unpub.).

Figure 14. Epipalaeolithic artifacts from the Caspian area: Ali Tappeh I and Hotu Cave. 1–8; backed double ended microliths; 9–14: triangles; 17–19: notched scrapers on blades; 20: heavy flake tool; 21–22: end scrapers; 31–32: core scrapers. (1–16 from Ali Tappeh, McBurney 1968; 17–24 from Hotu Cave, Dupree 1952).

FIGURE 1

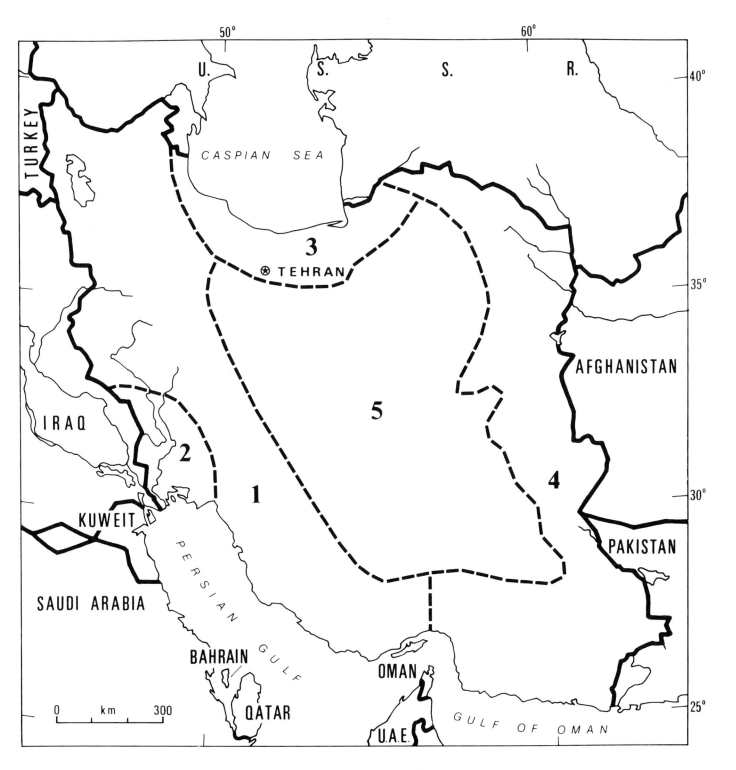

The Physiographic Units of Iran

1. Zagros Highlands
2. Khuzistan Lowlands
3. Northern Highlands and Caspian Lowlands
4. Eastern Highlands
5. Interior Desert Basin or Central Plateau

FIGURE 2

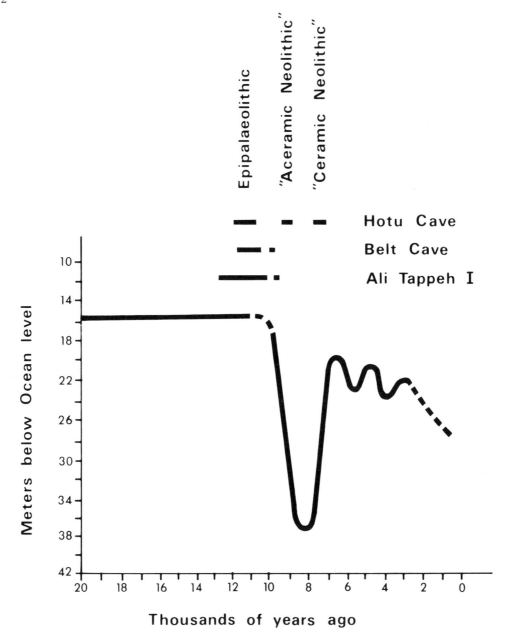

Late Pleistocene and Holocene fluctuations of the Caspian Sea (based on Dolukhanov 1977), with probable correlations of the Epipalaeolithic occupations on the Iranian foreshore.

FIGURE 3

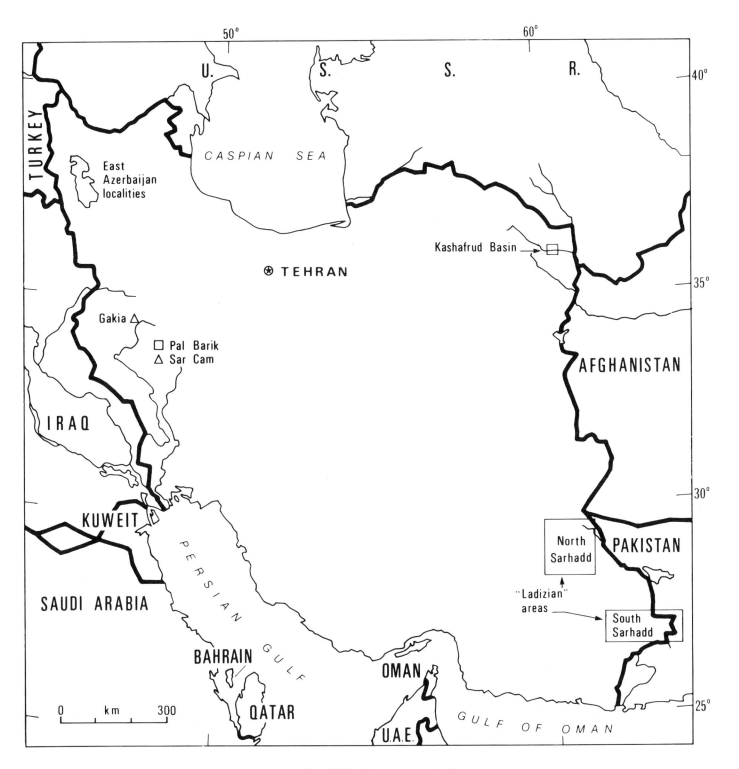

Lower Palaeolithic Occurrences in Iran

△ Isolated surface finds
□ Surface sites or localities

FIGURE 4

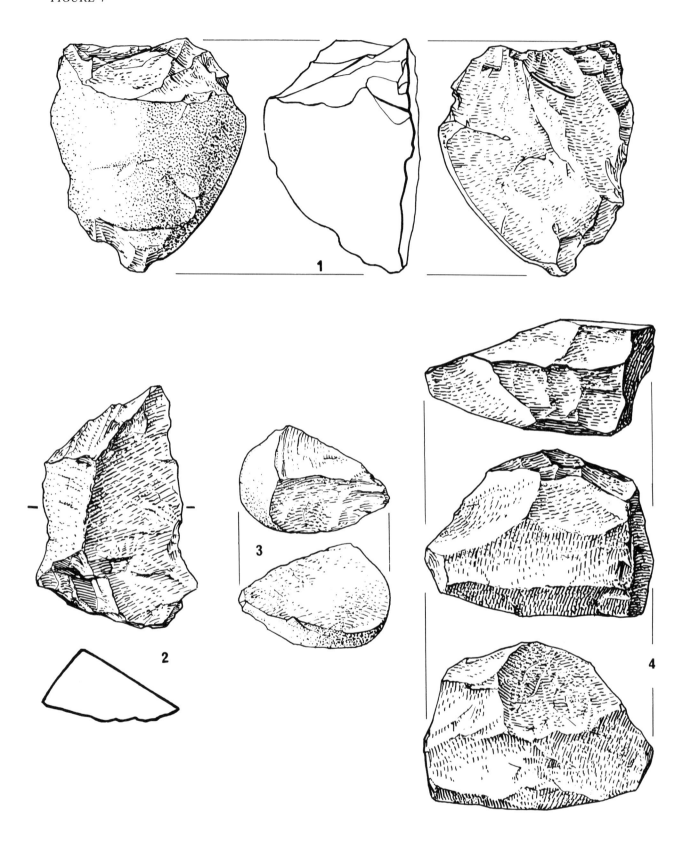

Lower Palaeolithic artifacts from the Kashafrud Basin, Khorasan.

FIGURE 5

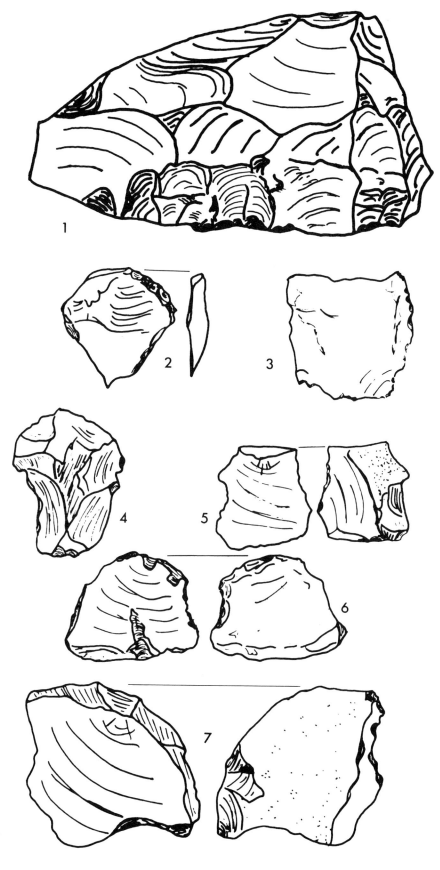

Lower Palaeolithic ("Ladizian") artifacts from the Sarhadd Plateau, Baluchistan.

FIGURE 6

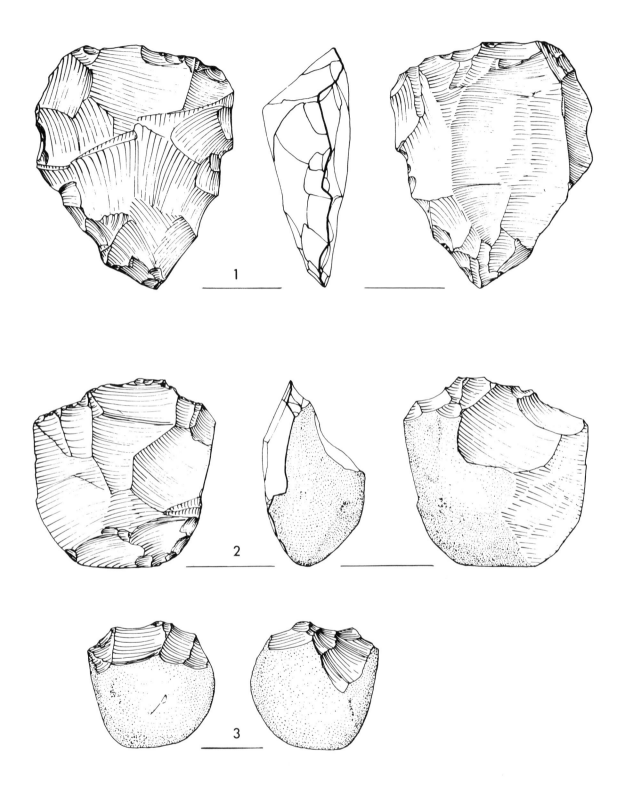

Lower Palaeolithic (Acheulian) artifacts from Pal Barik site, Hulailan Valley, Luristan.

FIGURE 7

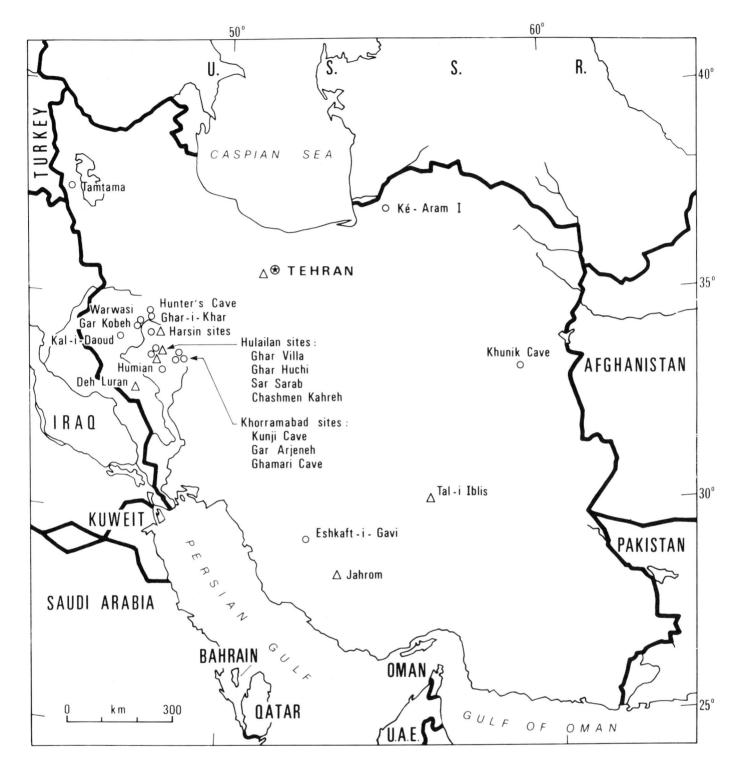

Middle Palaeolithic Occurrences in Iran

○ Cave or shelter occupation sites
△ Principal open air or isolated finds

FIGURE 8

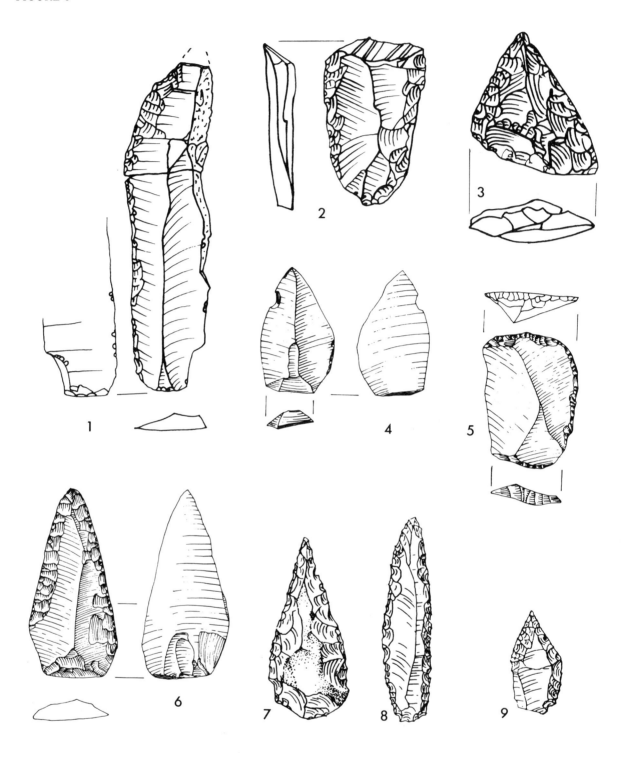

Middle Palaeolithic (Mousterian) artifacts from Ghar-i-Khar, Hulailan Valley sites and Khorramabad sites.

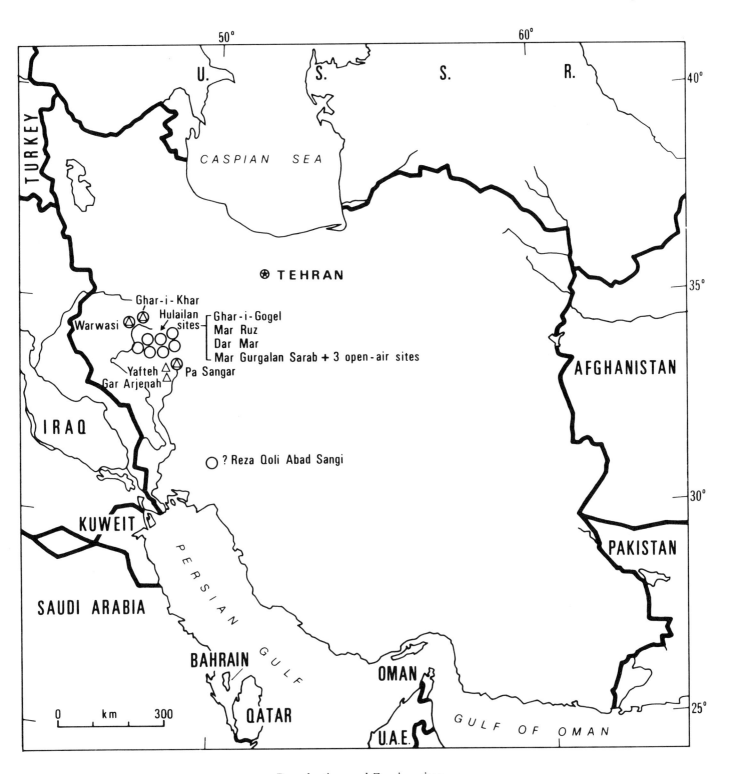

FIGURE 9

Baradostian and Zarzian sites

△ Baradostian
○ Zarzian
◉ Both Baradostian and Zarzian

FIGURE 10

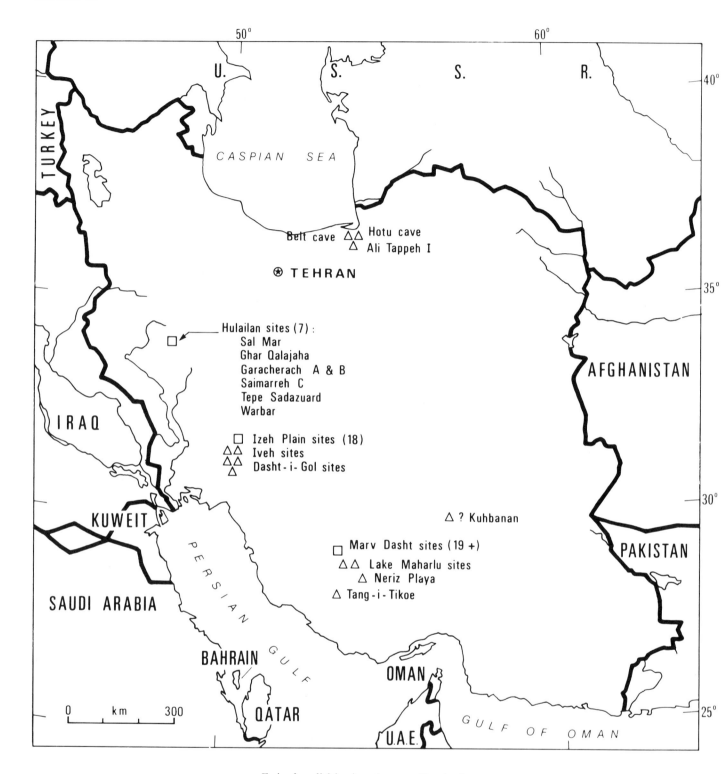

Epipalaeolithic sites (except Zarzian)

△ Site
□ Large group of sites

FIGURE 11

Years B.P.	Stages	Vegetation & Climate in Zagros
ca. 6200	Early Post-Glacial	Warm & dry especially summers. Forest steppe vegetation, slowly expanding trees esp. pistachio; also oak, almond. Less *Artemisia*
ca. 10,500	Late Glacial	Dry with higher temperatures than before, and perhaps more precipitation. Trees spreading in final phase (pistachio, little oak); less *Artemisia*, few grasses.
ca. 14,000	Upper — PLENIGLACIAL Colder and drier than today. Some strong fluctuations in temperature and/or humidity. Semi-desert vegetation, few grasses or trees.	Increasing aridity. Treeless in uplands; *Artemisia*. Some tamarisk & willow in valleys. Virtually no pistachio or oak.
		Scattered tree stands—oak rare. *Artemisia*, etc.
ca. 33,500		
ca. 37,000		Some oak, pistachio & maple but fluctuating & decreasing in numbers. *Artemisia*, Chenopodiaceae, Umbelliferae
ca. 40,000	Middle	Some oak, pistachio & maple present but environment is steppe or desert-steppe (*Artemisia*, Chenopodiaceae, Umbelliferae).

Late Pleistocene and early Holocene climates and vegetation in the Zagros (based on van Zeist and Bottema 1977).

FIGURE 12

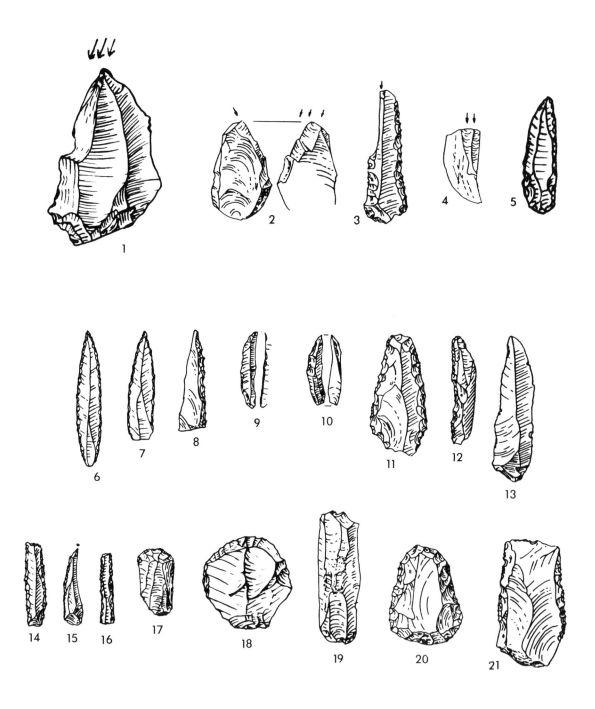

Baradostian artifacts from Ghar-i-Khar and Khorramabad sites.

FIGURE 13

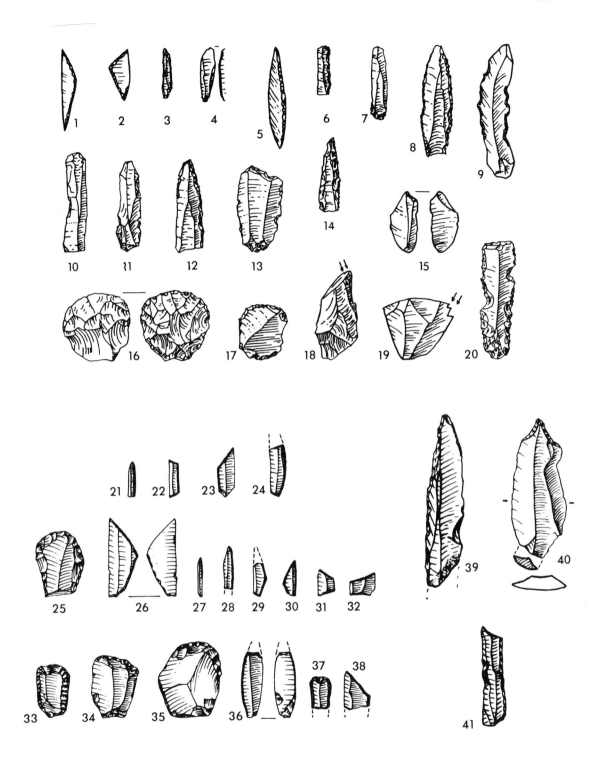

Zarzian artifacts from Khorramabad sites, Hulailan Valley site, and Ghar-i-Khar.

FIGURE 14

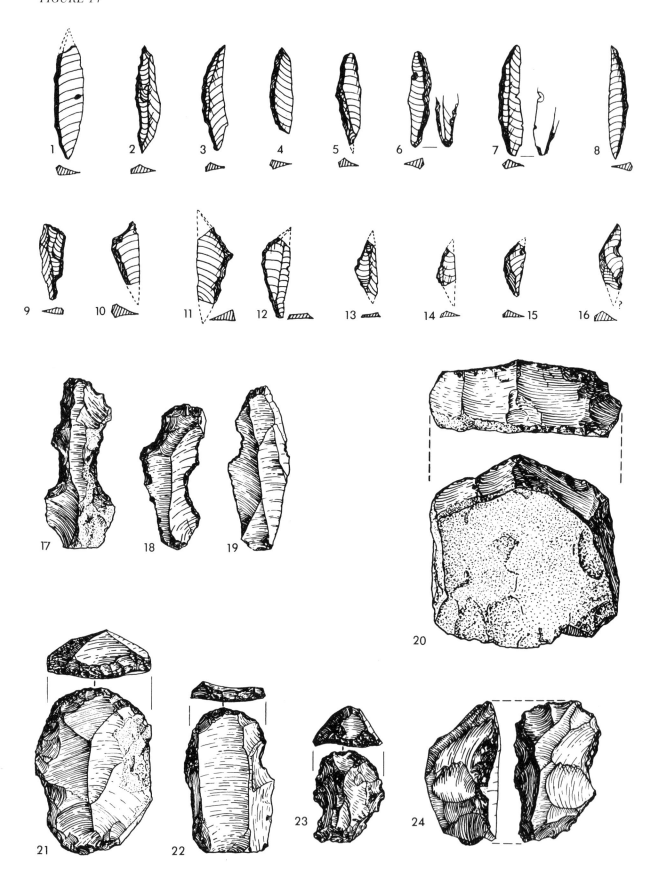

Epipalaeolithic artifacts from the Caspian area: Ali Tappeh I and Hotu Cave.

FIGURE 15

Years B.P.	Geological Periods	Cultural Periods		Zagros Highlands	Khuzistan Lowlands	Northern Highlands/ Caspian Lowlands	Eastern Highlands	Central Plateau
10,000	Holocene	Neolithic		Iveh sites Izeh sites Dasht-e-Gol Warwasi Ghar-i-Khar Pa Sangar Hulailan sites	?	Hotu Cave Belt Cave Ali Tappeh I	?	Kubhanan?
18,000	Upper Pleisto-cene	Epi-Palaeolithic	Zarzian, etc.					
40,000		Upper Palaeolithic	Baradostian	Arjenah Yafteh Pa Sangar Ghar-i-Khar Warwasi	?	?	?	?
80–100,000	Last Glacial	Middle Palaeolithic	Mousterian	Khorramabad sites Jahrom Humian Ghar Villa Ghar Huchi Warwasi Hunter's Cave Ghar-i-Khar Gar Kobeh Tamtama?	Unnamed surface sites	Ké-Aram I	Khunik Cave	Tehran Plain? Tal-i-Iblis?
150,000	Inter-glacial	Lower Palaeolithic	Pebble Tools?—Acheulian	Pal Barik? ? East Azerbaijan Terraces?	?	?	Sarhadd Plateau? Kashafrud Basin?	?
700,000	Middle Pleisto-cene							
1,800,000	Lower Pleisto-cene							

"Ladizian"?

A synthesis of the Iranian Palaeolithic. Chronological subdivisions are not to scale and positions of individual sites within the cultural periods are only approximate.

مقـــــدمــــه :

این مقاله بمنظورشرح وتشخیص وضعیت وچگونگی دیرینهسنگی درایران برشتهتحریردرآمده است . بعلت محدودیت موجوددرمدارک مربوط بدین دوران شایدانجام این وظیفهتا اندازهای آسان بنظرمیرسدولی این محدودیت با عث گردیدهکهقسمتهای تاریک ومبهم زیادی درطول دوران دیرینه سنگی هنوزبچشم میخوردودرنتیجهپیچیدگی وابهام خاصی دروضعیت ایران دراین دوران پیـــش ازتاریخ موجودمیباشد .

با وجودیکهمدارک واطلاعاتی دربارهاین دوران ازنقاط مختلف ایران بدستآمدهولی بطور عمومی وکلی وضعیت این دوران درایران بهروشنی مناطقی ما نندا روپا یا منطقهلوانت (سواحــل شرقی دریای مدیترانه) درغرب قارهٔآسیا ویا بعضی ازقسمتهای افریقا ویا حتی شبهقا رههندنمی ـ باشد . چون بنظرمیرسددرآیندهای چندان نزدیک تغییراتی درحجم اطلاعات ومدارک موجوددربا ره این دوران حاصل گرددا فسوس برا این فقدان معلومات نتیجهای ندا شتهومنطقی ترا ست بهشرح و ـ بررسی همین مدارک محدودنا قص پرداختهوبرروی نکات مبهم دوران نهای تاریک ونا رسا ئیهــای موجودتا کیدنما ئیم . با توجهبهنکات فوق دراین سطوربهتفسیروتعبیرمدارک موجودا زنظرتحولات انسانی دراین منطقهوا رتباط ومقا یسهآن با مدارک مربوط بهدوران دیرینهسنگی کهدردیگـــر نواحی بدستآمدها ست مبادرت نمودهونظرا ت وپیشنهادا تی تا هنگا می کهمجددا "فعالیتهـــای با ستا نشنا سی درایران شروع گرددعرضهمینما ئیم .

عموما "نظرات وفرضیات نسبت بهچگونگی وضعیت دوران دیرینهسنگی ناپایدا روبی دوام ـ میباشندوکشفیات جدیدهموا رهتغییرا تی درآنها بوجودمیآورندولی درشش سال گذشتهدرا یران کـه فعالیتهائی دراین زمینها نجام نگردیدهاین فرضیهها را ثابت وبدون تغییرگذا ردهومعلوم نیست تا چهمدتی نیزدرآیندهبهمین منوال باقی بمانند .

جای هیچگونهتردیدی نیست کهبررسی وتحقیق دربا رهوضعیت دوران قدیم ودیرینه سنگی درایران بهتنهائی بدون درنظرگرفتن وضعیت مناطق همجوا را مکان پذیرنمیباشد . ایـن موضوع دردوران دیرینهسنگی کهبشرزندگانی خودرا ازطریق شکا روجمع آوری آذوقهتا مین مینموده حتی بیش ازدوران نهای تاریخی ضروری بودهومصداق پیدا میکند . مدارک بدستآمدها زبقا یـــــای چندین میلیون سال گذشتهدرا رتباط با دوران دیرینهسنگی حاکی از آنست کهعموما "خصوصیا ت و نحوهزندگا نی درهرا جتما عی بهمنا طق مجا وروحتی دورترسرا یت نمودهوا زحدودآن ا جتماع بخارج

گسترش نموده و بتدریج به تمام مناطق جهان راه یافته است . بنا براین جای تعجب نیست اگر منطقه ایران نیز از این قاعده مستثنی نبوده و دراین مدار ارتباطی مواردی را کسب نموده و یا با لعکس بخارج انتشار داده باشد . با وجودیکه وضعیت جغرافیایی ایران این منطقه را تا اندازه ای دردوران دیرینه سنگی بسته تر و محدودتردرمقام مقایسه با بعضی نواحی دیگرجهان قرارداده ولی این سدهای طبیعی و زمینی به هیچ وجه دردوران کا ملا "جلوگیری از روابط اجتماعات انسانی ننموده اند . دراین مقاله خواهد گردیدکه دوران دیرینه سنگی درایران دررابطه با مناطق همجوار آن در قاره آسیا و بخصوص با مناطق همسایه و نزدیک و مجاور مورد بررسی قرار گیرد .

با ستا نشناسان همواره مفید دانسته اند خصوصیات هرتمدن ی را کا ملا "مشخص نما یند . درست است که هرمنطقه ای درطول زمان هرتحت تا ثیر وضعیت جغرافیائی مخصوص بخودبتدریج درباف ت خاصی خصوصیات منطقه ای پیدا میکند و این نکته ای است که با ستا نشناسان و مورخین درگذشته آن را شخصیت منطقه ای نامیده اند و لی بنظر میرسدکه دراین راه تا اندازه ای درگذشته افراط گردیده و بیش از حدِ واقعی این خصوصیات منطقه ای را از یکدیگرمستقل و مجزا دانسته و به یک محل خاصی نسبت داده اند .

به هرحال بنظر میرسدکه ایران بعلت وضعیت جغرافیایی خودنقش خاصی را دردوران دیرینه سنگی از نظر ارتباط قاره ها روپا و آسیا ایفا نموده و درضمن بعلت خصوصیات اقلیمی و منطقه ای خودباف ت خاصی را در اجتماعات خودنیز بوجود آورده است .

حاجت به تذکراست که دراین مقاله بعلت محدودیت مدارک وا طلاعات مربوط به دوران حجرایران نظریه وباف ت خاص و منحصری برای منطقه ایران پیشنها دنگردیده که منحصر به طرززندگانی ساکنین این دوران دراین منطقه با شد بلکه به بررسی مدارک موجوددراهنا حیه مبا درت نموده و امکان چنین نظرات و یا فرضیه ها ئی را به کشفیات جدیددرآینده و جمع آوری مدارک بیشتری موکول مینما ئیم .

کمبودونقصان اطلاعات ما راجع به باستا نشناسی دوران دیرینه سنگی درایران مربوط به چند عامل است که به شرح بعضی از آنها میپردازیم .

یکی از عوامل مهم دراین قسمت تعدادا نگشت شما رحفا ریها و بررسی های علمی مربوط به این دوران درایران میباشد . علاوه براین حتی گزارش این حفا ریهای محدودنیز تا کنون بطورکامل مـــل انتشار نیا فته و فقط گزارشهای مقدما تی درباره آنها منتشرگردیده است . با وجودیکه وضعیـــت

---

1. Eurasian land

طبقا ت ودورا نها ی با ستا نی دیرینه‌سنگی درمنا طق دیگرجها ن ما نندلوا نت (منطقه‌سوا حل شرقـــی دریا ی مدیترا نه) نیزکا ملا"روشن ومشخص نیست ولی ا زا ین لحا ظ ا یرا ن دروضعیت مبهم تــــرو تا ریک تری قرا ردارد . ا زنوزده‌نمونه‌آزما یش تا ریخ گذا ری بوسیله‌کربن ۱۴ که‌درا یرا ن ا نجـــام گردیده‌وتا ریخ آ نها معلو م میبا شدفقط بعضی میتوا ندمورد‌قبول بوده‌وبه‌رحا ل همگی قدمتـــــی مربوط به‌حدودپنجا ه‌هزا رسا ل گذشته‌ویا بعدا زآ ن را معرفی مینما یند . بنا برا ین چندا ن ا طلاعا ت کا فی مربوط به‌دورا نها ی قدیمتر‌عصرحجردرا یرا ن ویا نمونه‌آزما یشها ی علمی دیگری ما ننـــد پطا سیم آ رگون[2]ویا ترمولومنیستــــن[3]ویا جهت قطب مغنا طیسی[4]ویا ا ورا نیوم توریم[5]که‌درنقا ط دیگر جها ن با موفقیت برا ی تا ریخ گذا ری دورا نها ی دیرینه‌سنگی بکا ررفته‌هنوزدرا یرا ن موردا ستفاده قرا رنگرفته‌ا ست .

وقا یع مربوط به‌دورا ن پلیستوسین ودورا نها ی زمین شنا سی که‌درحدوددومیلیون سا ل پیش شروع گردیده‌درا یرا ن بعلت عدم ا طلاعا ت کا فی هنوزمبهم وتا ریک میبا شد .آ ثا روشوا هدزمیـــن شنا سی مربوط به‌وقا یع ا قلیمی ما نند‌دورا نها ی یخ بندا ن وبا را نی ونوسا نها ی آ نها بسیـــــار محدودبوده‌وبه‌همین علت بسیا رمشکل ا ست که‌بتوا ن نسبت به‌طول ومدت دورا ن هریک ا زفرهنگها ویا تمدنها ی دیرینه‌سنگی درا یرا ن به‌دقت ا ظها رنظرنموده‌ویا را جع به‌تحولات ودگرگونیها ی آ ن هـــــا بطورصریح پیشنها دا تی نمود .

علاوه‌برا ین همین محدودیت مدا رک درزمینه‌وضع ا قلیمی ومنطقه‌ای دورا ن دیرینه‌سنگـــــی مشا هده میگرددودرمقا م مقا یسه‌با سا یرمنا طق ما نند‌ا روپا ویا لوا نت ویا ا مریکـا ی شما لی که‌درا ین موردبررسیها وتحقیقا ت بیشتری ا نجا م گردیده‌فلات ا یرا ن درمحدودیت بیشتری قرا رگرفته‌ا ست .اگر چه‌بررسیـها ی جا لبی بخصوص درزمینه‌گرده‌شنا سی با ستا نی[6]با نتا یج‌مفیدی درمنطقه‌ا نجا م گردیـده ولی چون تعدا دآ نها بسیا رکم ومحدود‌میبا شدهنوزبمرحله‌ای نرسیده‌ا یم که‌بتوا نیم تا ثیــــــر

---

1. Levant
2. Potassium Argon
3. Thermoluminescence
4. Magnetic polarity chronology
5. Uranium Thorium
6. Palynology

اجتماعات انسانی دوران حجر را در تغییرات فت طبیعی محیط حتی در نواحی جبال زاگرس کـــه بیشتر این بررسیها انجام گردیده ارزشیابی نمائیم .

نتیجه این عدم توانائی ارزشیابی بحدی است که نمیتوان تغییرات وتفاوتهای موجود بین دوران پلستوسین ومحیط فعلی را بررسی نمود . ولی بهرحال میتوان تصور نمودکه یقینا "تفاوتهای کلی در وضع طبیعی وظاهری ایران وجود داشته است وا حتما لا"این تفاوتهای بین منطقهای در آن ـ دوران بیش از عصر حاضر موجود بوده اند . بنا براین میتوان تصور نمودکه تفاوتهای کلی در بافت ومنابع تهیه احتیاجات زندگانی در دوران حجر نیز وجود داشته است . بنظر میرسد اجتماعات انسانی که در آن دوران در نواحی کرمان ویا بلوچستان میزیسته اندا حتما لا"دارای نحوه وبافت زندگانی شبیه به آنچه امروز بومیان صحراهای استرالیا دارند دا شته وا جتماعاتی که در مناطق زاگرس بوده اند شبیه به اجتماعات بومی شکارچیانی هستندکه در نواحی غربی امریکای شمالی ما یحتاج زندگانی خودرا از طریق شکار وجمع آوری آذوقه تامین مینمایند .ویا اجتماعاتی با ستانی که در کرانه های جنوبی بحرخزر میزیسته اند بطور کلی طرز زندگانی دیگری که بتواند آنها را آماده برای بهره برداری از منابع غذائی دریائی علاوه برمنابع زمینی بنما یداشته اند . متاسفانه فقدان مدارک مستند علمی وبررسیها وتحقیقات بحدی است که نمیدهد در اینمواردپای فراتر از حد تصور وگمان ـ گذارده وا ظهارات ونظریه های قطعی در حال حاضر پیشنها دنمود . درحقیقت میتوان در اینجا به سهولت بدین نکته اشاره نمودکه چون در حال حاضر در نواحی ایران وحتی منطقهء آسیای غربی نمـــونهء اجتماعاتی که از طریق شکار وجمع آوری آذوقه میزیسته باقی نمانده وبکلی از بین رفته اندا مکان اینگونه ارزشیابیها برای با ستان شناسان دوران حجر در این منطقه تقریبا "میسر نمیبا شد . در منطقه ایـــران (برخلاف مناطقی ما ننداندافریقا ،آسیای جنوبی ،سیبریه ودنیای جدید) بنظر میرسدا ینگونه اجتماعات شکارچی وجمع آوری کننده آذوقه در حدودا وا خردوران نهای پیش از تا ریخ از بین رفته وا مروز چگونگی زندگانی آنها را فقط میتوان از طریق مدارک بدست آمده در حفاریهای با ستان شناسی که در عین حال بسیار محدود میبا شند مورد بررسی وتحقیق قرار دا د .

درخا تمه ، حاجت به تذکرا ست که اطلاعات مربوط به وضع جسمانی افرادا نسانی که مسئول اصلی چگونگی با فت این گونه فرهنگهای دوران حجر میبا شند بسیار محدود بوده وهما نطورکه در صفحات بعـد شرح دا ده خواهدشدفقط مقدار بسیار کمی آثار مربوط به اسکلت انسانهای دوران حجرتا کنون در ـ مناطق مختلف ایران بدست آمده است . بنا براین پیشنها دنظرات وفرضیه هائی در بارهء چگونگـــی هویت جسمی ، تداوم زیستی ویا چگونگی زندگانی آنها موکول به بررسیها وتحقیقات بیشتری در ـ

آینده خواهد بود. نتایج بررسی فسیل وسنگواره ها ئی که درایران جمع آوری گردیده وبوسیــــله پروفسور سندرالاند[1] درسال ۱۹۶۸ میلادی عرضه گردیده تقریبا "بدون تغییرات کلی امروزنیز معتبــر بوده وفقط بعضی سئوالاتی درموردنظرات ایشان موجودمیباشد .

_____
1. Sunderland, 1968

۶

دوران دیرینه‌سنگی

نظـــرات عمومـــی :

پیش از آنکه به‌شرح دوران دیرینه‌سنگی[1] در ایران به‌پردازیم بهتراست راجع به‌چگونگی و تقسیمات این دوران بطور عمومی اشاره‌ای بنما ئیم . واژه‌وکلمه پال اولتیک درقرن نوزدهم میلادی برای اصطلاح عصرحجرقدیم یا دیرینه‌سنگی موردا ستفاده قرار گرفت . دراین دوران ادوات سنگی بطریق ابتدائی وخشن وبدون صیقل ساخته میشدوما نندآنچه دردوره‌های بعدیعنی دردوران - حجرجدیدیا نوسنگی[2]تولید میگردیدنمیبا شند . درقاره اروپا بعدا "یک دوران تحولی برای تغییر از دوران قدیم به‌جدیدبنا م حجرمتوسط یا میان سنگی[3]پیشنها دگردیده وبکا ر گرفته‌شد . بعدها این نظریه‌دوران میان سنگی درخا ورمیا نه‌نزدیک نیزبکا ربسته‌شد . بعضی از با ستا نشنا سان پیش از - تاریخ ترجیح میدهندا صطلاح دوران روی دیرینه‌سنگی ، اپی پال اولتییک[4]را برای دوران بعد از دیرینه‌سنگی که‌مقارن با شا نزده‌هزار سال پیش ویا کمی قدیمترا ست وا حتما لا "به‌دورا نها ی اولیه کشا ورزی منجرمیگردد بکا ربرند . بزودی ضرورت تقسیمات بیشتری برای دوران دیرینه‌سنگـــی در بررسیها وتحقیقا ت با ستا نشنا سی محسوس‌گردیدودرا روپا وآسیای غربی این دوران طویـــــل را به سه‌دوره‌تقسیم نمودند : اول دیرنیه‌سنگی عمیق که‌ا زابتدای استفاده‌ادوات سنگی درحدودا واخـــر (؟) دوران پلستوسین عمیق تا حدودیکصدهزا رسا ل (۱۰۰۰۰۰) پیش را شا مل بوده‌وبنوع ادوات خشن وسا ده‌سنگی بخصوص تبــرهای دستی سنگی[5]مشخص میگردد ،دوم دورا ن دیرینه‌سنگی متوسط که‌ا زحدود یکصدهزا رسا ل پیش‌شروع وتا حدودچهل هزار (۴۰۰۰۰) سال پیش را شا مل بوده‌وبنوع ادوا ت سنگـــی کوچکتروظریفتری با انواع مختلف مشخص گردیده‌ا ست ،وسوم دوران دیرینه‌سنگی مرتفع وروی - دیرینه‌سنگی[6](یا با لای دیرینه‌سنگی)که‌تا حدودده‌هزا ر (۱۰۰۰۰) سال پیش درخا ورنزدیک ا دا مــه دا شته‌وبه‌نوع ادوا ت سنگی تیغه‌های مختلف ا لانداز ه‌که‌غا لبا "بسیا رظریف وکوچک وهم چنین در -

---

1. Palaeolithic
2. Neolithic
3. Mesolithic
4. Epipalaeolithic
5. Stone hand axe
6. Epipalaeolithic
7. Microlithic

بعضی مناطق ادواتی ساخته‌شده از استخوان ویا شاخ حیوانات ویا عاج با تنوع زیاد و تفاوتهای منطقه‌ای بیشتری مشخص گردیده است . بسیار مشکل است که بطوردقیق تداوم نوع ادوات را از ـ دورانی به دوران دیگر بطوریک نواخت ویکسان وهمزمان برای مناطق مختلف بطورعموم مشخــص نمود .

این تقسیم بندی بطورکلی برای مناطق ایران ویا سایرنواحی خاورنزدیک وهم چنین آسیای مرکزی ، ودرسالهای اخیربرای مناطق هندوپاکستان نیزا عمال گردیده است وبا وجودنواقصی کــه دا ردبهرحال برای تحقیقات علمی از نظرمقایسه و را بطها این فرهنگها با یکدیگر مورد استفاده می ـ با شد .

<u>فعالیتهای علمی تحقیقات وحفاریهای مربوط به عصرحجردر ایران :</u>

تحقیقات وبررسیهای علمی مربوط به دوران دیرینه‌سنگی در ایران مانندکشورهای ترکیــه و عراق، وافغانستان خیلی دیرتر از مناطق سوریه و فلسطین درخاورنزدیک انجام گردید .علت این ا مررا شایدبتوان دربعدمسافت ایران از اروپا ویا انحصار فعالیتهای باستانشناسی بوسیلـــه فرانسویان از سال ۱۸۹۰ تا   ۱۹۳۰ میلادی در ایران جستجونمود .[1]

در اواخرقرن نوزدهم پروفسورژاک دمورگان رئیس هیات حفاری فرانسوی گزارش وجودادوات سنگی را که درلایه پلستوسین قرا ردا شتندد رحوزه بحرخزر انتشا ردا دولی اظهارداشت که بقیه ایران در این دوران بوسیله یخچالها ودریا چه‌ها پوشیده بوده است . (مورگان ۱۹۰۷) .دردهه٬ ۱۹۳۰آثا رسطحی مربوط به دوران دیرینه‌سنگی درفا رس درنزدیک شهرشیرا زبدست آمد (فیلد ۵۵-۵۵۳: ۱۹۳۹میلادی) . اولین حفاری مربوط به دوران دیرینه‌سنگی در سال ۱۹۴۹ میلادی بوسیله پروفسورکوون انجــام گردید (کوون ۱۹۵۱) .این استاد ا مریکائی در ابتدا درغا رشکا رچیا ن بیستون وسپس درغا رتمتمـــه درنزدیک دریا چه رضا ئیه وپس از آن درغا رخونیک درجنوب خراسان درنزدیکی مرزا فغانستان حفاری نمود . درهمان سال نیزدربقایای دوران میان سنگی درغا رکمربندنزدیک بهشهرودرسال ۱۹۵۱   در غا رهوتودرنزدیک غا رکمربندحفا ری نمود . بزودی آشکا رگردیدکه ایران نیزدا را ی آثا روبقا یا ی مربوط به دوران دیرینه‌سنگی متوسط ومیان سنگی بوده وشا ثرتما یدبرا ثرتما دف پروفسورکوون به آثار مربوط به دیرینه‌سنگی مرتفع که بعدها در ایران آشکا رگردید (وبعنوا ن فرهنگ با را دوستیان[2]مشخص گردیده) دست یا بی پیدا ننموده .اوگزا رش دقیق کا روخوددر ا کا روخوددرکتاب هفت غا ر[3]درسال ۱۹۵۷ به‌چا پ

---

1. Negahban, 1981−82
2. Baradostian culture
3. Coon, 1957

رسا نید .

ا ز آ ن سا ل بـه بعد فعا لیتها ی مربوط بـه با ستا نشنا سی عصر حجر بوسیلـه با ستا نشنا سا ن خا ر جـی ا ز کشورها ی کا نـا دا ،دا نما رک ، فرا نسه ، ا نـگلستا ن ،ا یتا لیا ۺ ا مریکا درا یرا ن ا نجا مگزدیده ا ست . گروه پروفسور بریدوود درچند غا ر مربوط بـه دورا ن دیرینـهسنگی متوسط ومرتفع درکرما نشا ه (نا م فـعلی با خترا ن) درسا ل ۱۹۶۰-۱۹۵۹ ،پروفسورهول وفلانـری درپنج محل درنزدیک خرم آ با د درلرستا ن درسا لـهای ۱۹۶۵،۱۹۶۳ وپروفسورسپت ادا مها ین کا ررا در ۱۹۶۹ ادا مهدا د .نویسنـــــده (پروفسورا سمیت)ترا نشهکوچکی درغا رخا رخا ردربیستون درسا ل ۱۹۶۵ درغا ریکهقبلا "بوسیلـه پروفسور کرون دیدهشدهولی حفا ری نشدهبود حفا ری نمود . پروفسورمک بورنی درسا لـها ی (۱۹۶۴و ۱۹۶۸) در غا رکی آ را م درما زندا را ن دربقا یا ی دورا ن دیرینـهسنگی متوسط ودربقا یا ی میا ن سنگی درعلی تپـهنزدیک بهشهردرحوزهبحرخزردرسا لـها ی ۱۹۶۲ و ۱۹۶۴ وسپس درسا ل ۱۹۶۹ دربقا یا ی دوران دیـرینـهسنگی متوسط درغا ری درلرستا ن بررسی وتحقیقا ت نمود .درسا لـها ی ۱۹۶۶ و ۱۹۶۷ پروفسور هیوم درمنا طق بلـوچستا ن بررسی وآ ثا رسطحی درچندمحل مربوط بـه دورا ن دیرینـهسنگی وسپـس پروفسورمروچک درا ین منطقهدرسا لـها ی ۱۹۷۴ و ۱۹۷۵ کا ررا ا دا مهدا د .پروفسورپیرنو درآ ثا ر سطحی تپهای کهدرسا ل ۱۹۶۹ بوسیلـه پروفسورزامنر گزا رش شدهبودبررسی نمودهودرسا ل ۱۹۷۴ را جـع بـهتیغههای سنگ چخما ق مربوط بـه دورا ن دیرینـهسنگی مرتفع دریک پنا هگا هسنگی درنزدیک شیرا ز گزا رش نمودها ست .

درسا ل ۱۹۷۶ پروفسورر ا یت درآ ثا ر وبقا یا ی عصر حجردرچندمحل درشما ل خوزستا ن بررسینمود. درشما ل غربی ا یرا ن خا نـم پروفسورهندکوروس آ ثا روا دا وا ت سنگی دررا بطهبا دورا ن دیرینـهسنگی

1. Braidwood, 1960
2. Hole and Flannery, 1967
3. Speth, 1971
4. Young and Smith, 1966
5. Hume, 1976
6. Marucheck, 1976
7. Piperno, 1972
8. Wright, H.T., 1979

درلایه پلستوسین زمین شناسی درآ ذربایجان شرقی'وهمچنین پروفسورآریایی وپروفسورتیبالت۲ درخراسان بررسیهایی نموده وآثاری که احتمالا"مربوط به قدیمترین مدارک دررابطه با زندگانسی انسان درایران میباشد بدست آوردند .هم چنین آثارمربوط به عصرحجردرچندناحیه ازلرستان بوسیله پروفسورمورتنسن وبررسی۳دیگری بوسیله نویسنده وپروفسورمورتنسن درسال ۱۹۷۷ میلادی درنزدیک هرسین درکرمانشاهان انجام شدویک کارگاه بزرگ تولیدا دوات سنگی مربوط به دوران حجردرقسمتی از دشت کشف گردید .هم چنین بررسیهای دیگری مربوط به این دوران درمناطق شمال غربی ایران وبخصوص آذربایجان بوسیله پروفسورسولکی۴وهم چنین بوسیله پروفسورسینگروویمر۵انجام گردیده اسـت .

1. Sadek-Kooros, 1974
2. Ariai and Thibault, 1975–77
3. Mortensen, 1974a; 1974b; 1975
4. Solecki, 1969
5. Singer and Wymer, 1978

وضعیت طبیعــی : حا ل وگذشتــه :

آنچه مسلم ا ست بشرا ولیه که زندگا نی خودرا بشکا روجمع آ وری ما یحتــا ج خودا زمنا بع طبیعـی تا مین مینمودها رتبا ط بسیا رنزدیکی با طبیعت همجوا رخوددا شتهو آ ثا را رقیما نده مربوط بدیـــن دورا ن ا زا ین منا بع طبیعی بدست آ مدهو آشنا ئی بوضعیت طبیعی آ ن دورا ن بهترین را هنمـــــای آشنا ئی با ا ین ا جتما عا ت که مدا رک محدودی ا زآ نها با رقیما نده ا ست میبا شد .

وسعت ا یرا ن درحا ل حا ضردرحدود ۱۶۴۸۰۰۰ کیلومترمربع بودهودرا ین منطقها نوا ع وا شکـال مختلف طبیعت ، لایهها ی زمین ومنا بع طبیعی ، رشتهجبا لها ی مرتفع ودشتها ی همـوا روکویـــر ومنا طق سا حلی دریا ها وجوددا رد . بگفتهیکی ا زا ستا دا ن گیا هشنا سی کمترمما لکی درمنطقها روپـا وآ سیا هستندکه درقسمتها ی شما ل منا طق معتدل وحتی سردسیرودرقسمتها ی جنوب منا طق آ ب وهـوای ا ستوا ئی دا شتهبا شند وتما م ا ین ا نوا ع مختلف آ ب وهوا ها فقط درفا صلهیا زده درجه عرض جغرافیائـی درکشورا یرا ن قرا رگرفتها ند . [1]

بطورخلاصها یرا ن دا را ی رشتهجبا لها ئی ا ست که منا طق مرتفع بین ۳۰۰ تا ۱۲۰۰ متـرا ز[2] سطـح دریا بصورت دشتها درما بین آ نها بوجودآ مدهوا زبعضی آ نها که رجا هبخا رج دا رندرودخا نهها ئی بطـرف دریا ی خزریا خلیج فا رس جریا ن دا رودرنتیجهدا را ی آ ب وهوا ها ی مختلف حا شیهکویری ویـــــا با را نهای موسمی درقسمت جنوب میبا شد . [3] بجزمنطقهسوا حل دریا ی خزربقیها یرا ن بطورکلـی دا را ی آ ب وهوا ی خشک میبا شد ومقدا رنسبتا "کم ومحدودی دربین ما ههای مهرتا ا ردیبهشت با رندگــی در فلات ا یرا ن وجوددا ردوا ین وضعیت ا حتما لا"دردورا نهای پیش ا زتا ریخ نیزوجوددا شتها ست . ا یـــن منطقه ا زنظرآ تش فشا ن وزلزله همیشه فعا ل بودهوبا فت ومنظرطبیعی فعلی آ ن دا را ثرا ین عوا مـــل با ضا فها ثرا ت آ ب وبا دبوجودآ مدها ست .

با وجودیکه منطقها یرا ن ممکن ا ست بهمنا طق مختلف جغرا فیا ئی وطبیعی تقسیم بندی گـرد د ولی درا ین مقا لهبهپنج منطقهبهشرح ذیل طبقهبندی گردیدها ست (شکل شما ره۱) .

۱ـ منطقهرشتهجبا ل زاگرس که درنوا حی غربی ا یرا ن ا زحدودآ ذربا یجا ن تا خلیج فا رس وتنگه هرمزدرحدود ۱۶۰۰ کیلومترا دا مهدا رد . ا ین رشتهجبا ل که درا بتدا درا ثرفشا رها وعوا مل ا رضــــی مولـودا زبحرا حمربوجودآ مدها مروزها زلایهها ی موا زی سنگ آ هگی که بعضی ا زآ نها حدود ۴۰۰۰ متـــــو

1. Zohary, 1963
2. Bobek, 1968
3. Bobek, 1968

ارتفاع دارند تشکیل میگردد . دربین این ارتفاعات دره هائی قرار گرفته که درآنها بستر رودخانه هائی مانند خانبور ، سمیره ، کرخه ، کارون ، دز ،زاب بزرگ وزاب کوچک ،دیاله در ایران وعراق جاری هستند .وضع اقلیم و آب وهوا در این منطقه شدید تراز منطقه مدیترانه ای بخصوص در ایام زمستان میباشد .در این منطقه ما مروزهم نگونه که احتمالا "در دوران پلستوسین نیز مشابه آن وجود داشته آب وهوا های مختلف مشاهده میگردد .دامنه غربی رشته جبال زاگرس بیش از دامنهء شرقی که سردتر است با رندگی دارد .ریزش برف در این ناحیه سنگین بوده و براساس اختلاف و چگونگی آب وهوا وارتفاع در دزه های مختلف نباتات و گیاهانی مانند بلوط ، پسته ، بادام ،گندم وجو وحشی روئیده وحیوانا تی مانند بزکوهی ، گوسفند ،خرس ، آهو ،غزال هنوز زندگا نی مینمایند .این منطقه مروزه درحدودیک سوم منطقه جغرافیائی ایران را فرا میگیرد و پرجمعیت ترین مناطق ایران است .آثار مربوط به عصر حجر نیز بیشتر در این منطقه زاگرس بدست آمده اند .

۲ـ دشت خوزستان که بصورت دشت رسوبی وازفرسایش ارتفاعات مشرف بدان بوجودآمده امروز بصورت کاملا "هموارمشاهده میگردد . این دشت ازدامنه های جبال زاگرس تاکرانه های شمالـــی خلیج فارس امتداد میابد و بوسیله پنج رودخانه بزرگ کرخه ،کارون ، دز ، جراحی وزهره مشروب می ـ گردد .بعضی نواحی این دشت با طلاقی ولی بیشترآن بصورت استپها ی نیمه خشک میباشد .زمستـــان ملایم تراز منطقه زاگرس وتابستان گرمترازآن میباشد .نباتات و گیاهان این استپ وبیابان وچـرا ـ گاهها ومراتع غنی درفصل زمستان وجوددارند .حیوانا تی مانند غزال ،گاو ،آهو وگرازوحشی بنظر میرسدما نند امروزدردوران نهای پیش ازتاریخ نیزوجودداشته وبزدردامنه کوهها مشاهده میگردد .ماهی وپرندگان دریائی و لاک پشت در رودخانه ها وبا طلاقها زندگانی مینمایند .

۳ـ ارتفاعات شمالی رشته جبال البرز که درجنوب بحرخزرقرارگرفته و درحدود ۹۶۰ کیلومتـر بصورت قوس هلالی ازآستارا درمغرب تا جاجرم درمشرق ادامه دارد .این رشته جبال شامل بلندترین کوه آتش فشان ایران قله دماوند نزدیک تهران میباشد .! مروزه یخچالهای کوچکی هنوز درآن باقی ـ ما نده ولی دردوران پلستوسین این منطقه بیش ازرشته جبال زاگرس یخبندان بوده است .بعلـــت ارتفاع زیا درطوبت حاصله ازبحرخزردردامنه های شمالی سدگردیده و بارندگی ، دراین قسمت زیاد میباشد شده و چندرودخانه مانند سفیدرود به دریای خزرجریان دارند .برودت هوا درزمستان بیش ازمنطقه زاگرس میباشد .درنواحی کم ارتفاع هوا ملایم بوده و حدمتوسط باران دراین نواحی درحدود دوهزار میلیمتردرسال میباشد .نباتات و گیاهان جنگلی مختلف مانند بان گنجشگ ،زیزفون یا نمدار ، نارون ، گردو ، افرا ، آلش ،ممرزدراین منطقه میروید .علاوه بربزوگوسفند ،حیوانات مشخص دیگری

در این منطقه ما نندخوک دریا ئی بحرخزروببروجوددا رندکه احتما لا"نسل ببرا زبین رفته ا ست .

۴ـ نا حیه سیستا ن وا رتفا عا ت شرقی ا یرا ن که ا زخرا سا ن تا بلوچستا ن ا دا مه دا ردوشا مـل نوا حی مکرا ن وسوا حل شما لی دریا ی عما ن نیزمیگردد . ا ین نا حیه شا مل کوهها ودشتها ئی کـه بعضی درحدود ۹۰۰ متر ا رتفا ع دا رندوبوده ودریا چه ها وبا طلاقها ئی ا زرودخا نه ها ئی ما نندهیرمنـد مشروب میگردند میبا شد . آب وهوا ا ین منطقه متغیر بوده وتا بستا نها ی گرم وزمستا نها ی سرددا رد . نبا تا ت ا مروزی شا مل جنگلها ی بلـوط، عرعر، پسته وبا دا م میبا شد .حیوا نا ت ا مروزی شا مل ، بز ، قـوچ وحشی ، گرا ز ،غزا ل وخروحشی بوده که ا حتما لا"دردورا ن دیرینه سنگی نیزوجوددا شته ا نـد . ا لبته حیوا نا ت دورا ن پلستوسین بخصوص دربلوچستا ن کمترشنا خته شده ا ند .

۵ـ فلات مرکزی ویا کویرمرکزی که نیمی ا زوسعت ا یرا ن درحدود ۷۸۰۰۰۰ کیلومترررا فرا گرفتـه ا ست [1] . ا ین کویربزرگ بوسیله رشته جبا لها ئی درا طرا ف محصورگردیده ا ست ومجرا ئی به خا رج ودریا ندا ردوشا مل دوکویربزرگ یکی دشت کویردرشما ل ودشت لوت درجنوب میبا شد .درا ین دوکویـــر دریا چه های آب شورونمک وهم چنین رشته جبا لها ئی وجوددا رد . با رندگی درا ین منا طق بسیا رکـم وکمترا ز۱۰۰ میلی متردرسا ل میبا شد . آب وهوا ی تا بستا ن بسیا رگرم وزمستا ن بسیا رسردمیبا شد . نوع نبا تا ت صحرا ئی ا ستپ مشا هده میگرددوحیوا نا تی ما نندعزا ل وخروحشی (گورخر) درا ین منطقه وجوددا رند .

هما نگونه که قبلا" ا شا ره گردیدآب وهوا ی ا یرا ن (بجز منطقه حوزه بحرخزر) دا را ی تا بستـان خشک وگرم وزمستا ن سردومرطوب میبا شد ومقدا ربا رندگی بیشتردرشما ل وشما لغرب وبسیا رکمتـــر وحتی هیچ درسا یرنوا حی مملکت وجوددا رد . با دمدا وم درفلات تا ثیردرجه برودت ویا حرا رت را شدیـد ترمینما ید . رشته جبا لها ئی که درا طرا ف فلات قرا ردا رندا زورودرطوبت دریا ی مدیترا نه ،بحرخـزر، ویا خلیج فا رس ویا با را نهای موسمی شبه قا ره هندوپا کستا ن به دا خل فلات جلـوگیری مینما یننـد .در زمستا ن هوای سردسیری سیبریه درتما م منطقهٔ ، هوا ی مدیترا نه ا ی درشما ل غربی (نا حیه زا گـــرس وا لبرز) وآب وهوا ی صحرا ئی درمنطقه فلات تا ثیرگذا رده ورویهمرفته آب وهوا ی متغیری بــــرای قسمتها ی مختلف ا یرا ن بوجودمیآ ورند .[2] بنا برا ین تغییرا ت هوا درفصول وقسمتها ی مختلف ا ها لـی ا یرا ن درتا بستا ن به منا طق سردترومرتفع ودرزمستا ن به منا طق گرمترمسا فرت مینما یندولی هنـوز

1. Fisher, 1968, fig. 3
2. Fisher, 1968

مدارکی موجود نیست که آیا اجتماعات دوران عصر حجر نیز بدینکار مبادرت می‌ورزیده‌اند .جای تردید نیست که از نظر بافت آب و هوا وضع مشابهی در دوران پلستوسین نیز وجود داشته است[1].

سوال حل بحر عمان احتمالاً در دوران یخبندان به نظر میرسد بیشتر در منطقه دریا پیشرفتگی داشته و این سوال در زیر آب قرار گرفته اند ممکن است محل زندگانی اجتماعات عصر حجر بوده با شدولی تحقیقات و بررسیهائی در این مناطق انجام نگردیده است . احتمالاً بررسیها و تحقیقات با ستا نشناسی در این نواحی منجر به کشف آثار و مدارکی از این دوران خواهد بود[2] .اما حیه مکران نیز احتمالاً محل مناسبی برای اینگونه تحقیقات میتواند باشد[3] .

وضعیت دوران پلستوسین در مناطق مرتفع شمال ایران هنوز کاملاً مشخص نیست .مسلمــــاً یخچـالهای بیشتری در دوران سرد وجود داشته است . وجود زندگانی انسان در این ارتفاعات البرز بدانگونه که در مناطق زاگرس مشخص گردیده هنوز مسلم نیست . تاکنون شواهدی از زندگانی انسان در دوران دیرینه سنگی از منطقه جبال البرز بدست نیامده ولی تصور می‌رود چنین منطقه مناسبی با شکارگاههای فراوان در حداقل در فصول گرم تر بدون استفاده نمانده با شد .

حوزه بحر خزر به همانگونه که امروز کاملاً منحصر بخود میبا شد در گذشته نیز همین وضعیت را داشته است . سطح آب دریا که امروز در حدود ۲۸ متر از سطح دریاهای آزاد پائین تر است در گذشته نوسانهائی داشته و گاهی بالاتر (در حدود ۱۶ متر) و گاهی پائین تر (در حدود ۴۰–۳۰ متر) از سطح دریای آزاد بوده است .سطح بحر خزر به علت تبخیر متفاوت و وصول حجم متفاوت آب رودخانه‌ها در دوران پلستوسین نیز متغییر بوده است . کرانه‌های مرتفع تری تا حدود ۹۰ متربالاتر از کرانه‌های امروزی بوسیلــــه دانشمندان در اطراف این دریا مشخص گردیده است . بنظر می‌رسد سطح بحر خزر در دوران یخبندان بالاتر از سطح کنونی بوده است (شکل ۲)[4]. در دوران‌های گرم سطح دریا به مقدار قابل ملاحظه‌ای نقصان حاصل نموده است . در دوران هلوسین[5] سطح دریا چندین باربه بالاتر یا پائین ترتغییـــــر نموده ولی بهر حال احتمالاً هیچگاه به ارتفاع قبلی آن نرسیده است[6] .وضع نوسانها وتغییــــرات سطح بحر خزرتا کنون در دوران‌های مختلف کاملاً مشخص نگردیده و از این نظربرای تحقیقات دورانهای باستانی مشکلاتی بوجود می‌آورد .آنچه مسلم است محل اجتماعات مربوط به دوران متوسط و مرتفـــع پلستوسین که در آن وقت در نزدیک کرانه‌های فعلی دریا قرار گرفته بوده‌اند امروز در زیر آب قـــــرار

1. Zohary, 1963
2. Field, 1956
3. Hume, 1976
4. Dolukhanov, 1977
5. Holocene
6. Gerasimov, 1978

گرفته اندو با درزیرطبقا ت زمین وا قع شده ا ند . بنظر میرسدمنا طق جنگلی وسعت بیشتری دا شتـــه
ا ست . [1]کا هش درجه حرا رت برف بیشتری دردورا ن یخبندا ن درحوزه بحرخزربوجودآ ورده ا ست . [2]بـــا
رسیدن دورا ن های گرمترسطح دریا پا ئین تررفته وغا رها ئی که دردا منه های ا لبرزقرا ردا شتنـــد و
قبلا"درزیرسطح آ ب پنها ن بودندا ززیرآ ب درآ مده وبرا ی سکونت ا جتما عا ت ا نسا نی موردا ستفا ده
قرا رگرفتند .وبا لاخره با فت وشبکه نبا تا ت وحیوا نا ت ا مروزی نیزبتدریج بوجودآ مد .

با وجودیکه بنظرمیرسدحیوا نا تی که غذا ی ا ین ا جتما عا ت را تا مین مینمودندا حتما لا"همیـــن
ا نوا ع ا مروزی حیوا نا ت بوده با شندولی نسبت به نوع حیوا نا ت دورا نها ی قدیمترنمیتوا ن ا ظهار
نظرنمود . آ نچه مسلم ا ست ا ینکه حیوا نا ت سردسیری وقطبی ما نندگوزن شما لی ویا ما موت پشمدار
ویا حیوا نا ت ا ستو ا ئی درا ین مـنطقه وجودندا شته ا ند .حیوا نا تی که بمنظورتا مین منا بع غذا ئـی
بوده اندشا مل گا و ، گوسفند ،بز ،خوک ،خروحشی ،آ هو ،غزا ل ، حلزون وصدف ودرا وا خردورا ن   —
پلستوسینوا یل دورا ن هلوسین علاوه برآ ن ما هیها وپرندگا ن موردا ستفا ده قرا رگرفته ا ند .دراوا خر
دورا ن پلستوسین خوک آ بی درسوا حل بحرخزرشکا رومورد ا ستفا ده قرا رمیگرفته ا ست . حیوا نا ت وحشی
گوشتخوا رما نندخرس ، گرگ،روبا هشکا روا زپوست آ نها برا ی لبا س ا ستفا ده نموده ا ند .ا طلاعا ت مـــا
دربا ره نبا تا ت ومیوه درختا ن دردورا ن پلستوسین درا ین نا حیه ا زنظرمنا بع غذا ئی ا جتما عـــا ت
ا جتما عی بسیا رمحدودونا قص میبا شد .شرح نبا تا ت ا مروزی ا یرا ن بوسیله پروفسورظهری[3]ممکن ا ست
تصویرمشا بهی نسبت به نبا تا ت با ستا نی درا ختیا رما بگذا رد .

شا یدبتوا ن ا ظها ر دا شت که دروضع فعلی شا یدیک سوم وسعت ا یرا ن برا ی شکا روجمع آ وری   —
آذوقه مسا عدبوده [4]وبقیه نا مسا عدمیبا شدودرگذشته نیزا ین منطقه با نوسا نها ئی دردورا ن هـای
مختلـف موردا ستفا ده ا جتما عا ت با ستا نی بوده ا ست . تخمین تعدا دجمعیت دورا نها ی با ستا نی در--
ا یرا ن ا مکا ن پذیرنیست . مسلما "ا ین تعدا دنیزدردورا نها ی مختلـف متفا وت بوده وبتدریج ا ز --
دورا ن دیرینه سنگی به نوسنگی روبا فزا یش رفته ا ست . بنظرمیرسددرا بتدا ا ین ا جتما عا ت ا نسا نـی
ا زیکدیگرمتفرق بوده ولی بتدریج درا وا خردورا ن پلستوسین کمی قبل ا زدورا ن تولیدمحصـــولات
غذا ئی وکشا ورزی به گروهها ی بزرگ تری تبدیل گردیدند .بنظرمیرسددردوره ها ئی که آ ب وهوا مسا عد
نبوده جمعیت روبه نقصا ن رفته ومنا طقی ما نندرشته جبا ل زا گرس که برا ی زندگا نی مسا عدتربوده ا ند

1. van Zeist and Bottema, 1977
2. Krinsley, 1970
3. Zohary, 1963
4. Flannery, 1969:94

دارای جمعیت بیشتری بوده اند . در اینجا ضروری بنظر میرسد به تقسیما ت دورا ن پلستوسین نیز اشاره ای گردد .

دانشمندان زمین شنا سی ا ین دورا ن را به سه (وبعضی چهار) دوره اصلی تقسیم مینما یند . (شکل شما ره ۳) . پلستوسین عمیق که از زما نی درحدود دو میلیون سا ل پیش شروع وبدون تردید ادوا ت سنگی بوسیله اجتما عا ت ا نسا نی درقاره افریقا سا خته شده و حتی شواهدی را جع به پیش ا زاین زما ن نیز موجود میبا شد . ا ین ! جتما عا ت بتدریج از نظرفرهنگ وجسم تکا مل یا فته وبه قا ره ا روپا وآسیا نیز توسعه یا فت . دورا ن پلستوسین میا نه در حدود هفتصد هزا رسا ل پیش شروع گردید ودورا نی کوتا هتر ا زدورا ن قبلی بودوفعا لیتها ی یخبندا ن وهم چنین تغییرا تی دروضع حیوا نا ت درآ ن ـ مشا هده میگردد . هم چنین تغییرا تی درنوع ا دوا ت سنگی درآ ن بوقوع پیوست وتبرها ی دستی سنگی درا ین دورا ن آشکا رگردید . دورا ن پلستوسین مرتفع درحدود ۱۲۵۰۰۰ سا ل پیش شروع گردیده ودراین دورا ن تحولاتی دروضع ا نسا ن وحیوا نا ت مشا هده میگردد . ا نسا نها ی نوع نئا ندرتا ل جا یگزیـــن نوع قبلی هوموا رکتوس گردیدندوبتدریج نوع ا نسا ن هـو موسا پین (که ا حتما لا"درحدود یکصدهزا رـ سا ل پیش درا فریقا ظا هرشده بود) جا یگزین ا نسا نها ی نئا ندرتا ل دردورا ن پلستوسین مرتفــــع گردید . با وجودیکه ا ین تقسیما ت سه گا نه دورا ن پلستوسین بطورکلی از نظرلایه ها ی زمین شنا سـی ودورا نها ی ا قلیمی بوده ولی بهرحا ل تقسیم بندی مفیدی برا ی دا نشمندان با ستا نشنا س دورا ن پیش ا زتا ریخ برا ی طبقه بندی فرهنگها مورد ا ستفا ده قرا رگرفته است . جا ی بسی تا سف ا ست که مدا رک مستندی مربوط به ا ین دورا نها ی طویل بعلت محدودیت تحقیقا ت وبررسیها ی با ستا نشنا سی هنوز بطورکا مل درحا ل حا ضردرا یرا ن وجود ندا رد . فقط دورا ن پلستوسین مرتفع درا یرا ن تا ا ندا زه مشخص وروشن گردیده وآ خرین قسمتها ی آ ن درزما ن دوره٬ سردترکه همزما ن با دوره یخبندا ن وورم [1] که دورا ن قبل آ ن تقـریبا "درحدود هشتا دتا یکصدهزا رسا ل پیش به پا یا ن رسیده بود بطورجزئـــــی مشخص گردیده ا ست . ا لـبـته شوا هدی وجود دا ردکه بتوا ن تصورنمود منطقه درا ین هنگا م موردسکونــت اجتما عا ت ا نسا نی بوده ا ست .

---

1. Würm Glaciation

دوران دیرینه‌سنگی عمیـــق :[1]

هنـوزکاملا"روشن نیست اولین انسانها ازکجا و؛ زچه‌جهتی به‌منطقه ایران وارد گردیده‌انـــد . چون احتمال ندارداایران ویا قسمتهای دیگرخاورنزدیک گهواره‌تمدن بشری بوده‌باشند ،بایدتصور نمودکه اولین اجتماعات بشری دراین منطقه ازخارج بدان مهاجرت نموده‌انـــد .متاسفانه‌هنـوز مبداء اصلی ویا نوع فرهنگ ووضع جسمانی این اجتماعات اولیه ایران به‌علت عدم وجودمدارک ــ مربوط به‌دوران دیرینه‌سنگی عمیق دراین منطقه مشخص نگردیده‌است .اگرچه‌باکشفیات باستانشناسی درمنطقه‌لوانت درعبیدیه‌درده‌اؤردن دراسرائیل منطقی به‌نظرمیرسدتصورنماﺌیم دردوران پلستوـ سین عمیق درحدودیک میلیون سال پیش اجتماعات انسانی با ادوات سنگی مشخص خودبتدریج از ــ افریقا مهاجرت نموده‌وبه‌مناطق اروپاوآسیای غربی مانندلوانت وجنوب عربستان را ه‌یافته‌وسپس بتدریج به‌نواحی بین النهرین وایران مهاجرت نمودندولی مسیراین مهاجرت هنوزازحدودحـدس وگمان خارج نمیباشد .این احتمال نیزوجودداردکه‌اولین اجتماعات انسانی درایران ازطریـــق شمال ازآسیای مرکزی ویا ازراه‌قفقازبه‌ایران مهاجرت نموده‌باشندبه‌نظرمیرسدمنطقه‌جنوب روسیه درحدودیک ربع میلیون سال پیش درهنگام دیرینه‌سنگی یعنی درحدودپلستوسین میانه[2]مـــورد سکونت اجتماعات انسانی بوده‌است . همچنین احتمال داردکه‌این مهاجرت ازجهت شرق ازشبه‌قاره هندکه‌آثاری مربوط به‌دوران پلستوسین میانه‌درحدودنیم میلیون سال پیش درآن بدست آمـــده صورت‌گرفته‌باشد ،به‌هرحال دروضع فعلی تاﺌیدهیچیک ازاین نظریه‌ها با محدودیت شواهدومـــدارک باستانی درایران (وعراق) میسرنمیباشد .

حاجت به‌تذکراست که‌دردنیای قدیم (افریقا ،لوانت ، اروپای غربی وشبه‌قاره‌هند)دوگـروه ادوات سنگی دردوران دیرینه‌سنگی عمیق بدست آمده‌است .گروه‌اول ادوات سنگی خشن که‌ازقلـوه سنگها ویا تیغه‌های خشن ساخته‌شده‌است .گروه‌دوم یا جدیدترکه‌احتمالا"ازگروه‌اول مشتق گردیـــده شامل ادوات سنگی دوطرفه‌ماننندتبرهای دستی سنگی[3]وتیشه‌ها یا شکاف دهنده‌های سنگی[4]میبا شـــد . گروه‌اول وقدیمتردرحدودتقریبا "یک میلیون سال دوام داشته‌وعموما "بنام اولدوان[5]خوانده‌شده

1. Lower Palaeolithic
2. Ranov and Davis, 1979
3. Hand axe
4. Cleaver
5. Oldowan

وگروه دوم که درحدود دویست تا یکصدهزار سال ژ٠ ش خ ا تمه یا فته عموما "بنا م آشولیا ن[1] نا میــــده شده است .سازندگان گروه اول بنا م انسا نهای آسترالوپیستین[2] که از انسا نهای اولیه بوده خوانده شده اندوساکنندگان زندگان نوع دوم ادوات سنگی از انسانهای هموارکتوس[3] بوده اند .

وضعیت ایران بعلت عدم شواهد ستا نشنا سی دوران دیرینه سنگی عمیق وگروهها ی دوگانه ادوات سنگی مبهم میبا شدوفقط چندتبردستی سنگی درسطح زمین تا کنون بدست آمده وا حتمــا لا" ممکن است این تبرهای سنگی مربوط به دوران دیرینه سنگی متوسط وحتی دوران نوسنگی بـاشد. بنظر میرسداستعمال تبرهای دستی درمناطق شرقی کمترا زمناطق غربی خاورنزدیک موردا ستفاده بوده است .[4]معلوم نیست به چه علت اجتماعات دوران آشولیان که درتما م منطقه از افریقا تا انگلستان فعالیت داشته وآثاری برجای گذارا ده اند دارای شواهد مستندی درا یران وعراق نمی ـ با شند .احتما لا"آثار آنها در این منطقه درزیرلایه ها ی دیگرهنوزمخفی بوده وکشف نگردیده است .

درحا ل حاضرکلیه مدارک مربوط به دوران دیرینه سنگی عمیق درایران درسطح زمین جمع آوری گردیده وآثاری ا ز این دوران درغا رها وپناهگاههای سنگی با ستانی بدست نیا مده است (شکـــــــل شماره ۳) وبا وضعیت آثار مربوط به این دوران درمناطق آفریفا ،هندکه درمحلهای روبا زبدست آمده شباهت دارد وبنظر میرسدغارها وپناهگاههای سنگی تا اواخراین دوران بندرت موردا ستفاده قرار میگرفته اند .

احتما لا"قدیم ترین محل مربوط به دوران دیرینه سنگی عمیق درایران درنا حیه خراســان میبا شدکه درسال های ۱۹۷۴ و۱۹۷۵ بوسیله پروفسورآریا ئی وتیبالت کشف گردیده است .[5]تعـداد ی درحدودشصت عدد ادوات سنگی دربسترردخانه کشف رودرفا صله چهل تا یکصدکیلومتری مشهدجمع آوری گردید .دریاچه ای درا ین منطقه دردوران پلیوسین وجودداشته وبتدریج پرشده است .احتمـــــــالا" اجتماعاتی از انسانهای قدیم دراطراف این دریاچه سکونت مینموده اندوادوات سنگی مختلــــف خشن وبزرگ وهمچنین کوچکترشا مل تیغه ها ورنده ها وچاقوهای سنگی از آنها به یا دگار باقیما نده است (شکل شماره ۴)

---

1. Acheulian
2. Australopithecines
3. *Homo erectus*
4. McBurney, 1950:178
5. Ariai and Thibault, 1975—77

این ادوات با ادوات بدست آمده درهیمالیا وآسیای مرکزی ،افریقا وآنت قالبل مقایسه هستند . کاشفین این آثار آنها را مربوط بهدوران قبل از آشولیان دانسته ودرحدود هشتصد هزار سال قدمت آنها را تخمین زده اند .

ادوات سنگی مشابهی درسالهای اخیر درمنطقهبلوچستان درنزدیک لادیزو مشکید بدست آمده وبنام فرهنگ لادیزیان[1]بوسیلهپروفسورهیوم[2]نامگذاری گردیده اند وقدمت آنها را همزمان با دوران یخبندان وورم دردوران پلستوسین میانه ومرتفع دانسته ودورانی استعمال آنها را درحدودیکصد هزار سال پیشنهاد نموده است . این ادوات درمحوطهء کارگاههای سنگی بدست آمده وشامل رنده ها ، تیغه ها میباشد (شکل شماره ۵).با وجودیکهشواهدی درباره وضع محیط واقلیم وحیوانات ونباتات بدست نیامده ولی کاشف این آثار را اظهار میدارد که حیوانا تی مانند خروحشی ،غزال ومرال بوسیله این اقوام شکار گردیده ومورد استفاده قرار گرفته اند .اخیرا "آثاری مشابه با این ادوات درناحیه خاش درفلات سرحد بوسیلهپروفسور مروچک[3]نیز گزارش گردیده است .

دربقیهایران بقایای مربوط بهدوران دیرینهسنگی عمیق بسیار محدود بوده ومنحصرا "دررشته جبال زاگرس بدست آمده اند .اتفاقا "بهترین شواهدا زناحیهبردا بالکا[4]درسرحدایران وعــــــراق درمنطقهکردستان عراق بدست آمده است . این محل کهدارا رتفاع ۷۰۰ متری دردهچمچال[5]دردا منه غربی زاگرس میباشد فقط بررسی شده وهنوز حفاری نگردیده است . ۵ ادوات سنگی شامل قطعات سنـــگ آهکی وتیغه های سنگی ̈ تعدادزیادی تبرهای سنگی کوچک شبیهبهتبرهای آشولیان جمع آوری گردید .بقایای استخوانهای حیوانا تی مانندفیل ،کرگدن،آهو ،گوسفندوبزوخروحشی نیزدرایـــن مکان وجودداشت .بنا برپیشنهاد کاشفین این آثار درحدودیکصدهزار تا هفتادهزارسال قدمت دارند . بنظر میرسدآثاری مشابه با این آثار درنواحی قفقاز ̈،گرجستان ،آذربایجان ،ارمنستان وجنوباوستیا ونواحی دیگر درعراق وایران وجودداشته با شد .شایدمحل پلبا ریک[6]درمنطقه هلیــــــــلان در لرستان کهدرآن چنــــــــدتبردستی کوچــــک درسطح زمین با قطعا ت شکستها دوا ت سنگـــی

---

1. Ladizian
2. Hume, 1976
3. Marucheck, 1976
4. Barda Balka
5. Chemchemal
6. Wright and Howe 1951; Braidwood and Howe, 1960
7. Pal Barik

(شکل شما ره ۶) بدست آمدنیزمربوط به این اجتما عا ت با شد! همچنین تبرهای سنگی دستی شبیه به تبرهای سنگی آشولیا ن درمنطقه کرما نشا ه درتپه گاکیا[2] بوسیله پروفسوربریدوود[3] وتبرسنگی دستی دیگری درآذربا یجا ن[4] نیزاز همین قبیل با شند .دربررسی های علمی درآذربا یجا ن شرقی درمشرق دریا ی ا ورومیه که بوسیله خا نم پروفسورهندکوروس ا نجا م گردیده هم چنین آثا روا دوا ت سنگی بدست آمده که[5] احتما لا"ا زهما ن نوع ا دوا تی ا ست که درخرا سا ن نیزکشف گردیده بود .بهرحا ل وضعیت مدارک وشوا هدمربوط به دورا ن دیرینه سنگی عمیق درا یرا ن بنحوی ا ست که نمیتوا ن ا ظهار ا ت قطعی را جع به ا جتما عا ت ا نسا نی وتا ریخ ورودآ نها ،مبدا ء ومحل ا ولیه آ نها ویا وضعیت جسمی آ نها ویا ا نوا ع ا دوا ت سنگی تولیدشده بوسیله آ نها عرضه نمود .

---

1. Mortensen, 1975
2. Gakia
3. Braidwood, 1960
4. Singer and Wymer, 1978
5. Sadek-Kooros, 1976

دوران دیرینه‌سنگی متــــوسط^۱ :

وضعیت مدارک وشواهدمربوط به‌ای‌ن دوران به‌ترو‌کا ملترازدوران قبلی بوده‌وآثاری ازاین دوران درغارها ،تپه‌ها وسطح‌زمین بدست آمده‌که‌تاانداز‌ه‌ای چگونگی ای‌ن اجتماعات ووضع نباتات ومحیط وحیوانات موجودرا روشن ترنمایید .علاوه‌براین ازنظرقدمت این دوران دربعدزمانی قرار داردکه‌میتوان آزمایشهای کربن ۱۴ برروی آثاربدست‌آمده‌انجام داده‌واطلاعاتی را راجع به‌قدمت آثارکسب نمود .بنظرمیرسددرای‌ن اجتماعات قابل ملاحظه‌دررشته‌جبا‌ل زاگرس سکونـــــت مینموده‌ولی معلوم نیست‌سایرنوا‌حی ایرا‌ن نـیزهمین وضع را داشته‌است .

تقریبا "درحدودبیست مکان باستانی مربوط بدین دوران درا‌یران مشخص گردیده‌وعلاوه‌براین نیزآثاری جسته‌گریخته‌درمحل های دیگری یافت گردیده‌است (شکل شما‌ره ۷۵).

بیشترای‌ن مکان‌ها دررشته‌جبا‌ل زاگرس قرارگرفته‌وتعدادی نیزدرنوا‌حی دیگرنیزمشا هـــده میگردند .مهمترین محل باستانی مربوط به‌این دوران غار شانیدر^۲میبا شدکه‌درنزدیک مرزا ی‌را‌ندر کردستا‌ن عراق نزدیک رودخا نه‌ذاب بزرگ قرارگرفته‌است . دراین غار علاوه‌براثار تنها اسکلت کامل مربوط به‌دوران دیرینه‌سنگی متوسط که‌تاکنون درایران وعراق بدست آمده‌آشکا رگردیـــد.^۳ مکان‌های باستانی مشابهی نیزدرایران ما ننده‌غار خار دربیستون (که‌به‌وسیله‌نویسنده‌درسال ۱۹۶۵ آزمایش گردیده)نیزوجوددا رندکه‌هیچکدا م تاکنون کا ملا"حفاری نگردیده‌ویا مدارک وشواهدی ما ننده‌غار شانیدر عرضه‌ننموده‌اند .با توجه‌به‌مدارک وشواهدبدست آمده‌ازای‌ن محلها ی باستانـــی میتوا‌ن تا اندازه‌ای را راجع به‌چگونگی محیط ویا آب وهوا‌واقلیم ای‌ن دوران وبخصوص درا وا‌خـــر آن درمنطقه‌زاگرس با قا طعیت بیشتری اظها رنظرنمود .همچنین مسلم است که‌درای‌ن دوران انسا‌ن نئاندرتال درایرا‌ن سکونت داشته‌ونسبت به‌عقا یدوا فکا رآ ن نیزمیتوا‌ن اظها رتی نمود .

با وجودیکه‌نمیتوا‌ن بطوردقیق شروع دورا‌ن دیرینه‌سنگی متوسط را درا‌یرا‌ن تعیین نمـــود ولی با درنظرگرفتن مدارک موجوددرا‌ین منطقه‌ازآسیا شا یدبتوا‌ن اظها ردا شت که‌ای‌ن دوران در ایران نیزدرحدودیکصدهزارتا هشتا دهزارسال پیش شروع گردیده‌است . بنظرمیرسدا‌ین دورا‌ن همزما ن با وقتی است که‌آ ب وهوا متعا دل تروخنک ترگردیده‌ونوسا نها ئی دروضع هوا وبخصوص رطوبت

---

1. Middle Palaeolithic
2. Shanidar Cave
3. Solecki 1955; 1963; 1971

درفاصله ما بین ۶۲۰۰۰ تا ۸۰۰۰۰ سال پیش ویا ۴۲۰۰۰ تا ۵۶۰۰۰ سال پیش بوجودآمده است[1].تحقیقاتی درغارشانیدربرای تشخیص این نوسانهای اقلیمی ورطوبت بوسیله بررسی های گرده گیاهان انجام گردیده است[2]. گرده هائی که از دریاچه زریبار در غرب ایران که در حدود چهل هزار سال قدمت دارند (شکل شماره۱۱)جمع آوری گرده شان میدهدکه هوای سردتروخشک تری از دوران حاضرکه قابل مقایسه وشبیه به آب وهوا ومحیط صحرا واستپ بوده در منطقه زاگرس در آن زمان وجود داشته وتعداد معدودی درختان بلوط پسته وافرا وکمی علف ولی بیشترگیاهان استپی مانندآرتمیزیا[3] وگیاهان خشک در این منطقه میروئیده اند[4].

حیوانات موجوددرآنوقت تقریبا "شبیه به گروه حیوانا تی بوده اندکه امروزنیزدراین منطقه وجوددارد.درآثار حیوانا تی مانندبز ،گوسفند ،آهو ،خروحشی،گاو ،خوک وحیوانا ت درنده مختلف بدست آمده است .نسل فیل بنظرمیرسیداز بین رفته بوده وکرگدن درقسمت شمال شرقی ایران هنوز وجودداشته است .آنچه مسلم است آتش در این وقت وجودداشته است ولی نوع استفاده از آن هنوز کاملا"روشن نیست .

بیشترادوات وصنایع وتولیدات سنگی دوران دیرینه سنگی متوسط را (ولی نه تمام آن را) بعنوان نوع موستریان[5]میتوان طبقه بندی نمودواین نوع بطورکلی از غرب اروپا تا شمال افریقا وخاورنزدیک تا آسیای مرکزی گسترش داشته است .دراین نوع ادوات سنگی بزرگ گذشته ما نند تبرهای دستی ، شکاف دهنده ها ویا ادوات قلوه سنگی تقریبا "وجودنداشته وازبین رفته اند .ادوات ظریف تری ما نندرنده ها ،ادوات نوک تیز ،مته های سنگی ازنوع متداول این دوران میبا شند .نوع وروش لوالوا[6]برای تهیه تیغه ها از سنگ ما دردر منطقه زاگرس کمترراایج بوده ولی دردشت خوزستان درمکانهای روبا زدردشت بیشترموردا ستفاده قرارگرفته است .تقریبا "تمام اجتماعات مسکون دراین دوران را میتوان درگروه موستریان طبقه بندی نمودوشباهت کاملی به نوع مشخص موستریان دراروپا دارند .البته تفاوتهائی بین اجتماعات مسکون درغارها ویا درهوای آزاد ودشتها دریافت زندگانی آنها مشاهده میگرددکه مولودوضع محیط مجاورویا منابع سنگی موجوددر اطراف ایـــن

1. Farrand, 1981
2. Solecki and Leroi-Gourhan, 1961
3. Artemisia
4. van Zeist and Bottema, 1977
5. Mousterian
6. Levallois

اجتماعات میباشد .

مدارک کافی برای پیگیری این نکتهکهآیا این دوران دیرینهسنگی متوسط درایران ادامه
دورا ن دیرینهسنگی عمیق در ا ین منطقه بوده و یا از خار ج بدین ناحیه و ا رد شده است در حا ل حا ضر
وجود ندارد .وجودتبرهای دستی کهدررشتهجبال زاگرسدرنواحی مختلف ما نندحاضرمرد ،بردا با لکا
و یا سا یرنواحی آ ن بدست آمده یدتوا ندد لیلی براداله دورا ن گذشته با تحولات و تغییرا تی بـــه
صورت ا ستمرار به دورا ن میا ن سنگیدرهمین منطقه با شد .

زما ن شروع دورا ن موستریا ن در ا یرا ن هنوزکا ملا "بطرزدقیق مشخص نیست .پروفسورمکبورنی
برا سا س توزیع نباتات ،آثارباستانی کی آرام اول درما زندرا ن را مربوط به آخرین فا صلـــه
بین یخبندا ن ها و یا ا و ا ئل آخرین دورا ن یخبندا ن دا نسته\(و پروفسورسلوکی آثا رعمیق موستریـان
را درغار شا نیدرمربوط به حدودیکصدهزا رسا ل پیش تخمین زده است ؟

همچنین مراحل تحولی دردورا ن موستریا ن کا ملا "روشن نبوده و فقط درچندمحل لایه هـــای
مختلف ا ین دورا ن بررو ی یکدیگر بدست آمده و کا فی نیست که بتوا ندا زا ین نظربطورروشن مـــورد
ا ستفا ده قرا رگیرد .ا ین مسا ئل نه فقط در منطقه زا گرس و ا یرا ن وجود دارد بلکه درتما م نوا حی آ سیا
و ا روپا موجود میبا شد .همچنین تا ریخ دقیق خا تمهفرهنگ موستریا ن در ا یرا ن روشن نیست و ا حتمالا'
ا ین فرهنگ درحدودچهل هزا رسا ل (۴۰۰۰۰) پیش ا زمیلادمسیح پا یا ن پذیرفته است .بنا برا یـــن
منطقیبنظر میرسدطول ا ین دورا ن را مدتی درحدودما بین شصت هزا رتا پنجا ه هزار (۵۰۰۰۰ـ۶۰۰۰۰   )
سا ل تصورنما ئیم .

رویهمرفته یک همآهنگی ویک نوا ختی خا صی دربین ا دوات مربوط بدین دورا ن درمنطقـــه
زا گرس و سا یرنوا حی ا یرا ن مشا هده میگردد .بطورکلی درسا خت ا دوا ت نوک ، تیزکه بعنوا ن سرنیـزه
میتوا نسته ا ند موردا ستفا ده قرا رگیرند تشدیدبیشتری گردیده ا ست .رندههای سنگی جا نبی و مته های
سنگی نیزرا یج بوده ا ند .بررویهم ا دوا ت سنگی دورا ن مـــــــــــــــموستریا ن ا یرا ن و عـــــراق
بنظر میرسدیک نوع منطقه ای از ا ین فرهنگ را معرفی مینما یند .ا دوا ت ا ستخوا نی و شا خی بنـــدرت
بدست آمده ا ست .

محلهای با ستا نی مربوط به ا ین دورا ن بیشتردرمنا طق جبا ل زا گرس درنوا حی آ ذربا یجـان
کردستا ن ولرستا ن بوده و فقط یک محل درما زندرا ن ، یک محل درخرا سا ن وچندمحل درخوزستـــان
وا قع میبا شند .دردا خل فلات نیزیک ا ثردرحوا لی تهرا ن ویکی دیگردرکرما ن بدست آمده ا ست .در ـ

1. McBurney, 1964
2. Solecki, 1963

ناحیه‌بلوچستا ن که‌مرکزفرهنگ لادیزیا ن میبا شدهنوزآ ثا ری مربوط به‌موستریا ن بدست نیا مـــده
ا ست . با وجودیکه‌مشکل ا ست تعدا دکلیها این نقا ط را مشخص نمودولی بررویهم درحدودشا نزده‌غـا ر
یا پنا هگا ه‌سنگی وچها رمحل روبا زکه‌محل کا رگا ه‌تولیدا دوا ت سنگی مربوط بدین دورا ن‌بوده‌ودر‌ـ
نقا ط دیگری فقط ا دوا تی که‌بطورمتفرق پرا کنده‌بوده ا ندمشخص گردیده ا ند .

ا حتما لا"نقا ط با ستا نی درنزدیک خرم آ با ددرلرستا ن که‌بصورت غا رها وپنا هگا ه‌های سنگـی
درکنا رچشمه‌آ ب قرا ردا رندبهترین نمونه‌ا جتما عا ت مربوط بدین دورا ن میبا شند .ا ین محلـها در
سا لـهای ۱۹۶۳ و۱۹۶۵ بوسیله‌پورفسورهول وپروفسورفلانری موردبررسی قرا رگرفتند[1] . سه‌غا رازا ین
مجموعه‌موردبررسی وآ زما یش قرا رگرفت . یکی غا رکنجی (که‌بعدها نیزبوسیله‌پروفسورسپت حفا ری
گردید[2]ولایه‌ها ی آ ن کا ملا"مغشوش و مضطرب گردیده‌بود)ودیگری‌غا ریا درواقع پنا هگا ه‌سنگی ا رجنــد
وسومی غا رقمری که‌کا شفین تا ریخ‌آنها[!] درحدودبین پنجا ه‌تا سی وهشت هزا رسا ل (۳۸۰۰۰ تا ۵۰۰۰۰)
پیش ا زمیلادمسیح تعیین نموده ا ند .چندنمونه‌آ زما یش کربن چها ردها زغا رکنجی تا ریخی قدیمترا ز
چهل هزا رسا ل پیش (۴۰۰۰۰) را تعیین کرده ا ست .ا دوا ت سنگی شا مل قطعا ت شکسته‌سنگی ما نــند
رنده‌ها ی جا نبی ،نوک تیزهای مثلثی شکل ،مته‌ها بوده‌روش لوا وا بکا رگرفته‌نشده ا ست .به‌علـــت
محدودیت آ ثا را ربا فت وطرززندگا نی ا ین ا جتما عا ت چندا ن مشخص نمیبا شد .درمحل دیگری درلرسـتان
که‌آ ثا رموستریا ن درنا حیه‌کوهدشت نزدیک کوه‌سرسحون بدست آ مده‌سبک زندگا نی موسمی وفصلـــی
موقتی را نما یش میدهد .پنا هگا ه‌سنگی بنا م هـومیا ن درسا ل ۱۹۶۹ بوسیله‌پروفسورمک بورنــــی
موردبررسی قرا رگرفت[3].ا ین پنا هگا ه‌درا رتفا ع دوهزا رمتری ا زسطح دریا قرا رگرفته‌ودرزمـــره
مرتفع ترین آ ثا رمربوط به‌عصرحجردرخا ورنزدیک میبا شد .ا ین آ ثا رمربوط به‌یک ا جتما ع موقـت
موستریا ن درفصل تا بستا ن میبا شدوا حتما لا"برا ی سکونت شکا رچیا ن درا ین فصل موردا ستفا ده‌قرار
میگرفته‌ا ست وا ین شکا رچیا ن با ا جتما عا ت نوا حی خرم آ با دوهلیلان درا رتبا ط بوده ا ند .درنا حیه
دره‌هلیلان که‌درا رتفا ع ۹۳۵ متری قرا ردا ردپروفسورمورتنسن هفت محل با ستا نی مربوط به‌دوره ــ
موستریا ن را که‌درنزدیک محل با ستا نی پل با ریک مربوط به‌دورا ن ا شولیا ن قرا رگرفته‌بودنـــد
مشخص نمود .دوعددا زا ین محلها که‌به‌ا سم غا رویلاوغا رهوجی نا میده‌میشوندپنا هگا ه‌سنگی‌بودو پنـج
محل دیگردر محوطه‌روبا زدرسطح زمین واقع میبا شند .ا دوا ت سنگی شبیه‌به‌ا دوا ت سنگی یا فت شده

1. Hole and Flannery, 1967
2. Speth, 1971
3. McBurney, 1970; Bewley 1984

درغارهای خرم آبا دبودهولی دراینجا ازروش والوا برای تولیدتیغهها استفاده نموده موجـــود میبا شد (شکل شماره۸) . احتمالا"ا ین محلها نیزسکونتهای موقتی فصلی را معرفی مینما یند .[1]

درحدودهفتا دتا هشتا دکیلو متربطرف شمال درا رتفا عا ت بیشتری (درحدود۱۴۰۰–۳۰۰،متراز سطح دریا) یک گروه دیگرآ ثا را ستا نی مربوط بهدورا ن دیرینهسنگی متوسط درحا شیه شهرکرمانشا ه درمحل تنگ کنشت آ ثا ری از دورا ن موستریا ن درزیرطبقا ت مربوط بهدورا ن دیرینهسنگی مرتفـع درسا لهای ۱۹۵۹ و ۱۹۶۰ بوسیلهٔ هیا ت پروفسوربریدوودکشف وبوسیلهپروفسورها وحفاری گردیـد .[2] ا دوا ت سنگی بدست آ مده دراین محل شبیهنوع موستریا ن منطقهزا گرس میبا شد .بقا یا ی حیوا نـات کهبدقت بررسی گردیدهشا مل حیوا نا تی ما نندخروحشی ،آ هو ،گا ووبزوگوسفندمیبا شد .شوا هدی وجود دا ردکها ین محل بعنوا ن محل ا ستقرا رشبا نهبرا ی شکا رچیا ن خروحشی (گورخر)بودها ست ودردورا ن های بعدی دیرینهسنگی مرتفع بههمین منظورموردا ستفا ده قرا رگرفتها ست .[3] آثا روشوا هدی نیـــز درغا رکبهدرنزدیک کرما نشا ه وکل هوکل دا ودردرسرپل زها ب ا زا ین دورا ن بدست آ مدها ست .درنزدیـــک کتیبهبیستون اولین حفاری دریک غا رموستریا ن درا یرا ن درغا رشکا رچیان بوسیلهپروفسورکـــوون درسا ل ۱۹۴۹ میلادی ا نجا م گردیـد .[4] آثا ربدست آ مده دراین محل شبیهبها دوا ت سنگی ا ست کــه در واروا سی بدست آ مدها ست . درا ین محل یک تکها ستخوا ن با زوی ا نسا ن کهبوسیلهکا شف مربوط بــه ا نسا ن نئا ندرتا ل تشخیص دا دهشدهبدست آ مد .درنزدیک همین محل غا رخا ردرسا ل ۱۹۶۵ بوسیلـــه نویسنده بررسی و آزما یش گردیـد .[5] ا ین غا ر عمیق وطویل بودهوا حتما لا"محل دا ئمی ا ستقرا را جتماعا ًا موستریا ن بودها ست .محل دیگری درنزدیک هرسین بوسیلهنویسندهوپروفسورمورتنسن درسا ل ۱۹۷۷ درمنطقهروبا زدشت کشف گردید (شماره۱۶بررسی)کها حتما لا"محل ا ستخراج سنگ برا ی ا دوا ت سنگـــی بودها ست .همچنیـن درهمیـن نزدیکـی هرسیـن درنقطهدیگری (شما ره۱۷بررسی)آ ثا رسنگی مربوط بدین دورا ن جمع آ وری گردید .دربقا یا ی با ستا نی درزیرلایهها ی دورا ن نوسنگی درگنجدرهتیغهها یسنگی

1. Mortensen, 1974a:15; 1974b; 1975
2. Braidwood, 1960
3. Turnbull, 1975
4. Coon, 1951
5. Young and Smith, 1966

احتمالاً مربوط به‌دوران دیرینه‌سنگی متوسط نیز بدست آوردیم.[1]

در منطقه‌های شمالی و جنوبی رشته‌جبال زاگرس آثار پراکنده و متفرقی مربوط به‌دوران
دیرینه‌سنگی متوسط بدست آمده است .در جهرم در فارس در سال ۱۹۶۹ پروفسور زامنر آثار و ادوات سنگی
زیادی در سطح زمین که احتمالاً محل کارگاه تولید ادوات بوده است مشخص نمود ،احتمالاً این
ادوات نوع خاص محلی این دوران را معرفی می‌نمایند.[2] اگرچه پروفسور هیوم آنها را مربوط به
فرهنگ لادیزیان دانسته است.[3] آثار سطحی دیگری در نزدیک شیراز[4] و در ده رود کر[5] نیز بدست آمده‌اند.
چندنمونه ادوات سنگی شبیه به موستریان بوسیله پروفسور کالدول در محل تل ابلیس در کرمان گزارش
گردیده است.[6] همچنین آثار پراکنده‌ای در شمال شرق خوزستان در منطقه دشت گل[7]، در ایوه و درا یذه
جمع آوری گردیده‌اند .همچنین آثار دوران دیرینه‌سنگی متوسط در قسمتهای پست دشت خوزستان
هم در ایران و هم در عراق وجود دارد ولی از طرز زندگانی این اجتماعات و چگونگی آن اطلاعات
زیادی در دست نیست .در یکی از این محلها در نزدیک دهلران سنگ ما در تیغه‌های سنگی به روش لوا و
بدست آمد.[8]

در قسمت شمالی جبال زاگرس پروفسور کوون در غار تمتمه در آذربایجان در نزدیک دریاچه
اورومیه آثار و ادواتی که احتمالاً مربوط به‌دوران موستریان می‌باشند بدست آورد.[9] در بقیه
قسمتهای شمال ایران تقریباً آثار دیگری از این دوران دیرینه‌سنگی متوسط بدست نیامده است.
چندنمونه ادوات سنگی از مناطق رسوبی دشت تهران بوسیله پروفسور ریبن گزارش گردیده است.[10] در
غار کی آرام اول در ماز ندران نیز آثار ریزمشا به‌با آثار موستریان جبال زاگرس بدست آمده است.[11]

1. Smith, 1975
2. Piperno, 1972
3. Hume, 1976: 250
4. Field, 1939
5. Sumner, 1980
6. Caldwell, 1967
7. Wright, 1979
8. Coon, 1951
9. Rieben, 1955
10. McBurney, 1964
11. Coon, 1949

استخوان حیوانات بدست آمده شامل آهوی قرمز، گاو و کرگدن میباشد. همچنین درغار خونیک در
خراسان نزدیک بیرجند آثار موستریان بدست آمده است. درسواحل مُکران ادواتی که به روش لوآ وا
بدست آمدنیز جمع آوری شده است.[1] زبقایای اسکلت انسان فقط یک استخوان بازوی انسان
نئاندرتال درغار شکارچیان بیستون بدست آمده ولی شواهد غارشانیدرنیز تا ئیدمینماید که انسان
نئاندرتال وجودداشته و شواهد دیگری که وجودنوع تنومند هوموسا پین را نیزدراین دوران
درمنطقه اشاره مینماید. خصوصیات نوع انسان نئاندرتال غارشانیدربوسیله پروفسور ترینکاس[2]
وطرزرفتارآن بوسیله پروفسورسولکی[3] بررسی گردیده است. اظهارات زیادی درموردا صل وسرچشمه
انسانهای نئاندرتال ویا سابقه آنها درمنطقه ویامهاجرت آنها از محل دیگری بمنطقه با مدارک
موجودچندان امکان پذیرنیست. آخرین اسکلت غارشانیدربوسیله آزمایش کربن 14 درحدودچهل
وچهار هزارسال (۴۴۰۰۰)قبل تاریخ گذاری شده است.

1. Vita-Finzi and Copeland, 1980
2. Trinkaus, 1983
3. Solecki, 1971

<u>دوران دیرینه‌سنگی مرتفع[1] وروی (یا بعد از)دیرینه‌سنگی[2] :</u>

با وجودیکه بنظر میرسد مدارک بیشتری از این دوران با یددربیشترنقاط ایران بدست
آمده با شدولی بیشترآثارمکشوفه درمنطقه رشته جبال زاگرس جمع آوری گردیده (شکل‌های شماره ۱۰ و
۹) وشاید دربعضی موارد محدود ترا زدوران قبلی باشد .

ولــی بهرحال اطلاعات بیشتری از این دوران درباره وضعیت آب وهوا ومحیط موجود میباشد[3]
واین شواهد روشنگرمنطقه‌ء وسیعتری نیزمیگردند (شکل ۱۱) .طرزتوزیع نباتات نشان میدهدکه در
حدودچهل هزار سال پیش (۴۰۰۰۰)آب وهوا سردوخشک بوده ودرحدودسی هزار سال پیش این وضعیت
شدیدتر گردیده و تا دوازده هزار سال پیش نیزدوام داشته است . درحدودده تا نه (۹۰۰۰ تا ۱۰۰۰۰)
هزار سال پیش درجه حرارت با لاتررفته وگرم ترشده است .مدارک وشواهدبا ستا نشنا سی آغا زفعالیتهای
کشاورزی وتولیدآذوقه درا ین دوران را درهمین اوا ن تائیدمینما یند .دربعضی از غارهای با ستا نی ما نندا رجنه
درنزدیک خرم آباد،واروا سی نزدیک کرما نشا ه ،غا رخا ردربیستون ،وقفه وفاصله[4] ی بین آثـــار
اجتماعات دوران دیرینه‌سنگی متوسط ومرتفع مشا هده نمیگرددواین وضعیت احتما لا"بیانگرا یـــن
نکته‌است که بتدریج تحولاتی درنوع ا دوات وطرززندگا نی ا ین دودورا ن درمنطقه زا گرس بوجود
آمده است .ا ین وضعیت وتحولات آثار وا دوات بوسیله پروفسورگا رد[4] وپروفسورمک بورنی[5] وهمچنیــن
وضعیت تحولات جسما نی وبوجودآمدن ا نسا ن هوموسا پین درمنطقه بلوچستا ن درحدودفاصله هزار
تا سی هزا ر (۳۰۰۰۰-۶۰۰۰۰) سا ل پیش بوسیله پروفسورها نتنگین[6] بررسی گردیده است .تحقیقا تــی
درباره اصل وسا بقه فرهنگ دیرینه‌سنگی مرتفع بوسیله پروفسورمک بورنی[7] وپروفسورکوون[8] درمورد
ا ین نکته که آیا ایران مبداء بوجودآمدن فرهنگ نوسنگی بوده ویا ا ین فرهنگ قرا ردا شتـــه
ا نجام گردیده است .

1. Upper Palaeolithic
2. Epipalaeolithic
3. van Zeist and Bottema, 1977; 1982
4. Garrod, 1938
5. McBurney, 1964
6. Huntington, 1938:435
7. McBurney, 1964:398
8. Coon, 1957:127

یکی از خصوصیات دوران اخیردیرینه‌سنگی تحول سریع وتنوع زیاد ادوات سنگی درا ین مدت نسبتا "کوتاه (سی هزارسال) نسبت به‌دورانهای پیش میبا شد .علاوه‌براین درا ین دوران خصوصیات محلی ومنطقه‌ای تا اندازه‌ای درنحوهٔ ساخت ادوات ظاهرگردیده‌که مسلما "درا ثرا قلیم ومحیـــــط ومنابع طبیعی موجوددرهرنا حیه‌بوده‌است . بهرحال درا ثرا ین خصوصیات محلی ونوع ادوات سنگی میتوان آنها را درا یران به‌دوفرهنگ یا گروه‌با را دوستیان[1] وزا رزیا ن[2]طبقه‌بندی نمود .ا یـــــن دوگروه‌درمنطقه‌رشته‌جبا ل زاگرس وبخصوص درقسمتهای شما لی ومرکزی آ ن مشا هده‌میگردند .وضعیت ا ین دوفرهنگ دربقیه‌نوا حی ا یران بدین روشنی نمیبا شد .دقا یق ا ین تقسیم بندی وا رتبا ط ا ین دوفرهنگ با یکدیگرحتی درمنطقه‌زا گرس ویا نوا حی مجا ورا مدا رک موجودهنوزکا ملا "مشخص نمیباشد . نحوه‌وبا فت زندگا نی ا جتما عات دوران دیرینه‌سنگی مرتفع ومبا رزه‌با عوا مل طبیعی ما نندسرما و گرما وسا یرامور درمقا یسه‌با وضعیت ا جتما عات ا ین دوران درسا یرنوا حی ا روپا ٓ وآ سیـــا کمترروشن میبا شد .بعضی ا ز دا نشمندا ن پیش ا ز تا ریخ ا ظها رمیدا رندکه‌ا رتبا ط ا ین ا جتما عـــات با یکدیگربیشتربوده‌وا زپیشرفتها ی ساخت ادوات ویا ا ستفا ده‌ا زمنا بع طبیعی یکدیگرا ستفـــا ده بیشتری نموده‌ا ند .شوا هدمربوط به‌عقا یدوا فکا را ین ا جتما عات نیزکا ملا "محدودبوده‌وا مکـــان پیشنها دنظرا تی را میسرنمی نما یدولی با توجه‌به‌ا جتما عات سا یرمنا طق درا ین دوران شا یـــــد با فت مشا به‌ی را برا ی نا حیه‌ا یران نیزبتوا ن تصورنمود .تا کنون درآ ثا روبقا یا ی دوران دیرینه سنگی مرتفع درا یران نقا شی غا رها وصحنه‌هائی مربوط به‌طرززندگا نی ا ین ا جتما عات ویا ا شیـــاء وا دوات هنری که‌بتوا ندنما یشگرعقا یدمذهبی وا فکا رآ نها با شدبا ندا زه‌کا فی بدست نیا مده‌ا ست . تقسیم بندی ا ین دوران به‌دوفرهنگ با را دوستیان وزا رزیا ن فقط برا سا س نوع ادوات وآ ثـــار سنگی آ نها بطورعموم ا نجا م گردیده‌وخصوصیا ت دیگرا ین ا جتما عات درنظرگرفته‌نشده‌ا ست.

وا ژه‌وا صطلاح با را دوستیان ا بتدا بوسیله‌پروفسورسولکی برا سا س غا رشا نیدردرکوههای با را دوست شما ل عرا ق نا م گذا ری گردید .ا گرچنا نچه‌آ زما یش ها ی کربن ۱۴ برا سا س نمونه‌هـــای لایه‌ج غا رشا نیدرونمونه‌غا رریا فته‌درنزدیک خرم آ با دلرستا ن درست ومـــوردا عتما دبا شدا یـــن فرهنگ دوران دیرینه‌سنگی مرتفع درحدودیا سی وسه (۳۳۰۰۰)هزا ریا سی وشش (۳۶۰۰۰) هزا رویـــا ا حتما لا "سی وهشت (۳۸۰۰۰) هزا رسا ل پیش وجودداشته‌ا ست . تا کنون درحدودشش ا جتماع دوران —

1. Baradostian
2. Zarzian

با را دوستیا ن پنج عدد آنها درا یرا ن ویکی درعرا ق مشخص گردیده ا ند .ا لبته بعلت ا ینکه ا بتــدا
آثا را ین فرهنگ درکوههای با را دوست بدست آ مده ا ین ا ن مگذا ری گردیده ونا مگذا ری های دیگـری
ما نندبیستونیا ن یا لادیزیا ن وما زندرا نیا ن برا سا س محلـها ی دیگری کـه ا ین آ ثا ربدست آمـــده
بوسیلـه دا نشمندا ن دیگرپیشنها د گردیده ا ست .

فرهنگ با را دوستیا ن مشخص بهسا ختن تیغه های سنگی وبخصوص ا دوا ت بسیا رریز[1] میبا شد (شکـل
١٢) .ا لبته ا دوا ت بزرگ ترنیزتولید گردیده ا ند . ا دوا ت ا ستخوا نی بندرت سا خته شده ا ند .برا سا س
آثا ربدست آ مده درنا حیه خرم آ با د ا ین دورا ن بهدودوره تقسیم بندی شده ا ست[2]. یکی دوره با را دو-
ستیا ن قدیم کهدرحدودسی وهشت تا سی هزا ر (٣٠٠٠٠-٣٨٠٠٠) سا ل پیش ا زمیلادمسیح ودیگـری دوره
با را دوستیا ن جدیددرحدودسی هزا رتا بیست هزا ر (٢٠٠٠٠-٣٠٠٠٠) سا ل پیش ا زمیلادمسیح تا ریــخ
گذا ری شده ا ند .هما نگونه کهزما ن شروع فرهنگ با را دوستیا ن بدقت معلو م نیست تا ریخ خا تمــه
آ ن نیزکا ملا"روشن نمیبا شد وا حتما لا"محلـها ئی ما نندغا رشا ن نیدردرحدودبین بیست وشش هــــزا ر
تا دوا زده هزا ر (١٢٠٠٠-٢۶٠٠٠) سا ل پیش ا زمیلادمسیح متروک گردیده ا ند .

ا حتما لا"هما ن نوع حیوا نا ت کهدردورا ن موستریا ن وجوددا شتندما نندبز،گوسفندوآ هوی قرمز
وگا ووخروحشی درا ین دورا ن نیزوجوددا شته وشکا رمیشده ا ند .

با وجودیکه نبا تا ت وغلات وجوددا شته ولی کمتر موردا ستفا ده قرا رگرفته ا ند .بنظر میرسدهمانگونه
کهپروفسورهول وپروفسورفلانری[3] ا ظها ردا شته ا ند ا ین ا جتما عا ت درمحلی برا ی مدت قا بل ملاحظه ا ی
مستقربوده وشکا رچیا ن برا ی شکا ربا طرا ف میرفته ا ند .

شما لی ترین نقطه ا ی کهآ ثا ردوره با را دوستیا ن درمنطقه ا یرا ن درآ ن آ شکا رگردیده غا رخـار
دربیستون میبا شدکهدرآ ن بقا یا ی دورا ن با را دوستیا ن بهضخا مت یک مترما بین آ ثا ردورا ن مو –
ستریا ن وزلارزیا ن قرا رگرفته ا ست .[4]

همچنین در غا روا روا سی درنزدیک کرما نشاه بقا یا ی با را دوستیا ن درطبقه ا ی ما نندغا رخـار
بدست آ مدوبقا یا ی ا ستخوا ن حیوا نا ت ا ستقرا رشکا رچیا ن را درا ین محل آ شکا رمینمود .[5]

---

1. Microlith
2. Hole and Flannery, 1967
3. Hole and Flannery, 1967
4. Young and Smith, 1966
5. Turnbull, 1975

احتمالا"آثاری ازبار ادوستیان دردره‌هلیلان درلرستان نیزوجوددارد. اوضع این دوره‌درخرم آباد درغا رهای یافته ، ارجنه ،پا سنگرکها دوات سنگی شرح دا ده‌شده‌روشن ترمیبا شد .[2]بزکوهی بنظر میرسدبیشترشکا رگردیده‌وگل اخری نیزا حتما لا"برای تزئین بدن زیا دموردا ستفا ده‌قرا رگرفته‌است. صدفهای دریا ئی[3]که‌درغا رپا سنگربدست آ مده‌دلیل را بطها ین اجتما ع با نواحی دوردست تا حدود دریا میبا شد .چندتکها ستخوا ن انسان که‌با گل اخری پوشیده‌شده‌بودنیزبدست آ مد .[4]

آثاری نیزکمی جنوب تردرفا رس درغا رشکفت قدبر میشور ،همچنین درا طراف دریا چه مها رلو نزدیک شیرا زپرا کنده‌درسطح زمین[5]،همچنین درکرا نه‌های دریا چه‌تا شک درفا رس[6].وآثاری دیگری که‌کا ملا"هنوزنسبت آنها به‌دوران دیرینه‌سنگی مرتفع تعیین نگردیده‌درغا رشکفت گاوی درنزدیک رودکر[7]بدست آ مده ا ست .به‌عقیده‌نویسنده‌آثاری مربوط به‌دوره‌با رادوستیان ازخوزستان گزا رش – نگردیده ،اگرچه‌پروفسوررا یت ازشش محل مربوط به‌دوران نوسنگی دردشت ا یذه‌گزا رش دا ده‌است . محلی که‌درآ ن آ ثا ردوره‌با رادوستیان بدست آ مده‌با شددرشرق جبا ل زاگرس درا یرا ن تا کنون گزا رش نگردیده ا ست .

نا گفته‌نما ندبا وجودیکه‌قا عدتا "با گسترش اجتما عا ت بشری میبا یست شوا هدبیشتری ازدوره – با رادوستیان نسبت به‌دوره‌قبلی یعنی دوران موستریان درنقا ط مختلف ا یرا ن بدست آ یدولی بعکس درمنطقه‌فلات کمترمحل ها ئی ا زا ین اجتما عا ت بدست آ مده‌وشا یددلائل ا قلیمی وآ ب وهوای سردردفلات منطقه‌را برا ی ا دا مه‌زندگا نی نا مسا عدنموده‌وموجب ا ین وضعیت گردیده‌با شد .

وا ژه‌وا صطلاح زا رزیا ن بوسیله‌پروفسورگا رودپس ازحفا ری ا ودرسا ل ۱۹۲۸ میلادی درمحله‌ای درعرا ق معرفی گردید . این آثا رمربوط به‌دوره‌بعدا زویا روی دیرینه‌سنگی[8]میبا شند .فرهنگ

---

1. Mortensen, personal communication, 3-23-1981
2. Hole and Flannery, 1967
3. Salt-water-scallop shells
4. Hole and Flannery, 1967
5. Piperno, 1974
6. Krinsley, 1970:224
7. Sumner, 1980
8. Epipalaeolithic

این اجتماعات در اروپا و افریقا و آسیای غربی درحدودبعداز شانزده هزار (۱۶۰۰۰) سال پیش از ـ
میلادمسیح (وکمی قدیمتربنظربعضی ازدانشمندان)ظاهرگردیده و تا دوران نوسنگی واجتماعات
اولیه تولیدآذوقه وکشاورزی تا اوایل دوره هولوسین[1] ادامه داشته است .ادوات سنگی مربوط بدین
دوران مشخص به ادوات سنگی ظریف وکوچک بوده و به اشکال هندسی مانندمثلث ،هلال وذوذنقه
ساخته شده اند .این اجتماعات تماماً قبل به تولیدمحصولات کشاورزی داشته اند .درایران وعراق دوره
زارزیان بهترین دوران شناخته شده مربوط به اجتماعات دوره بعداز (یا روی)دوران دیرینه سنگی
میباشند .

اظهارنظردرباره شروع دوره زارزیان ویا اصل ومبدا آن بعلت فقدان مدارک کافی امکــان
پذیرنیست ولی آنچه مسلم است درحدودسیزده هزار (۱۳۰۰۰) سال پیش ازمیلادمسیح وجودداشته وتــا
حدودیازده تا ده هزارسال پیش ازمیلادمسیح ادامه داشته است .احتمالاً این دوران برای مدتــی
با دوره با ردوستیان همزمانی وهمزیستی داشته است ویا چنانچه پروفسورهول اظهارمینمایـــد
احتمالاً از آن دوران درحدودبیست هزار (۲۰۰۰۰) سال پیش ازمیلادمسیح مشتق گردیده است.[2] فقدان
تاریخ گذاری دقیق دربین بیست وپنجهزار تا سیزده هزار (۱۳۰۰۰–۲۵۰۰۰) سال پیش ازمیلادمسیـح
بوسیله آزمایش کربن ۱۴ امکان اظهارنظرقطعی را مشکل نموده است .اطلاعات تقریباً کافی بـرای
نمایش وضعیت اقلیم وآب وهوای زارزیان درمنطقه زاگرس درحدودقبل ازدوازده هزار رســـال
پیش ازمیلادمسیح تقریباً "موجودمیباشد (شکل شماره ۱۱) وبنظرمیرسدآب وهوا خشک تروسردتربوده و
درحدوددوازده (۱۲۰۰۰) هزارسال پیش ازمیلادمسیح گرمترومرطوب ترگردیده ودرختانی ماننـــد
بخصوص پسته وهمچنین بلوط درحدودنه تا هشت هزار (۹۰۰۰–۸۰۰۰) سال پیش ازمیلادمسیح درمنطقــه
تزایدیافته وگسترش حاصل نموده ونوع علفهای مربوط به منطقه استپ روبه نقصان گذارده و ازبیـن
رفته است .[3] احتمالاً "غلات وحشی نیز از اوائل دوره زارزیان روبگسترش وتزایدگذارده اند .

برروی هم ادوات سنگی دوره زارزیان کوچکتروظریف تراز ادوات دوره با ردوستیان میباشنـد
(شکل شماره ۱۳) .انواع تیغه های سنگی رایج ترگردیدوادوات ظریف با شکل ظریف هندسی مثلـثی
شکل ومته ها رواج یافته اندوعموماً "برروی دسته های چوبی یا استخوانی ویا شاخی نصب میگردیـده

1. Holocene
2. Hole, 1970
3. van Zeist and Bottema, 1977

80

۳۲

وبعنوان سرنیزه، پیکان وچاقو مورد استفاده قرارمیگرفته‌اند. همچنین ادوات استخوانی ما نند درفش رواج یافته‌است. عموما "نوع سنگهای محلی بکاررفته‌ولی ازشیشه معدنی[1]نیز از منطقه‌آناتولی واردگردیده‌وازآثاربدست‌آمده‌درعراق درزاگرزی و پال گارا اوشا نیدرمشاهده میگردند.

رویهمرفته‌توزیع نوع حیوانات درا ین دوره‌شبیه‌به‌دوره‌با دوستیان میباشدوفقط موارد تازه‌ای مشاهده‌میگردد. بقایای حلزون زمینی[2]بوفوردرغارهای زاگرزی وشا نیدروجوددارد. در مکانهای دیگرخرچنگ آبی[3]،نوعی صدف[4]،لاک پشت‌ودرغارزاگرزی برای اولین با ردرمنطقه‌ازاگرس بقایای استخوان ماهی مشاهده‌میگردد. سگ‌که‌ظاهرا "ازنوع گرگ اهلی شده‌بوده،درحدوددوازده‌هزار (۱۲۰۰۰) سال پیش ازمیلادمسیح وجودداشته‌است[5].(اگرچه این تشخیص بوسیله‌جانورشناسان دیگر تائیدنگردیده‌است)[6]. ثا رپرندگانی مانندکبک کوهستانی، مرغابی ،لک‌لک ،عقاب ،نوعی باز[7] نوعی ردک وحشی[7]نیزدربقایای باستانی بدست‌آمده‌است. آیا تا چه‌حدودغذاهای نباتی وغلات مورداستفاده قرارمیگرفته‌اندهنوز کاملا"روشن نیست، ولی شواهدی وجوددارد[8].

بنظرمیرسددراین دوران تحولی دربافت تامین آذوقه‌ایصورت شکارتوام با تولید واستفاده اززنبا تات‌وغلات بوجودآمده[9]وا دوات سنگی برای خردنمودن غلات ونگاهداری آنها درحفاریها بدست‌آمده‌است[10]. علت بوجودآمدن این تحول دربافت زندگانی کاملا"روشن نیست ،ولی نظراتی دراین زمینه‌که‌بعنوان سابقه‌تولیدآذوقه‌دردوره‌هلوسین میباشد پیشنهادگردیده‌است.

پروفسورگارود[11]درحدودسال ۱۹۲۸ اظهارداشت‌که‌تحولاتی درنوع ادوات سنگی بدست‌آمده

1. Obsidian
2. *Helix Salomonica*
3. Water crab
4. Clam
5. Turnbull and Reed. 1974
6. Herre and Röhrs, 1977
7. Kestrel
8. Sheldrake
9. Wahida, 1981
10. Flannery, 1969
11. Hole and Flannery, 1967
12. Garrod, 1930

درزا رزی مشا هده میگرد دوحفا ری ا خیردرزا رزی ا ین نکته را تا ئیدمینما ید .[1] بنظر میرسدهمیـــن تحول درپا ل گا را [2] ودرغا رخا رنیزبتدریج بوقوع پیوسته ا ست .

محلـها ئی کهدر آ نها آ ثا ردوره زا رزیا ن بدست آ مده تقریبا "هما ن منا طق دوره هبا را دوستیـا ن میبا شند .فقط غا رپا سنگردرخرم آ با دا زمحلـها ئی کهآ ثا را ین دوره را دربردا رندتا کنون حفا ری شده ا ست . در هلیلان درچها رغا رهما رروز ،ما رگورگلان سرا ب ،دا ر ما رۆغا رگوگل وهم چنین سه محل روبا زآ ثا ردوره زا رزیا ن آ شکا رگردیده ودرشش محل دیگرکه هنوزمعلوم نیست آ ثا را آ نها بطوریقیـن بـها ین دوره تـعلـق دا شته با شد شوا هدوآ ثا ری بدست آ مده ا ست .[3] با وجودیکه آ زما یش کربن ۱۴ ا ز محلها ی در ه هلیلان ا نجا م نگردیده ولی نوع ا دوا ت تعلـق آ نها را بـها وا خردوره زا رزیا ن مشهودمیـ دا رد .ا حتما لا "غا رها ی هلیلان محل ا ستقرا رثا بت ا ین ا جتما عا ت بوده ومکا نها[4] روبا زدرا طرا ف سیمره بـعنوا ن قرا رگا ههای موقتی برا ی شکا رموردا ستفا ده قرا رمیگرفته ا ند .[4] نکته ء جالب ا ینکه،در محل گنج در ه نزدیک کرما نشا هده درحدودهزا رهشتم جوقبل ا زا هلی نمودن حیوا نا ت کشت میگردیده ا ست.[5] همین وضعیت کشت غلا ت قبل ا زا هلی کردن حیوا نا ت درتپه چا یا نودرجنوب شرقی ترکیه که تقریبا " مقا رن با همین زما ن ا ست مشا هده میگردد .[6]

دوا م وا ستمرا ردورا ن زندگا نی شکا رچیا ن وخا تمه آ ن درخا ورنزدیک کا ملا "روشن نیست وبنظر میرسدکه ا ین ا جتما عا ت شکا رچیا ن تا زما نی نیزبهمرا ه ا جتما عا ت ا ولیه کشا ورزی بـهطرززندگا نـی خودا دا مه دا ده وحیوا نا ت شکا رکرده را با محصولا ت کشا ورزی تولیدشده بوسیله ا جتما عا ت ا ولیـــه کشا ورزی مبا دله مینمودند .بـهرحا ل بنظر میرسدکه تا ا وا خردورا ن پیش ا زتا ریخ بدین طرزبـــــه زندگا نی خودا دا مه دا ده ا ند .

شوا هدومدا رک مربوط بـه آ خرین ا جتما عا ت شکا رچیا ن درا یرا ن بیشتردرحوزه بحرخزردرسوا حـل ما زندرا ن بدست آ مده ا ست .بقا یا ی ا ین ا جتما عا ت کمی شما ل تردرسوا حل شرقی بحرخزردرروسیه نیز

1. Wahida, 1981
2. Braidwood and Howe, 1960:155
3. Young and Smith, 1966
4. Mortensen, 1974a; 1974b; 1975
5. Mortensen, 1979
6. Braidwood et al. 1981

بــا قیما نده ودرمحل دا م دا م چسمه اول ودوم[1] جبل[2] ،کا یلیا[3]وحا جا سوا ول[4]درغرب ترکمنستــا ن مشا هده میگردد .[5]

با وجودیکه احتما لا"ا جتما عا ت بیشتری درمنطقه حوزه بحرخزردردورا ن دیرینه سنگی میزیسته ا ند ولی آثا رکمی ا زآنها بدست آمده ا ست .ا حتما لا"آثا روبقا یا ی مربوط به ا ینا جتما عا ت ا مروزدرزیر لایه ها ی رسوبی دردا منه ء کلووویوم[6]ما زندرا ن یا دربقا یا ی لوس[7]درگرگا ن پنها ن گردیده ا ست .درمحل پا ئین زرا ندین درنزدیک بهشهرا دوا ت سنگی بدست آمده ا ست [8] ا حتما لا"درغا رها ی مرتفع تری نیز دردا منه ها ی ا لبرزممکن آ یین بقا یا وجوددا شته با شد .پروفسورکوون اظها رمینما ید[9]که دره ه ـــز ا ر جریف درنزدیک رودنکا ا حتما لا"محل خوبی برا ی جستجوی ا ین آ ثا رمیبا شد .

درحا ل حا ضربقا یا ی ا ولین ا جتما عا ت ا نسا نی درحوزه بحرخزردر چندغا ردرنزدیک بهشــهر بدست آمده ا ست که مربوط به دورا ن روی دیرینه سنگی میبا شند (با وجودیکه پروفسورکوون کا شـف آ نها ا ین آثا ررا مربوط به دورا ن میا ن سنگی میدا ند)ودورا ن ا ین ا ستقرا ردر آ نها درحدودده هزا ر وپا نصد (۱۰۵۰۰) سا ل پیش ا زمیلادمسیح شروع گردیده ا ست .ا ین غا رها عبا رتندا زغا رکمربندوغـار هوتوکه بوسیله پروفسورکوون درسا ل ۱۹۴۹ و ۱۹۵۱ حفا ری گردید [10]وعلی تپه ا ول درنزدیک آ نها کـه درسا لهای ۱۹۶۴،۱۹۶۲ بوسیله پروفسورمک بورنی[11]بررسی گردید .ا ین غا رها ا مروزدرفا صله ۸ تا ۱۳ ـ کیلومتری کرا نه فعلی دریا وا قع میبا شند .ا ولین آثا رمربوط به وجودا نسا ن درعلی تپه ا ول در ـ حدود۱۰۵۰۰ سا ل پیش ا زمیلادمسیح درهنگا میکه آ ب وهوا ی مسا عدتروگرمتروجوددا شته وسطح دریـا پا ئین تررفته مشا هده میگردد (شکل شما ره ۲۵) .کمی بعدیعنی درحدودده هزا رسا ل پیش (۱۰۰۰۰)ا زمیلاد مسیح بنظرمیرسدغا رها ی کمربندوهوتونیزموردسکونت قرا رگرفته ومنا بع غذا ئی منطقه مجا ورآ نها ا زقبیل نبا تا ت وحیوا نا ت وپرندگا ن زمینی ودریا ئی موجودموردا ستفا ده ا ین ا جتما عا ت ا نسا نی

---

1. Dam Dam Chesme I, II
2. Djebel
3. Kailia
4. Hadja-Su I
5. Masson and Sarianidi, 1972
6. Colluviums
7. Loess
8. Keraudren and Thibault, 1973
9. Coon, 1952:236
10. Coon, 1951; 1952; 1957
11. McBurney, 1968

قرارگرفته است[1].درحدودتقریبا "نه‌هزارسال (۹۰۰۰) پیش ازمیلادمسیح بنظرمیرسدعلی تپه‌متروک گردیده وغارهای کمربندوهوترنیزکمی پس ازآن درحدوداواسط هزاره‌ششم ویا هفتم نیزدرهنگامی که‌سطح دریا پائین تررفته‌بودازاین اجتماعات خالی مانند.

ادوات سنگی بدست آمده درغارهای کمربندوعلی تپه‌اول عموما "ادوات ظریف[2]وکوچک بوده وبا آثاردورهزارزیان درمنطقه‌زاگرس مشابه‌میباشندوعلاوه‌برآن درضمن هم چنین ادوات سنگی برزگ تروسنگین تروسنگ سایها نیزموجودبوده اند (شکل ۱۴) .دردوران میان سنگی غارهوتوآثارادوات ظریف وکوچک وجودندارد وبیشترقطعات بدون شکل هندسی بوده (شکل شماره ۱۴)وبرای مشخص نمــودن آنها اصطلاح نوع مازندوانیان پیشنهادشده است[3].

درحدودنیم دوجین اسکلت انسان درغارهای کمربندوهوتوبدست آمدکه عموما "مربوط بــــه ۷۲۰۰–۶۶۰۰ سال ازمیلادمسیح میباشندواین ها تنها نمونه‌هائی هستندکه‌وضع جسمانی انسانهای دوران روی دیرینه‌سنگی[4] رادرایران نمایان میسازند.ازنظرجسمانی رسته‌انسان امروزی میباشند وبعضی دارای قدبلندونیرومندوازسلامت جسمی برخورداروتا حدودچهل سال عمرنموده‌اند[5].متاسفانه بعلت محدودیت مدارک هیچگونه‌اظهارنظری نسبت به‌ جداداآنها ویا تا آیرآنها درنسلهای بعـــدی اجتماعات ایران ازنظرجسمانی درحال حاضرمیسرنمیباشد .گل اُخُرئ برای پوشش مردگان بکاررفته واین قبورا اولین نمونهٔ دفن مردگان را معرفی می‌نماینداحتمالا"با بعضی ازقبورمربوط به‌اوائل دوران نوسنگی درمنطقه‌زاگرس همزمان میباشند.

گسترش این اجتماعات انسانی دردوره‌روی دیرینه‌سنگی درا این منطقه‌وتا آیرآن بررروی محیط وحیوانات وغلاتی که‌دردوره‌بعدبصورت اهلی مورداستفاده‌قرارگرفته اندکاملا"روشن نیست .پروفسور مک بورنی[6] اظهار می‌نماید که‌احتمالا"بزوگوسفندوشا یدگندم وبعضی غلات محلی دیگردراین دوران اهلی گردیده‌اند.آیا اهلی نمودن حیوانات ونباتات دراینجا مستقلا"انجام گردیده‌ویا ازمنطقه‌دیگـــری

---

1. McBurney, 1968
2. Microlithic
3. Dupree, 1952
4. Epipalaeolithic
5. Coon, 1951; Angel, *in* Coon 1952
6. McBurney, 1968

مانند منطقه زاگرس بدین ناحیه وارد شده است آشکار نمی باشد . در اجتماعات بعدی که در این غار هـــا
در دوران نوسنگی چه قبل از دوران سفال و چه در آن دوران مسکون گردیده اند مدارکی که بتوانـــد
آغاز دوران تولید محصولات کشاورزی را بدقت مشخص نما یدبدست نیا مده ا ست . احتما لا "در بعضـــی
ا ز ا ین ا جتما عا ت ا نسا نی شکارچیا ن دوره روی دیرینه سنگی درکنا ر ا جتما عا ت ا ولیه کشا ورزا ن بـه
نوع وبا فت زندگا نی خود ا دا مه دا ده وبتدریج در ا جتما عا ت کشا ورزی مستحیل گردیده ا ند .

بهرحا ل بنظر می رسد در حدود پنج هزا ر سا ل (۵۰۰۰) پیش ا ز میلا د مسیح بکلی بقا یا ی زندگا نـــی
دوران دیرینه سنگی نیز برچیده شده و در تما م نواحی ا یرا ن نحوه وبا فت زندگا نی کشا ورزی و تولید
آذوقه جا یگزین آن گردیده ا ست .

ا ین نکته که آ یا با شروع زندگا نی کشا ورزی ا جتما عا ت ا نسا نی رو به تزا یدرفته ا ست موضـــوع
جا لب و مهمی ا ست که مورد بررسی و تحقیق دا نشمندان می با شد . ۱ با تعدا د محدود و آ ثا رو مکا ن هـــا ی
با ستا نی که تا کنون حفا ری و بررسی گردیده ا ند پا سخ قا طع بدین نکا ت وسئوا لات بسیا ر مشکـــل
ا ست . شروع و آ غا ز دوران کشا ورزی در ا یرا ن چندا ن روشن نیست ولی ا ز هزا ره ششم پیش ا ز میـــلاد
مسیح شوا هد و مدا رک مربـــوط بدا ن مشا هده میگردد . ا ین شوا هد در ا یرا ن ا بتدا در منا طق کردستا ن
ولرستا ن وخوزستا ن بدست آ مده ا ند .

_____
1. Smith and Young, 1983

ا یـــرا ن دردنیا ی دیرینـهسنگی

پس ا ز آ نکها نسا ن ا ولیهبهسا ختن ا دوا ت شروع نمودهوا زموطن ا صلی خود ا فریقا بهخــــــــارج گسترش یا فت فقط تعدا دمحدودی ا ز منا طق زمین درمعرض ا ین مها جرت قرا رنگرفتهودست نخـــــورده با قی ما ندند . ا ین گسترش با وجودیکهبسیا رکندوتدریجی بودهولی پس ا زگذشت هزا رهاسال،دربیشتـــــر نوا حی مسا عدد ا منهپید ا نمود . با محدودیت مدا رک موجودبسیا رمشکل ا ست کهبتوا ن درحا ل حا ضـــــر جهت ا ین مها جرت ها وهم چنین قدمت آ نها را د ر نوا حی مختلف تعیین نمود .

دا نشمند ا ن با ستا نشنا س دورا ن دیرینهسنگی کهبکا رتحقیقا ت وبررسیهای علمی در منطقــــــــه ا یرا ن مشغول میبا شندبا ید د ر نظردا شتهبا شندکه منطقه جنوب غربیآسیا چه د ِردنیای با ستا ن وچهدرعصر حا ضرهموا رهنقش را بط بین ا روپا ،ا فریقا ٔ ̄آ سیا ی مرکزی وآسیا ی جنوبی را د ا شتهووسیلهٔ ا رتبا ط ا ین فرهنگها بودها ست . در ا ین منطقها یرا ن بخصوص بعنوا ن شا هرا ههستهومرکزتما س ا ین فرهنگها بودها ست . ا یرا ن درشما ل با منا طق قفقا زکهدرا رتبا ط با ا روپا بودهوهم چنین با آ سیا ی مرکـــزی، درشرق وجنوبشرقی درا رتبا ط با ا فعا نستا ن وحوزههندوپا کستا ن ،درجنوب با عربستا ن ودرمغـــرب با فلات آ نا طولی ،بین ا لنهرین ولوا نت وبا لمآ ل با ا فریقا را بطهدا شتها ست . بهرحا ل برا ی درک ـــ وروشن نمودن دورا ن گذشتها یرا ن شنا خت تمدنها وفرهنگها ی گذشتههمجوا ردرآ سیا ی جنوبغـــــربی ضروری بنظر میرسد .

منطقی بنظرمیرسدکهدردورا ن دیرینهسنگی ما نند دورا ن های پیش ا زتا ریخ وتا ریخی ا یرا ن در معرض نفوذوتا ثیرفرهنگها ی مجا ورا زجها ت مختلف بودهودرضمن خصوصیا ت فرهنگی خودرا درجهات مختلف گسترش دا دها ست . ا لبتهدرحا ل حا ضرا ین نکتهبیش ا زیک فرضیهنبودهوبرا ی ا ثبا ت آ ن ـــ مدا رک کا فی ضروری میبا شد . دنیا ی دیرینهسنگی ا ز نظرا قلیمی ،آ ب وهوا وا مکا نا ت تا ا ند ا زها ی متفا وت با دورا نهای بعدیبوده وبنا بر ا ین عوا مل نفوذوگسترش فرهنگها نیزتا ا ند ا زها ی بـــــا موا زین دورا نهای تا ریخی ویا حا ل متفا وت بودها ست .

بهرحا ل برا ی شنا خت حجم ا رتبا ط ا یرا ن با سا یر منا طق مجا وربررسی وضع دورا ن دیرینـــــه سنگی درآ نها ضروری بنظرمیرسد . تا کنون درصفحا ت گذشتهد ر هرفصل تا ا ند ا زها ی د ر با رها رتبــــا ط ا یرا ن ومقا یسهآ ثا را ربا قیما ندهآ ن با آ ثا رمنا طق مجا ورموا ردی تذکرد ا دهشدها ست . ا ینک بهبررسی بیشتری درا ینمورددردورا ن دیرینهسنگی میپردا زیم . بررسی آ ثا ربدست آ مدهدرمنا طق مجـــــا ور درجهت مغرب وجنوب چندان آثار مشا بهی نشا ن نمیدهد . مدا رک دیرینهسنگی درعربستا ن وهمچنین د ر فـــلات

آ نا طولی بخصوص درنوا حی شرقی بسیا رنا شنا خته میبا شند .درقسمت جنوبی بین ا لنهرین دردشت
رسوبی آ ن مدا رک وشوا هدزیا دیتا کنون بدست نیا مده ا ست . در منطقه لوا نت درکرا نه ها ی شرقی
دریا ی مدیترا نه آ ثا رزیا دی مربوط بدین دورا ن درمحله ها ی مختلفِ بدست آ مده ا ست .بعضی از ـ
این آ ثا ر درحفا ریها ی علمی آ شکا رشده وا ز نظر طبقا ت با ستا نی وقدمت کا ملا"بررسی شده ا ند ولــــی
آ ثا ر آ نها موا رد مشا به زیا دی درباره آ ثا روا دوا ت بدست آ مده درا یرا ن نشان نمیدهند .البته موا رد کلــی
مشا بهی ما ننـد تقسیم بندی دورا ن دیرینه سنگی درهر منطقه برا سا س آ ثا ر بدست آ مده در دورا نــها ی
دیرینه سنگی عمیق ومتوسط ومرتفع ودوره روی دیرینه سنگی یکسا ن میبا شد و بعضی ا دوا ت وصنا یـع
سنگی بطور عمومی وکلی درهردوره قا بل مقا یسه هستند .دورا ن موستریا ن ا یرا ن با ا ین دورا ن در ـ
منطقه لوا نت شبا هت عمومی دا رد وفقط در نوع محلی وطرز سا ختن ا دوا ت تفا تها ی جزئی دا رنـد .در
دورا ن با را دوستیا ن شبا هتها ئی بین آ ثا روا دوا ت منطقه لوا نت با آ ثا را یرا ن را بعضی ا دوا ت خا ص
ملاحظه میگردد .مثلا"ا دوا ت نوک تیزغا ر ارجنه با ا دوا ت نوک تیزا لوا د [1]آ نتلیا ن[2]مشا به هستنــد .
همچنین بعضی آ ثا ر دوره زا رزیا ن با آ ثا رکبا ریا ن[3]در منطقه مشا بهت دا رند .

        منا طق مجا ور درجهت شما ل ویا شرق ا یرا ن آ ثا رو مدا رک مشا به ومربوط تری را در بعضی دوره ها
دربردا رند وا ز نقطه نظر مقا یسه وضعیت بهتری موجود ا ست .هما نگونه که بعضی ا ز دا نشمندا ن ا ظهــار
دا شته ا ند[4]موا رد قا بل مقا یسه ا ی بین دورا ن دیرینه سنگی ـ منطقه زا گرس با منا طق قفقا زوما وراء ـ
قفقا ز درجهت شما ل ما ننـد گرجستا ن ، ا رمنستا ن ،آ ذربا یجا ن وا وستیا[5]مشا هده میگردد .مثلا"با فِــت
وطرز زندگا نی درمنا طق کوهستا نی وکوچ نمودن به نقا ط مختلف برا ی مبا رزه با سرما وگرما ویـــا
بدست آ وردن شکا ر درفصول مختلف درتما م ا ین منطقه از نا حیه کوهها ی قفقا ز تا جبا ل زا گـــــرس
بطورکلی مشا به بوده ا ست .

        در منطقه تفقا ز ما ننـد منطقه زا گرس بعلت محدودیت مدا رک مشکل ا ست راجع به دوره ه دیربربنـــه
عمیق سنگی ا ظها را ت زیا دی نمود .آ ثا روا دوا تی ا ز قبـل ا ز دوره آ شولیا ن درآ نجا گزا رش نگردیـــده

---

1. Elwad
2. Antelian
3. Kebarian
4. Garrod 1938; Hole 1970; Solecki 1963; McBurney 1964
5. Ossetia

وبا ستأ نشنا سا ن پیش ا زتا ریخ روسیه وجودچندنمونه تبرهای سنگی دستی نوع آشولیا ن را درمحل ـ
ها ئی ما نندغا رآ ذیخ[1]درآ ذربا یجا ن شوروی ،محلها ی کودا رو[2] وبوب[3]درگرجستا ن ، وسا تا نیـدر[4]
درا رمنستا ن گزا رش نموده ا ند .ا لبته نظرا ت مختلفی را جع بقدمت وتا ریخ ا ین آ ثا ر[5]هما نگونـه
که دربا ره آ ثا ر ربا ردا با لکا درعرا ق وبا ریک درا یرا ن مشا هده میگردددا ینجا نیز مطـرح
میبا شد .

ا زدورا ن دیرینه سنگی متوسط درمنطقه قفقا زآ ثا ر وا دوا ت کا فی ما نندمنا طق زا گرس بدست
آ مده ا ست وبنظر میرسدا جتما عا ت گسترده ای درا ین دورا ن درا ین منطقه مستقربوده ا ند .بعضـی
ا زغا رها درا رتفا ت قرا ردا رندوا حتما لا"محل های ا ستقرا رموقت تا بستا نی را معرفی مینما ینـد .
ا نوا ع مختلف آ ثا ر موستریا ن درا ین منطقه مشخص گردیده ا ست .[6]موا ردمشا بهی دربین ا دوا ت بدست
آ مده درزا گرس ودرا ین منطقه بخصوص درنوع رنده های با ریک وا دوا ت نوک تیزمشا هده میگردد .آ ثا ر
روش لوا وا درسا ختن تیغه ها وا دوا ت سنگی بنا با ظها ربعضی دا نشمندا ن بیشتردرمنطقه قفقا زبکا ر
رفته ولی مدا رک کا فی برا ی تا ئیدا ین نظریه وجودندا رد .

همچنین موا ردقا بل مقا یسه بیشتری دردوره دیرینه سنگی مرتفع بین آ ثا ر ا یرا ن وقفقـا ز
مشا هده میگردد .بعضی عوا مل شبیه به با را دوستیا ن درمنطقه قفقا زدرمحلها ئی ما نندتا روکلده[7]وغا ر
ویرچو[8]درگرجستا ن ا زقبیل رنده ها وتیغه های یک طرفه ومته ها[9] (شکل ۱و ۲) مشا هده میگردد .همچنیـن
عوا مل وموا ردمشا بهی بین آ ثا ردوره ا زرزیا ن زا گرس ومنطقه قفقا زدرمحلها ئی ما ننددویس خورلی[10]
درگرجستا ن[11]وگوا رزیلاس کلده[12]مشا هده میگردد .[13]

---

1. Azikh Cave
2. Kudaro
3. Bub
4. Satani-Dar
5. Klein, 1966
6. Lyubin, 1971
7. Taro Klde
8. Virchow
9. Field and Prostov, 1936
10. Devis Khoreli
11. Golomshtok, 1938, fig. 33
12. Gvardzhilas-Klde
13. Field and Prostov, 1936, fig. 2b

این فرهنگ های دوره روی دیرینه‌سنگی در این منطقه که بنا م های ایمرتی[1] وشا ن کوبـــا[2]
بوسیله با ستا ن شنا سا ن شوروی[3] خوانده شده اند احتما لا" از نظر نوع ادوات با دوران روی دیرینــــه
سنگی جنوب بحرخزردر ایرا ن ارتبا ط دارند .جهت این روا بط هنوز ازمنطقه ای به منطقه دیگر کٔ ملا"
روشن نیست ولی احتما لا" فرهنگهای زا رزیا ن وبا را دوستیا ن ازجهت شما ل از منطقه ما ورأ قفقــاز
ودر اصل از منطقه دریای سیاه به جبا ل زاگرس را ه یا فته ا ند .

موا ردمشا بهی بین صنا یع سنگی شرق ایرا ن با آسیا ی مرکزی بخصوص درترکمنستا ن،ازبکستا ن
وتا جیکستا ن مشا هده میگردد .البته بسیار مشکل است شوا هد دوران دیرینه‌سنگی عمیق ما نند آثـار
ابتدا ئی لادیزین وکشف رود درخرا سا ن را با آثا رجا ها ی دیگر مقا یسه نمودولی بطورکلی عوا مـــل
وآثا ربدست آمده در ایرا ن با آثا ربدست آمده در آسیا ی مرکزی در این دوران شبا هت نزدیک دارنــد.
درهردو منطقه آثا رمربوط به دوره آشولیا ن بندرت یا بطورکلی بخصوص درمنا طق کوهستا نی موجــود
نمیبا شد وتحقیقا ت اخیــــر نشا ن میدهد که ادوا ت سنگی درتا جیکستا ن از حدود دویست وپنجا ه هزا ر
(۲۵۰۰۰۰) سا ل پیش شروع گردیده است .[4] در این دوران احتما لا" دره کشف رودار ا ه ارتبا ط بین فـلات
ایرا ن وترکمنستا ن بوده است [5]

دردورا ن دیرینه‌سنگی متوسط بنظرمیرسد این ارتبا ط برقرا ر بوده است وپروفسور مک بورنــی
عقیده دا رد که شبیه ترین آثا ر به بقا یای غا رکی آرا م اول درمحل تشک تا ش[6] در ازبکستا ن بدســت
آمده ا ند .[7] البته ادوا ت سا خته شده از قلوه سنگ دردوره موستریا ن درآسیا ی مرکزی شبا هتی به صنا یع
سنگی ایرا ن وآسیا ی غربی ندا رند .

دردورا ن دیرینه‌سنگی مرتفع نیزروا بطی بین این دومنطقه ا یرا ن وآسیا ی مرکزی وجود دا شته
وآثا ربا را دوستیا ن تا حدودی با آثا رآسیا ی مرکزی ارتبا ط دارد .عوا مل وآثا رمشا بهی با آنچــــه

1. Imeretie
2. Shan-Koba
3. Koslowski, 1979
4. Ranov and Davis, 1979
5. Ariai and Thibault, 1975 -1977:6
6. Teshik-Tash
7. McBurney, 1964:393

كه مربوط به اوائل دوران دیرینه‌سنگی مرتفع در قره‌کمر در شمال افغانستان بدست آمده و مربوط به قبل از سی هزار (۳۰۰۰۰) سال پیش میباشد در ایران هنوز بدست نیامده است.[1] در دوران میان‌سنگی[2] روی عوامل و آثار مشابهی بین ایران و آسیای مرکزی و افغانستان در شمال رشته‌جبال هندوکش مشاهده میگردد و حتی پیشنهاد گردیده که ادوات سنگی ظریف هندسی شکل از طریق ایران در حدود یازده هزار (۱۱۰۰۰) سال پیش از میلاد مسیح به آن منطقه وارد گردیده است.[3]

درباره ارتباط ایران در جهت شرق با حوزه پاکستان و هند ضروری بنظر میرسد درباره عده‌ای مدارک، بدست آمده در پاکستان و شمال غربی هند بررسی نمائیم. احتمالاً صحرا‌های شمال غرب هند و پاکستان در دوره‌های خشک موانعی در راه ارتباط این دو منطقه بوجود می‌آورده‌اند.

راجع به ارتباط این دو منطقه ایران و هند و پاکستان در دوران دیرینه‌سنگی عمیق شواهد و مدارک دقیق و قاطعی وجود ندارد ولی بطورکلی و عمومی شباهتی بین آثار رلادیزیا در شرق ایران و آثار رو در شمال شرق ایران و آثار رسوانیان[4] جنوب هیمالیا در هند و پاکستان مشاهده می‌گردد.

نوعی از دوران دیرینه‌سنگی متوسط در هندوستان مشخص گردیده که قدمت آن قبل از بیست و پنج هزار (۲۵۰۰۰) سال پیش از میلاد مسیح بوده و ادوات سنگی مانند نوک تیزها و رنده‌ها داشته و همچنین استفاده از زروش لوا و گاهگاهی مورد استفاده قرار گرفته و احتمالاً شبیه به موستریان میباشد. مقایسه آن با شواهد موستریان در منطقه زاگرس ویا غارکی آرام اول در شمال ایران چندان روشن نمیباشد.

بررسیهای اخیر در هند و پاکستان شواهد و آثاری از دوران دیرینه‌سنگی مرتفع که در حدود بیست و پنجهزار سال (۲۵۰۰۰) پیش از میلاد مسیح قدمت دارند آشکار نموده است. چند نمونه شواهد مسلم بین این آثار و آثار و ربا در دوستیان مشاهده میگردد. بیشتر این آثار در مرکز و جنوب هندوستان و تعداد کمتری در شمال غربی این منطقه که احتمالاً رابطه‌ای با ایران داشته بدست آمده‌اند. هنر دردوران دیرینه‌سنگی مرتفع در هندوستان بصورت مجسمه‌ها وحتی نقاشی دیواری وجود داشته که با ایران در این مورد تفاوت دارد.

1. Coon, 1957:217–54; Davis, 1978
2. Mesolithic
3. Ranov and Davis, 1979:259-60
4. Soanian

بنظر میرسد را بطهء بیشتری در دورا ن روی دیرینه سنگی مرتفع ویا میا ن سنگی در هنکا میگ....

ا ین ا جتما عا ت با ا دوا ت سنگی ظریف وکوچک مشخص بوده ا ندبین أ یرا ن وهندوپا کستا ن وجودا شته

ا ست ولی تا زما نیکه آ ثا رکا فی ا ز منطقه بلوچستا ن در جنوب شرق ا یرا ن برا ی ا ینگونه مقا یس....ا ت

بدست نیا مده بسیا ر مشکل ا ست که نظرا ت صریح ودقیقی پیشنها د نمود .با وجودیکه ا خیرا "آ ثا ری ا ز--

ا جتما عا ت ا ولیه کشا ورزی در حدودشش هزا ر سا ل (۶۰۰۰) پیش ا ز میلادمسیح در محل مهر گا ر خ[1] در --

بلوچستا ن پا کستا ن بدست آ مده[2] ولی با مدا رک موجودبسیا ر مشکل ا ست بتوا ن ا ظها ر نمودکه ا یــــن

ا جتما عا ت گسترش ا جتما عا ت کشا ورزی ا ولیه درا یرا ن بطرف شرق میبا شند .

بررسی آ ثا ر منا طق مجا ورا یرا ن که در سطور با لا بدا ن ا شا ره گردیدبا وجودیکه ا طلاعا ت زیـــا د

وروشنی درا ختیا ر قرا ر نمیدهدولی بهرحا ل در بعضی موا رد بعضی دورا نها همبستگی ا یرا ن بـــا

نوا حی ا طرا ف را بخصوص در نوا حی مجا ور یکدیگر ا شا ره مینما ید .نتیجه گیری منطقی ا ز ا ین بررسی--

یکی ا ینست که در دورا ن دیرینه سنگی عمیق ا یرا ن بخوبی با با فت ا ین دورا ن درآ سیا ی مرکز--ی

وجنوبی هم آ هنگی دا رد .ا ین هم آ هنگی در دورا ن دیرینه سنگی متوسط کمتربوده وحتی در دورا ن -

دیرینه سنگی مرتفع که ا رتبا ط بیشتری با منا طق قفقا زوما ورا[3] آ ن وحتی ا حتما لا "تا شما ل دریـــا ی

سیا ه برقرا ر گردیده نیزبه آ ن ا ندا زه دورا ن دیرینه سنگی عمیق وجودندا رد .

                                                                                                                    ا ی
علت ا ین وضعیت ا ینست که با گذشت زما ن وپیشرفت سا خت ا دوا ت سنگی خصوصیا ت محلی ومنطقه

بیشتر درآ ثا ر هر منطقه ظا هر گردیده هوا ا ین خصوصیا ت در دورا ن دیرینه سنگی مرتفع ودوره روی دیرینه

سنگی به حدکا مل خوددرا ین منطقه دنیا ی با ستا ن رسیده ا ست . درا ین زمینه ا یرا ن وسا یرنوا حـــی

جنوب غربی آ سیا شبا هت بیشتری با ا روپا وشما ل ا فریقا دا شته وتفا وتها ی زیا دقا بل ملاحظه ومهمـــی

با منا طق جنوبشرق ویا مرکزآ سیا دا رند .ا حتما لا "ا ین تفا وتها ویا همبستگیها درا ثر محیط ونــــوع

منا بع طبیعی موجوددرآ نها برا ی ا ستفا ده ا ین ا جتما عا ت ا ولیه بوده ا ست .

بطور خلاصه میتوا ن ا ظها ر دا شت که در دورا ن دیرینه سنگی ا یرا ن ا رتبا ط بیشتری با منا طـــق

شما لغربی ما نندما ورا ء قفقا زوشا ید کرا نه ها ی شما لی دریا ی سیا ه تا حدود منطقه کریمه ودر جهــــت

شما لشرق با آ سیا ی مرکزی وشما ل غربی حوزه پا کستا ن وهند تا منا طق دریا ی مدیترا نه وحتی قسمـــت

جنوبی بین ا لنهرین دا شته ا ست .ا ین وضعیت شا یدمتذکرا ین نکته با شدکه گسترش ونفوذا زرا ه صحرا ی

سوریه وبین ا لنهرین در دورا ن نها ی پلستوسین وا حتما لا "ا وا ئل هلوسین بطورقا بل ملاحظه ا ی بعلــل

نا معلومی وجودندا شته ا ست .

---

1. Mehrgarh
2. Jarrige and Meadow, 1980

نتیجـــــه‌گیـــــری

درخاتمه‌بنظرمیرسدارائه‌خلاصه‌ونتیجه‌ای ازاین بررسی مفیدواقع گـــردد .با محدودیت مدارک موجود وتعداد معدود مناطق بـــررسی ویا حفاری نتیجه‌گیری کلی چندان آسان‌نبوده‌ولی این نکتـــــه مسلم است که‌فعالیتهای باستان‌شناسان دراین راره‌هنوزقدمهای اولیه‌وابتدائی را میپیمایـــد . به مشکلات ونقصان مدارک دردوره‌ها ویا مناطق مختلف قبلا"اشاره‌گردیده‌وتکرارآن ضروری بنظــــر نمیرسد .احتیاج مبرم وشدیدی بمنظورنمایش تسلسل واستمرارردوره‌های مختلف دردوران دیرینه سنگی بچشم میخورد .تا زمانیکه‌ما قادرنخواهیم بودا زنظرزمان ظهورانسان درمنطقه‌واستقرار آن ،طول دوره‌های مختلف واستمرارآنها نظرات وفرضیه‌های قاطعی پیشنهانمائیم امکان جداول کوتاهیاطویل تسلسل دورانها میسرنمیبا شد .بررسی های گسترده‌ای درزمینه‌اقلیم ، محیط وآثار وادوات سنگی هنوزدرمناطق مختلف ایران لازم بنظرمیرسدتا بتوان درک بیشتری نسبت به‌وضعیت این دوران بدست‌آورد .ترکیب اطلاعاتی که‌ما مربوط به‌دوران دیرینه‌سنگی ایران دردست داریـم درشکل شماره ۱۵ نمایش داده‌شده‌است .

خلاها وحدفاصل های زیادی چه زنظرجغرافیا فیا یی وچه زنظردوره‌ها هنوزوجودداشته‌وبررسیها وتحقیقات آینده‌را ضروری مینماید .درضمن بررسیها ئی که‌بوسیله‌نویسنده‌درسال ۱۹۶۵ میلادی در جبال زاگرس درمناطق کردستان وآذربایجان انجام گردیدغارهای زیادی ملاحظه‌گردیدکه‌با وجودی که‌میتوانسته‌اندپناهگا ههای مساعدی برای زندگانی اجتماعات دوران دیرینه‌سنگی با شنـــــد ولی درآنها آثاری ازاین دوران باقی نمانده‌است . شایدا حتما لا"یا این غارها درآن دوران وجودندا شته‌ویا آثاربا قیما نده‌بوسیله‌اجتماعات بعدی ازبین رفته‌ویا دلایل دیگری برای عــــدم استفا ده‌از آنها وجودداشته‌که‌درحال حاضرروشن ومعلوم نیست .منطقه‌آذربایجان غربی با ستثنـای محل غارتمتمه‌درا ورومیه‌همین وضعیت را دا اردوغارهای آن موردا ستفا ده‌اجتماعات دوران دیرینـه سنگی قرارنگرفته‌اند .شایدا زنظرآب وهوا ویا علل دیگری این مناطق برای سکونت دربیشترایـــن دوران ویا قسمتی ازآن مساعدنبوده‌اند .[1]این مسئله‌ایست که‌برای روشن نمودن آن نیــــــــز بتحقیقات علمی درآینده میبا شد .

تحقیق وبررسی وضع توزیع حیوانات دردورا ن های مختلف دریک منطقه‌بسیا راهمیت دا شتـــــه

---

1. Solecki, 1969

ومیتوانندکاتی مانند ۱ـ آیا تغییرات قابل ملاحظه‌ای درتعداد و نوع حیوانات که مورد استفاده شکارچیان قرار میگرفته درطول زمان ، ۲ـ چه حیواناتی از نظر سن وسال ونرویا ماده بودن دریک رسته گلچین میگردیده‌اند ، و ۳ـ چگونه کشته وقطعه قطعه گردیده وبقیه اسکلت با قیمانده‌را روشـن نماید .این بررسیها میتواندشاخصی برای علت تولیداادوات مختلف سنگی برای استفاده وکاربردـ های مختلف درهم آهنگی با منابع موجود درمحیط باشد .همچنین اهمیت خاصی از نظر نحوه‌ء شکــــــار خواهدداشت .احتمالا"بین دوران بارا دوستیان زارزیان ازاین لحاظ استمراریبیش ازوقفه دربافت زندگا نی وجودداشته ولی تا ئیدآن احتیاج به نمایش مدارک بیشتری دارد .

همچنین نقطه‌ء ضعف دیگری که درباره بررسی دردوران دیرینه‌سنگی ایران وجودداردا ینست که کاشفین وحفاران وبررسی کنندگان این آثار هنوز بطوردقیق آثاربدست آمده را بررسی ننموده و آن را بطرق علمی دقیق انتشارنداده‌اند .حفاران منطقه خرم آباددرلرستان بدینکارمبادرت نموند[1] ولی متاسفا نه نمونه‌های بررسی شده محدودبوده وتعلق آنها به طبقات مختلف با ستا نــی کاملا"موردا عتما دنیست .مطلب دیگری که هنوز درباره آن چندان تحقیقات انجام نگردیده آنست که تا چه حدمنابع طبیعی موجوددرنحوه‌ء ساخت ادوات نفوذوتا ثیرداشته است . شایدعلت عدم استفاده ازروش لوا وا درمنطقه ازا گرس عدم وجودسنگ مادرمطلوب برای این نوع استفاده دراین منطقــه بوده است که دراین ناحیه بسیارنایاب میبا شددرصورتیکه درمنطقه‌ء لوا نت بسیا رفراوا ن است .

علی رغم محدودیت مدارک واطلاعات مربوط به دوران دیرینه‌سنگی درا یران شایدبتـــوان نسبت به چهاربافت[2] گونا گون برای استفاده ازمحیط وتعدیل آن اشاره نمودولی ترتیب آنها از نظر قدمت نسبت به یکدیگرهنوزمشخص نبوده وفقط میتوان اظها ردا شت دراوا خردوران دیرینه‌سنگـــی وجودداشته‌اند .

۱ـ یکی تنها بافت ونحوه‌ای که درتما م دوران دیرینه‌سنگی ازدوره دیرینه‌سنگی عمیـــق تا دوره روی دیرینه‌سنگی ادا مه داشته درمناطق مرتفع کوهستا نی وجودداشته ونمونه آن درزا گرس مشاهده میگردد .وجوداین بافت دردوران دیرینه‌سنگی درجبا ل البرزوارتفاعات شرقی (بجزدرغار خونیک) هنوزبا مدارک مستندمفعلی تا ئیدنگردیده ولی بعیدبنظرمیرسداین نواحی حداقل از ـ ـ

───────────

1. Hole and Flannery, 1967
2. Pattern

دوران دیرینهسنگی متوسط موردا ستفا دهقرا رنگرفتهبا شند .

۲ـ ازآ وا خردورهپلستوسین تا دوره هلوسین با فت دیگری مخلوط ا زنحوه ا ستفا ده ا زمنا بــــع زمینی ودریا ئی درسوا حل بحرخزروجودداشتهاست .ا بتداوشروع آ ن روشن نیست .ومدا رک مستنــد برای وجودآ ن درسوا حل جنوبی بحرخزردرا یرا ن هنوزبطورمبهم ا شا رهگردیده ا ست .درخلیج فـارس وسوا حل مکرا ن ا حتما لا"حیوا نا تی ما نندما هی یونس ۱ ،گرا زدریا یی۲ونهنگ وما هی قسمتی ا ز ما یجتا ج غدا ئی را تا مین مینمودها ند .

۳ـ با فت سوم کهنحوهزندگا نی ا ستفا ده ا زمحیط ومنا بع را درصحرا ها درنوا حی شرقی ومرکزی درمنطقهوسیعی فرا میگرفتهوهنوزکا ملا"ا زنظرمنا بع موردا ستفا ده چندا ن مشخص نیست ولی درصورتی کهتغییرآ ثا رمربوط بهفرهنگ لا دیزیا نها موردا عتما دوتا ئیدبا شدا ین با فت دردورا ن طویلــــی تقریبا "ا زدورهدیرینهسنگی عمیق بهبعدا دا مهداشتهاست .

۴ـ نسبت بهچگونگی با فت دیگری کهدرجنوب بین ا لنهرین ودشت خوزستا ن درمنـطقهرسوبی رودخا نهها وبا طلاقها ویا سطح زمین وجودداشتهوا زمنا بع طبیعی ا ین منطقها ستفا ده مینمـــوده ا شا رهای گردیده ا ست .متا سفا نهتا کنون مدا رک مستندموردا عتما دا زا یرا ن وعرا ق درا ین منطقــه کهبتوا ندشوا هدوا طلاعا تی را درا ختیا رقرارگذا ردبدست نیا مدها ست .درصورتیکهچنین با فتی درا یـــن منا طق وجودداشته ا حتما لا"شبیه بها فتی ا ست کهدرنوا حی مجا ورآ ن درقسمتهای جنوبی زاگـــــرس وجودداشتهوبهنحوموسمی وفصلی عملی میگردیده ا ست .

موا ردونکا تی کهتا کنون شرح دا ده شدبیشتربهوضعیت آ ثا رباستا نی ومسا ئل مبهم ودورا نهای تا ریک وخلا ها ی موجوددرا ین زمینهمربوط بودها ندکها حتما لا "میتوا ندرا هنما ئی برا ی فعا لیتهای آ یندهقرا رگیرد .آخرین نکتهدرا ین کتا ب مربوط بهفعا لیتها وبررسیها ی دورا ن دیرینهسنگـــــی درا یرا ن درآ یندهمیبا شد .

با ید ا ذعا ن داشت کهباستا نشنا سا ن ودا نشمندا ن دورا ن دیرینهسنگی کهدرا یرا ن فعا لیت مینمودها ندهنوزکا ملا"حق مطلب را ا دا ننمودها ند .ا گرچهدربعضی موا ردحفا ریها ی مطلوب ا نجــام گردیدهولی سطح تحقیقا ت بطورکلی بسیا رپا ئین ومحدودمیبا شد .منطقهٔ ا یرا ن بهمرا همنـاطـــق مجا ورخودترکیه ،عرا ق وا فغا نستا ن کهوضعیت مشا بهی را دا رندمیا ن محلی ا زجها ن ما نندلوانت ، قفقا زوآ سیای مرکزی وهندوستا ن وا قع شده ا ندکها کثرا موزهتحقیقا ت دا منهدا رو گستردهای با سرعتــی چشمگیرمربوط بهدورا ن دیرینهسنگی درآ ن نوا حی ا نجا م میگردد .درا یرا ن تحقیقا ت درا ین زمینه

1. Dolphin
2. Porpoise

اتفاقی وپراکنده وغیرمکفی درسطح کوچکی انجام میگیردولی علیرغم این وضعیت درمنا طـــق

مجاورا شارهشدهبرنا مههای منظم علمی برای روشن نمودن مسائل ومبهما ت مربوط بهدورا نهـای

گذشتها زطریق حفاریها وبررسیهای علمی درسطح وسیعی درجریان میباشد .

        نکتهدیگری کهاشارهبدان ضروری بنظرمیرسدا ینت کههرلحظها مکان ویرانی آثاروبقایـای

باستانی درا یران بعلل مختلف وبخصوص حفاریهای مخفیا نهوجودا رد .این خطردرضمن فعا لیتهای

دامندا رکشا ورزی ویا استخراج سنگ ا زمعا دن درمحلها ئیکهغا رهای باستانی وجوددا رندنیزموجود

میبا شدچنا نکهدرگذشتهغا ربا ستانی مهم هوتوقبل ا زحفا ری پروفسورکوون بوسیلهدینا میـــت

ویرا ن شدهبود .۱درسا ل ۱۹۷۷ درهٔ کوچکی درنزدیک کرما نشا نهکهپنا هگا هسنگی و٫ روا سی درآ ن وجود

دا ردبرا ی تعلیما ت جنگی وتوپخا نهموردا ستفا دهقوا رگرفت وسرنوشت غا روا روا سی درحا ل حا ضـــر

مبهم ونا معلوم ا ست .شا یدمنا سب ترین نحوپا یا ن دادن بهمطلب درا ین بررسی ا شا رهبهنظریـــه

پروفسوروفیشـروجغرافی دا ن مشهوربا شدکه میگوید ۲ " نقش ا یرا ن بطاورکلی تولید ،وصول ،تعدیــل

با نفوذمحلی و٫ نتقا ل فرهنگ خودوفرهنگها ی هم جوا ربوده ا ست ." نا گفتهنما ندشوا! هدومد! رکیکه

بتوا ندا ین نظریه٫را دردورا ن دیرینهسنگی ثا بت نما یدهنوزبا ندا زهکا فی موجودنیست وبرا ی درک٫

بهتروروشن ترنقش ا یرا ن فعا لیتها ی دامندا رتحقیقا ت ومطا لعا ت درآ یندهضروری بنظـــــر

میرسد .

                    "پـــــا یـــــا ن "

1. Coon, 1957:162
2. W. B. Fisher, 1968:740

بررسی دوران دیرینه‌سنگی در ایران

نویسنده :

فیلیپ اسمیت

تلخیص و ترجمه :

عزت الله نگهبان